LIBRARY
OKALOOSA - WALTON JUNIOR COLLEGE

D1255237

THE GOLD IN TIN PAN ALLEY

THE
GOLD
IN
TIN PAN
ALLEY

By HAZEL MEYER

J. B. LIPPINCOTT COMPANY
PHILADELPHIA • NEW YORK

ML
2511
M5
G6

Copyright © 1958 by Hazel Meyer

First Edition

Library of Congress Catalog Card Number 58-8670

Printed in the United States of America

LIBRARY
OKALOOSA - WALTON JUNIOR COLLEGE

For my mother, Carlotta Rosetta,
with words and music

11107

ACKNOWLEDGMENTS

As MUCH AS POSSIBLE in a book about people to whom song titles, copyright dates and name credits are very important, I have avoided lists. This forbearance cannot help but make the book incomplete—but, I hope, not listless.

But it is a more delicate reason than an aversion to lists which is responsible for the omission here of the customary honor roll of men and women from whom an author receives encouragement and assistance. There have been such rapid and revolutionary changes in the creating, marketing and exposure of popular songs in so brief a time that thirty, twenty or even ten years ago are dusty antiquity. Much of the material I was after has been stored in the memories of living people who were a vital part of those ancient times. Much of it is being lived right now. In the music business, everybody knows everybody else. Everybody is supposed to love everybody else, too, because of an affable interdependence that is unique in business competition. It would be indiscreet of me, I think, to thank by name, publicly, all the songwriters, publishers, contact men, disk jockeys, record company executives, performers and trade association officials who generously consented to talk or write to me privately—not only about themselves and their rivals, but also about professional colleagues whose continuing good will they cherish.

When I was briefly and unimportantly a part of the music business a dozen or so years ago, I don't think I had in mind that I would one day write a book about it. Several of the wonderful people I knew then are gone, now, but I remember them and am grateful to them for sharing with me their insight into the industry they grew up in. Most of all, I think, I miss Mose Gumble—that sweet, gentle dean of American song-pluggers who told me so many stories about the Tin Pan Alley of bygone days when he rode the horse-cars along Broadway, shouting songs through a megaphone. His last letter to me, written in answer to one of mine in which I suggested that he write a book, contained a postscript that said maybe he would, some day. He never did write his book. I hope this is one he would have liked.

Contents

1. *The Trail*

A HUMAN CREATURE ventured out of his cave one fine day and found two bones. He beat them together. His wife, crawling into the sunshine, gazed at him in admiration. Her husband was a songwriter!

Throughout recorded history and uncovered by the spade in diggings which are filling in history's gaps, it is evident that each of the world's progressive civilizations has produced its own popular music. The taut strings of hunting bows, notched reeds, shells and animal skins stretched across hollow tree stumps provided early instrumentation for melody; and when Man invented language, he added lyrics.

Down through the ages, the music of the people has been used to express their fears, supplications, hopes, loves and fantasies. Songs are the world's diary and its barometer, describing history's events and ideas and measuring the emotional climate of the brief periods we speak of as generations. You don't have to know a country's vocabulary in order to understand its tunes. You don't have to know musical theory in order to understand popular music. Speaking an international grammar, it communicates freely, accomplishing among nations what the nations' officials often cannot.

The message in popular music is universal, but there is a finicking tendency among modern devotees of nonclassical repertories to sort songs and dance tunes like artifacts unearthed by an archaeological expedition and file them away in pigeonholes carefully labeled as to date, origin, style, intention and function. These purists consider it not quite bright of you to speak of folk music, "art" songs, spirituals and gavottes in the same breath with sophisticated or sentimental love ballads, cowboy laments, sea chanteys and blues. It is a mark of barbarism not to know the difference between true jazz and its cooled-down, diluted or otherwise commercialized modulations.

These are good and true distinctions, as valid to dedicated collectors of "real" jazz or "real" folk music as special postage stamp issues are to philatelists; but particularism can be carried too far. Nowadays, songwriters who specialize in music for the stage resent having their works described as "popular music." A show tune may become as popular as all get-out, but its writers are inclined to flinch when it is called a popular song. To these writers, "popular" songs are written by a different breed of tunesmith altogether who travels a narrow path along the gutter side of Tin Pan Alley. Other categories of current music—Latin-American imports or imitations, country and Western rambles, syncopated gospel, rhythm and blues (or rock 'n roll, or rockabilly)—are also rigidly defined, their partisans unwilling to admit blood kinship with "pop" music except possibly by sneaky transfusion or illegitimate cousinship.

For the purposes of this book, which is more concerned with the business of songs than with their quality or classification, popular music will generally mean all—or most—music which is played, sung and enjoyed by people in a spirit of refreshment rather than reverence. Songs which have come down to us as an American legacy lived and breathed uncorseted in their own time, before time's passage honored them with labels. Just as today's precious antiques were yesterday's everyday furnishings and appliances, today's venerated art, folk and spiritual songs were yesterday's everyday music—popular music.

This country had songs that have been preserved, one way or another, and passed down as American, long before it had tradition, laws or even a permanent name. Like everything else American, the music was—and still is—a composite inheritance. Into our musical melting pot have gone the stock and seasonings of the world's ingredient cultures, flavored with a richness of lively new rhythms and an infusion of daring new ideas. In the American wilderness, men in sparse and often temporary colonies sang songs of homesickness for Holland, Spain, France, Sweden. In and around Jamestown, Virginia, a few high-born Londoners and greater numbers of less gently born but equally opportunity-seeking settlers sang the Elizabethan ballads and madrigals that reminded them of home. In New England a small band of refugees, determined to carve a homeland out of the formidable landscape, sang of thankfulness and faith—in God, in the new land itself, in the startling concept of freedom.

Before 1700, popular songs in the new world included lullabies and tuneful legends, drinking songs, love ballads and hymns. By 1770, popular music in thirteen American colonies struggling toward unity had added a brisk martial beat as men and women sang of impending revolt. Poetic patriots—not songwriters—borrowed melodies from the England whose tax demands they detested and wrote inflammatory songs of rebellion, urging Americans to join hands and respond to the call of liberty. Lyrical loyalists—not songwriters—countered with anti-revolutionary songs and parodies which mocked the idea of liberty for a land of greenhorns.

But then, as now, the scope of popular music could not be confined. The smell of cannon powder was in the air, but so were tender murmurings of love, praise for pretty girls, odes to homely objects and tribute for national heroes. In eighteenth-century drawing rooms and wayside taverns were heard lyrics about "Young Molly Who Lives at the Foot of the Hill" (better known as "The Lass with the Delicate Air"), "Sally in Our Alley," "The Spinning Wheel" and "Adams and Washington."

The subject matter for American songs hasn't changed very

much in three hundred and fifty years. Songs are written about everything and everybody, but they are written somewhat differently now, with motives that are less patriotic and poetic than they are pecuniary. One notable dissimilarity between the popular music of Revolutionary days and that of the atomic age is that America's earliest songwriters were amateurs. They could hardly have been anything else. There was little opportunity for professionalism in song writing because nobody made much money at song publishing, except possibly some English export firms. When songs were published here they were usually printed in newspapers and magazines or, rarely, in book collections.

Before and even after 1800, American "songwriters" were for the most part lyricists only, borrowing their melodies without apology from the old countries across the ocean. Our first acknowledged total songwriter, credited with original melodies as well as lyrics, was Francis Hopkinson (1737-1791), a signer of the Declaration of Independence, a representative from New Jersey in the Continental Congress and, later, a judge of the United States District Court. He, too, was not shy about appropriating existing melodies for his own words. He did compose and author a series of colonial love songs, but he also wrote a variant lyric to the tune now known as "Yankee Doodle," whose melodic origin is still vigorously disputed among musical historians. Claims are made that the tune is "indisputably" Dutch, Spanish, Hungarian, Irish, English, Scottish. For all that is known, the Russians may claim it, too. But "Yankee Doodle," whose familiar words have not been established, either, as the work of any one writer, American or otherwise, is called America's first popular song.

It is a contemporary of Francis Hopkinson who probably deserves to be cast in the role of America's first popular songwriter. This is William Billings (1746-1800) who certainly bore a more recognizable likeness to many of the modern-day song-writing clan than did the scholarly and dignified Mr. Hopkinson, who composed measured pieces for the harpsichord as well as other works reflecting his considerable accomplishments as an educated musician. Billings was what would today be called a character.

A rough and boisterous fellow, Billings looked into his heart, not his intellect, for music. Like many currently successful song-writers, he was somewhat lacking in musical education and he was, moreover, an aggressive and self-confident promoter of his own work. He was the prototype of the modern song-plugger.

A Boston-born tanner of hides by trade, Billings also served the New England community where he lived and worked with his enthusiastic and peremptory command: "Come on, everybody, *sing!*" His great vitality and irrepressible spirits found the colonial tradition of versified psalmody too tame and colorless for his liking, so he invented a rugged sort of musical counterpoint to which he cheerfully wrote his own ardent texts. He called his compositions "fuguing tunes." These hymns may not have been orthodox in either form or content but they were, to say the least, energetic.

It was the custom of early American writers to preface collections of their songs with laudatory prose descriptions of their contents. Billings' literary introductions sparkled with compelling "act-now-before-it's-too-late" phrases. He did not hesitate to extol his fuguing tunes as better, more powerful and effective than rival "old slow tunes." Although the prim elders of his time were horrified by the wild sounds he unleashed, the younger and more adventurous were delighted with his rocking, rolling rhythms.

The beginnings and borrowings that were American popular music enjoyed a leisurely life. We cannot possibly know accurately how many hearings any given song received in the years which preceded the tabulation systems devised by modern performance-rights societies, but it is reasonable to assume that songs were repeated endlessly, each in its own time and for years after its newness wore off. Those which survive in performance today from the colonial years are not necessarily the only ones worth preserving; it may be that only these were the songs whose bloom endured, or were published in permanent collections, or were distributed on paper not subsequently burned or thrown away.

A song introduced in Boston or Philadelphia in the early 1800s or before, had little mobility or grazing range. Its transportation from one place to another depended on itinerant musicians and casual wayfarers who traveled the long distances by sea packet or river boat, by land coach, horseback or afoot, stopping off along the way to perform in theaters and taverns. Then as later, a song was not properly "popular" until it was brought home to be worn into familiarity by frequent association.

Families gathered around the parlor harpsichord or organ, imported from England, to sing the decorous ballads of the era. In wayside inns and drinking places, earthier and more vigorous singing was joined, voices deepening and warming as they were lubricated by lusty brews.

It was in a tavern that the first public performance of "The Star-Spangled Banner" is supposed to have taken place. As most people know, what are now the words of our national anthem were written by a thirty-five-year-old poet and lawyer under highly dramatic circumstances. Few songs have ever been so spectacularly conceived under the stress of a man's emotion.

In September of 1814, toward the end of "Mr. Madison's War," Francis Scott Key was sent under a flag of truce to a ship of the British fleet off Baltimore to plead for the release of one Dr. William Beanes. The good doctor, it appeared, had got himself arrested after an exuberant spree during which he "captured" a few English soldiers.

The physician's patients preferred to have him home, in Upper Marlborough, Maryland, and his friends chose Key as their cause-pleader. With President Madison's permission to approach the enemy in the doctor's behalf, Key managed to persuade the British to release their now sobered prisoner and the two men were put aboard an anchored boat, from whose deck they watched the bombardment of Fort McHenry.

The sight of the American flag valiantly flying atop this battered fort in the early light of the following dawn roused in Key's heart a fierce pride. He was so moved by the sounds and sights of grim battle and by the fort's staunch resistance that he began to formulate a poem while watching the scene, its words to be written down later when he reached his lodgings ashore. He called his poem "The Defense of Fort McHenry," but a new and enduring title was soon discovered in the lines of the lyric itself.

The tune to which Key decided to set his poem was one already known by several other titles, the most popular being "To Anacreon in Heaven." So named, it was the theme song of a London society founded in honor of the Greek lyric poet, Anacreon, a gentleman much addicted—in verse, at any rate—to wine and women. The actual origin of the melody is still hotly disputed, claimed by a number of authorities to be the work of an equal number of composers. Whether deserved or not, credit for composing the melody of our national anthem is usually given to Massachusetts-born John Stafford Smith who voyaged to England in the mid-eighteenth century to continue his musical studies. While there, where he lived out his long life, he presumably either wrote, borrowed or adapted the tune to which the Anacreontic Society's president, Ralph Tomlinson, wrote (around 1775) a number of jolly stanzas.

Generally accepted acknowledgment for arranging "The Star-Spangled Banner" into its now familiar form is given to a Baltimore music-store proprietor named Thomas Carr, but by all accounts the melody had been well known and liked on both sides of the Atlantic for at least forty years before it became the vehicle for Mr. Key's stirring lyric. Key, himself, had used the same melody for an earlier poem of his own writing.

It could scarcely happen today, with our jealously enforced copyright laws, but in 1814 it was possible for two Baltimore newspapers to print the words of a poem and say to readers, "Sing this to the well-known tune, 'To Anacreon in Heaven.' " It was even possible to reproduce both words and music with no more than a casual mention of their source.

Sing the words the people did, and to the appropriated melody. They sang it in taverns and theaters in and around Baltimore, then farther afield, and they carried it home with them on their lips and in their hearts. In the years which followed the end of the War of 1812, "The Star-Spangled Banner" was a popular new patriotic song.

To those of us who have since childhood stood at attention, hands over hearts or at salute when the first notes are sounded, it seems incredible that this song, although soon adopted by the United States Army and Navy, was not officially designated as our national anthem until President Wilson issued an executive order in 1916, and not actually legalized until the order was confirmed by an Act of Congress in 1931.

Although local songwriters' bemusement with patriotism, politics, battle victories, lusty humor and current events received a fair share of crowd acceptance in the early years of the nineteenth century, polite parlor performers still fancied imported songs. America's favorite lyricist was Ireland's Thomas Moore. As set to suitable English or Irish melodies, his "Believe Me if All those Endearing Young Charms," "The Harp that Once, Thro' Tara's Halls," "The Minstrel Boy" and " 'Tis the Last Rose of Summer," were all hit songs before 1820. They were published in London.

The year 1823 can be marked as a popular-music milestone for America, because two things happened to bring music closer to the place where it has lived amiably ever since—home. The first was the establishment, in Boston, of America's first local piano manufacturing firm. Jonas Chickering made it possible for many Americans to own home instruments without the expense and waiting entailed by shipment from overseas. More pianos in American homes meant a greater market for published music. The second event was the publication, in Philadelphia and London, of a wildly popular song—"Home, Sweet Home."

"Home, Sweet Home" has been cherished possessively by succeeding generations who hold that the song is as American as New England clam chowder, but not even its words were grown on home soil. They were written in London by an American-born but expatriate actor and playright, John Howard Payne, for an Italian air adapted by the English composer, Sir Henry Bishop. The melody had first appeared in Bishop's opera *Clari*, *or the Maid of Milan* which in turn had been adapted from a French play.

There is an earlier date that is even more significant to the incubation, growth and prosperity of popular music in America than the 1823 publisher's imprint on "Home, Sweet Home" (George Bacon, Philadelphia, who neglected to credit Payne for the lyric). The date is 1789, the first Wednesday in March, which is the day on which the Constitution of the United States, duly ratified by the requisite nine fledgling commonwealths, was placed in effect as the law of the land.

The Constitution's significance to musical America is explicit in Article I, Section 8 of the original seven articles and also in the selfsame Fifth Amendment which, in recent years, has been so useful to a number of citizens who are not even remotely connected with music.

Before we had a constitution—which is to say, a government— there could be no valid national laws, hence no true copyrights. The lack of copyright protection, of course, made it risky for songwriters to submit their efforts to publishers who, in their turn, could not easily prevent other publishers from capitalizing on the works.

Article I, Section 8 gave impetus to our first statute concerned with copyright and it was modeled on the first English copyright act of 1710. Before the passage of this British act, the only protection an author had was one implied by common law, which forbade the publication of his original work without his permission. The moment an author granted such permission, however, the work passed entirely out of his control.

The earnest, frequently quarrelsome states' delegates to the Constitutional Convention, in drawing up the articles and amendments of our first federal laws, agreed that copyright protection was desirable. Therefore, Congress was empowered to "promote the progress of science and useful arts by securing for limited times to authors and inventors the exclusive rights to their respective writings and discoveries." The Fifth Amendment further provided that private property could not be taken for public use without just compensation.

It was the Constitution's protective provisions (for fourteen-year renewable copyrights) on which American songwriters and music publishers wobbled along precariously until 1909, when a more comprehensive copyright statute was enacted.

Nevertheless, the original Constitutional protection of authorship and composition made it profitable, for the first time, for American business firms to publish music. They embarked on this enterprise tentatively, often motivated by impulses that were perhaps more literary than commercial, and certainly they did not even dream of the industrial empire to which popular songs would one day belong. Some of our early nineteenth-century popular music was printed by American newspaper and book publishers and by specialists with facilities for reproducing musical notation, but much of it was not published at all.

Not published—in the sense of being submitted as manuscripts, edited, printed and circulated through sales or other means of distribution—were treasures of words and music which, to give them a general name, we know as American folk songs. These songs were not written down. Usually, the people who created and performed them would not have known how to write down c-a-t. Our folk tunes are pungent with the smell of freshly turned earth and of the sweating men who labored on the land. They are regional in flavor and expressed in colloquial accents. Typical of the American tradition for assimilation, they are stepping stones on which we can pick our way along the bright stream of naturalization.

From the several topographically different sections of the first settlements in the New World have come down to us distinctive songs bristling with clues as to their birthplaces and smudged with the thumbprints of the people who lived there. Just as in William Billings' hearty New England fuguing tunes can be heard the rough courage of untrained men who would crudely fight a rugged war, so can be heard in some of the folk songs of our southern mountain regions echoes of an old diction. "Hillbilly tunes" may be ever so quaintly and colloquially American, but they owe a good deal of their source material and sometimes their musical form, if not their semantics, to Shakespeare's England.

The mountains of New York State, Vermont, Kentucky and Tennessee resounded with local song-fests and play-parties. Natural rivers and man-made canals accumulated people along their banks and the people sang about their work and recreation and superstitions.

Out of an unhappy situation in our southern states came glorious songs of great beauty and variety, a gift from people to whom music was like a pulse in the blood. Sometimes these songs were spiritual in quality, seeking from a faraway heaven the solace denied on earth. Sometimes they were closely human and related to man's work and pleasures. At times they were funny.

Americans sailed the seas and waterways for food, fuel and commerce. They dug mines, felled trees, picked the plentiful crops of a fertile soil. They plodded in horse-drawn wagons across the plains and hills. They rushed out to discover gold, to gamble, to settle down, to land in jail. They drove railroad spikes and traveled noisily over the roadbed faster than they had ever traveled before. They strung the Western Union wire. They fought Indians and they fought each other. The country was stretching and its reaches were studded with spontaneous song, because whatever people did they sang about.

This was the music made by our folks. At times as uncouth and ungrammatical as the people who sang it, folk music tells tall tales and true ones, captures the sounds of pickaxe and mallet on wood and stone and metal, strains at ropes hauling sail and barge or hanging the careless horse thief, glistens with sweat purpling dark skins, celebrates the companionship of indulgent saloon ladies, croons babies to sleep in rough cradles.

The music made *for* our folks, meantime, was conceived somewhat differently by the purveyors of popular music, although much of it was bagged like nuggets from the raw vein and rubbed with commercialism until it shone with a slick new luster.

In 1828, a strolling actor-singer-comedian named Thomas Dartmouth Rice ("Daddy" Rice, in his poster billing) chanced upon a Baltimore stable attendant whose antics as he cleaned and curried horses fascinated the actor. The ragged little man sang to himself as he worked, the words of his song a stream of autobiographical comment. At intervals, he repeated a refrain: "I wheel about, I twist about, I do just so. Every time I turn about I jump Jim Crow." At the end of each chorus, the stable hand enlivened his performance with a hop, shuffle and jig.

"Daddy" Rice studied the Negro's actions until he could duplicate his foot-tappings and shoulder-twistings. He memorized the melody and copied down the words. The comedian had a new act to add to his repertoire, a characterization of a humorsome personality familiar to the residents of the Baltimore locality where he introduced it, wearing tattered clothes and blackening his face in caricature of the stable hand. His act stopped the show, a fact he put down to people's delight with a local joke. He soon found, however, that the appeal of his new specialty was not limited to Baltimore audiences. "Jim Crow"—the song and the blackface act—was an instantaneous hit in other cities as well. Rice enlarged his repertoire to include other similar routines.

This was a new kind of show business, and the song was a new kind of song. Music publishers, catching on to an idea they have held dear ever since, capitalized on the new trend with a rash of imitations, including "Pickaninny Nig," "Ching A Ring Chaw," "Clare de Kitchen" and "Zip Coon" (now known as "Turkey in the Straw"). Certain modern-day comedians are only following a time-honored precedent when they steal each other's gags; for, in imitation of "Daddy" Rice, entertainers of the 1830s began to haunt slave quarters for songs and dances to parody, to blacken their faces and costume themselves in odd garments—all calculated to caricature that amusing fellow, the underprivileged Negro.

From the first performance of "Daddy" Rice's entertainment

discovery, it was only a few steps and fifteen years to the beginnings of the American minstrel show. In 1843, the pattern was laid down by a quartet of players who called themselves "The Original Virginia Minstrels." The four included a tambourine player, a banjoist, a bones rattler and a violinist, and their act was played in dark make-up achieved by rubbing their faces with ham fat. According to one legend, it was this practice that gave rise to stage vocabulary's adoption of the word "ham" to describe an actor. Another legend, however, states that the theater's connotation of the word evolved from a biblical reference to Noah's son, Ham, because of his post-diluvian domain, Egypt, a land of dark-skinned people. Stage performers who darkened their skins were called "sons of Ham."

In "The Original Virginia Minstrels" quartet, the violinist was Daniel Decatur Emmett, who later achieved immortality as the composer of the piece now known as "Dixie," which he wrote as a walk-around piece to close a show with which he was connected. Although claimed by the South and used as a patriotic song by the Confederate States during the Civil War, "Dixie" was written almost two years before that war, by a Northerner, and had its first success well above the Mason-Dixon line.

Following the common practice of this early day in the history of the popular-music business, Emmett sold his song outright in 1860, when it was published as "I Wish I Was in Dixie's Land." He himself said he received $500 for the copyright, but other sources have placed his payment closer to $300. Emmett was forty-four years old when he composed his hit, and he lived to be eighty-nine. For forty-five years he was to hear his song played and sung everywhere he went, with enthusiastic embellishments and often with lyrics he never wrote. Other songwriters plagiarized or changed his words and claimed to be the composers, and at least a dozen publishers disregarded the original copyright and brought out profitable editions of their own. While all of this may have been gratifying to the heart of an old trouper, the memory of that total fee of $500 (or $300) must have been irritating.

The writing and publishing of the nation's songs were not yet what might be called big business in America, but in the years which preceded the Civil War there was one young man who established himself as the first in a long line of songwriters to make both a living and a lasting reputation from popular music. From 1844 (he was eighteen when he published his first song) to his death at the age of thirty-eight in 1864, Stephen Collins Foster turned out in the neighborhood of two hundred songs. A great many more of these were contemporary popular hits that have survived as the all-time Foster favorites everybody knows.

While the money he received during his most productive years was in no way ample or even fair payment for our handsome legacy of Stephen Foster melodies, the songwriter was not, as so many later insisted, the victim of unscrupulous music publishers. We have become so commercial and property-conscious in our thinking about popular music that we forget the facts about most nineteenth-century business practices. "Imagine! Foster sold the rights to 'Oh! Susanna' for *ten dollars*," we are told. "Never made another penny out of it, and the thieving publishers made millions."

Very possibly young Foster, at the age of twenty-two, did sell "Oh! Susanna" for ten dollars. It has been said that the song was included in a group of three he mailed out to various publishers, finally receiving $30 for the trio and being overjoyed to get it. But it is also said that "Oh! Susanna" was among a batch of untidy manuscripts the songwriter *gave* to a Louisville publisher, W. C. Peters, when he was trying desperately to break away from the hated bookkeeping career chosen for him by his family.

A persistent legend has grown up around the life story of Stephen Foster, in which he is pictured as a victimized genius forced into dark ways and driven too early to a pauper's grave by ruthless, profiteering publishers. In spite of the legend, Foster was not a rejected prophet, unhonored and unsung, who was "discovered" only after death. Plenty of people in his own time recognized his talents and were glad to pay him for them in cash and tribute. More than one admiring publisher carried him on the cuff, always ready and willing to hand over advances for songs yet to be written. Irresponsible and improvident, Foster was usually in debt to his publishers on financial arrangements that would be shocking today but were acceptable in the 1850s. Although he never came even close to getting what his songs would eventually earn for others, he was paid adequately by the reckonings of his era and profession.

Royalties of about $1,400 a year were not munificent for such songs as "Old Folks at Home," "My Old Kentucky Home" and other Foster classics, but this amount was by no means in the low-income bracket a hundred years ago, when rents were as low as three dollars a month and a seven-course dinner cost twenty-five cents. If he were living and writing his two hundred songs today, Stephen Foster would be a very rich man, because his earnings would be secured by protective copyright laws and performance-rights societies which did not exist in his lifetime. Whether or not he would be a happy man might be as uncertain now as it was then.

America's first full-fledged prolific writer of popular song hits was only thirty-eight years old when he was found, mortally ill, in a sordid flophouse in New York's Bowery section and taken to Bellevue Hospital, where he died. His death, as well as his life, has given a century of writers a mother-lode of source material for pathos. No imaginary scene need be added to the one which actually occurred when a police officer searched the ragged clothing of a man routinely described on the police station blotter as a "vagrant" and discovered a cheap purse containing thirty-eight cents and a soiled bit of paper penciled with the words, "Dear friends and gentle hearts."

Foster's legacy to popular music in the United States included more than just his output of salable, long-lived songs. His natural talent for expressing simple thoughts in singable melodies became a pattern for the songwriters who followed him. "The Foster touch" was sought after by imitators and publishers alike, and his songs' ability to make a great deal of money (for the publishers) opened up new vistas in the business of song publication.

When the Civil War broke out Foster was still alive and under obligation to a number of publishers, who judged that a competent songwriter should be as capable of turning out timely patriotic tunes as ballads and what he himself was pleased to call "Ethiopian songs." Obligingly, two years before his death, Foster wrote "We Are Coming, Father Abraham, 30,000 More" and "We've a Million in the Field." They did not match his previous successes.

Foster's ineptness at writing war songs to order and the Confederate soldiers' adoption of Emmett's popular "Dixie" as their very own prompted publishers to look to other songwriters for hits with a Union flavor. Several complied, and many of the fine songs written during—or about—the Civil War are still important to the literature of the nation's popular music.

One man combined songwriting with his own publishing effort. George Frederick Root, the writer of a number of successful songs, including "The Battle Cry of Freedom," "Just Before the Battle, Mother!" and "Tramp! Tramp! Tramp!" was a partner in the Chicago music publishing concern of Root & Cady which published the output of another brilliant contemporary songwriter, Henry Clay Work ("Marching Through Georgia" and the nonbelligerent "Grandfather's Clock," revived regularly by present-day recording artists). Competing with Root & Cady was another prominent music firm, Oliver Ditson & Company, of Boston, which had a tremendous hit in "The Battle Hymn of the Republic," whose famous lyricist had to be satisfied with honors in lieu of royalties and whose original composer, so far as is definitely known, received neither.

The stirring melody of "The Battle Hymn of the Republic" had earlier been sung as a religious camp-meeting rouser, "Glory, Glory, Hallelujah" and, as well, with words solemnizing the hanging of abolitionist-agitator John Brown. Although the melody is generally attributed to William Steffe who composed a number of camp-meeting hymns, it is believed by many to have been sung by Negro congregations long before it was written down.

There is no doubt, however, about the authorship of the words which have immortalized the borrowed melody. They were written with emotion by Mrs. Julia Ward Howe, the celebrated author and social reformer, soon after she had seen an army of tired but determined young Union soldiers go into battle near Washington singing, as they marched, "John Brown's Body" with its morbid lyrics and its pulsing chorus of hallelujahs.

Lax and untidy, the copyright laws of Civil War days were not often invoked on behalf of the authors or composers of the songs people sang. Publishers felt free to print and sell copies of song poems or music without worrying unduly about whose property they were. Half a dozen publishers did a thriving business with the battle hymn's music, set with half a dozen variant lyrics, and the Ditson company did extremely well with Mrs. Howe's poem, for which she had received four dollars when it was printed in the *Atlantic Monthly*.

When the Civil War ended, commercial profits in stage libretto and song publishing mounted, and a number of music-minded men established businesses to which they attracted increasing scores of topnotch composers and authors. The works of these successful post-bellum popular songwriters have passed into oblivion, seldom if ever heard outside of relatively obscure period-piece performances in salute to their time. Among these all-but-forgotten songwriters is William Shakespeare Hays who wrote upwards of three hundred immensely popular songs, few of them remembered now except by historians of popular-music publishing and a few program directors for glee club repertories.

The Irving Berlin of his day—in mood and quantity, if not in memorability and quality—Hays wrote song after song about home, love, log cabins, nature, Mother, places, weather and girls named Mollie, Nora and Nellie. They were enthusiastically published by J. L. Peters Company. During Hays' long and varied career as newspaperman and river boat pilot as well as songwriter, the aggregate sheet music sales of his prodigious output are said to have reached the astonishing figure of twenty million copies, some of his songs selling individually as many as 350,000.

Another great hit-writer of the period whose work as a lyricist for popular songs is forgotten did, however, leave a larger legacy to the American theater. Edward (Ned) Harrigan not only wrote words to the David Braham melodies which captured the ears and hearts of people during the 1870s and 1880s, but he and his young partner, Tony Hart, also developed for the American stage its first real musical comedy format.

Harrigan and Hart were producers and performers, and their names were boldly featured on billboards outside the theaters which drew crowds of enthusiastic fans to their rowdy Irish-American musical farces. It was Braham's melodies all America whistled for a while—"The Mulligan Guard," "Patrick's Day Parade," "Danny by My Side," published by William A. Pond. The glib, shamrock quality of the American team's tunes competed successfully for audiences and customers with the songs of two Englishmen named Gilbert and Sullivan. Now, of course, the songs of Harrigan and Braham are scarcely known to a music-loving America, while the British operettas are not only regularly performed but are also determinedly perpetuated by dedicated societies.

Music publishers were scattered all over the country in the last quarter of the nineteenth century. The great Chicago fire had wiped out that city's successful firm of Root & Cady, but C. M. Cady continued in business for several years. Boston had Oliver Ditson & Company and John F. Perry & Company, the latter firm doing the main bulk of its business with the beautiful songs of James A. Bland. In Philadelphia, Harry Coleman published the marching songs of John Philip Sousa until the composer switched to the John Church Company of Cincinnati. This firm also published the works of dialect comedian Joseph K. ("Fritz") Emmett who wrote, among other things, the famous "Lullaby," with its familiar "Go to sleep, my ba-hay-by."

But it was soon to be made clear that New York, the country's theatrical center, was the fitting location for a totally new kind of music business. There were several music firms already in New York, publishing all kinds of music. G. Schirmer and Carl Fischer were there, bringing out songs and scores of old and new music of artistic calibre, much of it imported from abroad. Willis Woodward and Company had established itself as an important specialty house for sprightly ditties of "Ta-ra-ra-*bom*-der-e" lilt, along with more sedate entries. The Pond company was doing fine with its long list of Harrigan and Braham tunes. Thomas and Alex Harms entered the field, publishing (as the firm of T. B. Harms & Company) a lion's share of the stage music of the 1880s and later, and had an 1892 hit with the novelty, "Daddy Wouldn't Buy Me a Bow-Wow," an English import.

But new names—young names—were about to make their appearance, and popular music as a separate entity was getting ready to sprint down the uncharted road that led to Tin Pan Alley.

2. *The Road*

Just before and following the bells and whistles which ushered in the year 1900, the emergent industry devoting itself to popular music showed twitchy symptoms of the instability by which it has been characterized ever since.

A new breed of songwriters developed, amiably pandering to the mutating moods of the era by writing songs that varied from mawkishly sentimental to slyly salacious. A new breed of publishers developed also, standing in relation to the songwriters as indulgent nursemaids, jealous guardians and mentors or, unhappily, as robber barons and receivers of stolen goods.

The nation's economy was expanding along with its population, and people were in holiday spirits. They wanted to be entertained. They accepted with equal relish the tear-jerking ballads incongruously sung by rouged barroom hoydens, the pure stanzas trilled on concert or operetta stage and the rowdy, ribald rondelays shouted across variety hall footlights.

Tunesmithing was beginning to resemble a full-fledged profession, with most of the era's durable hits written by stage and cabaret performers who plunged into song writing to provide themselves with exclusive material for their acts. Many an entertainer's success as a songwriter was a by-product, not the chief ingredient, of his occupation, and many of the songs so written were exploited by publishers who neglected to share the profits from them with their writers. Terms of payment were so loose and untidy that several songwriters set up shop for themselves out of rebellion against publishers who haggled over price, drove sharp bargains and were vague about royalties.

One of the first to recognize the value of publishing his own songs was Paul Dresser whose ballads, written while he was a singing end-man in the Billy Rice Minstrels, brought him little return at the same time they enriched his publishers. He became a partner in the publishing firm of Howley, Haviland & Dresser which published, among other great hits of the day, his "On the Banks of the Wabash."

Another was Charles K. Harris, who established his own publishing firm when he was hardly more than a boy bellhop and freelance banjo player, because he got mad at his own publishers, the Witmark brothers. The cause of his anger was the receipt of his first royalty check for a song the Witmarks did not much care for and, presumably, did not try very hard to sell. The check was in the amount of 85 cents and, according to the publishers, just about a fair exchange for the Harris ditty, "When the Sun Has Set."

Young Mr. Harris, however, took a dim view of the scornful treatment he was getting, and so he promptly went into business for himself, to the amusement and dire predictions of his estranged publishers. In about a year's time, the Witmarks were to regret having offended the hotheaded youngster, for in 1892 he composed, wrote, copyrighted and published "After the Ball."

The Witmarks' chagrin mounted as Harris followed this sensation of the '90s with a number of other hits, including "Break the News to Mother." This was a song Harris had written earlier without much success; hastily revamped at the proper time, it sold wildly during the Spanish-American War.

Writing—and publishing—a different sort of song was Carrie Jacobs Bond, author-composer of "Just A-Wearyin' for You,"

"A Perfect Day" and that melodic guest of almost every wedding, "I Love You Truly."

Mrs. Bond, a widow who turned to proprietorship of a students' boardinghouse after her husband's death left her without funds, was well educated in the artistic fields considered appropriately feminine in the years between 1895 and 1910. To supplement her meager income, she wrote a number of songs which she offered for sale to music publishers. These gentlemen, their attention on the success of less well-constructed ballads and novelties, considered her work much too arty for popular appeal. One or two, out of chivalry toward a struggling widow-lady, grudgingly purchased a few at the rate of $25 apiece. This, Mrs. Bond decided, was not very profitable.

With the financial assistance of a neighborhood druggist, Mrs. Bond invested in materials and equipment to turn her parlor into a publishing office. She not only wrote and composed her songs, but also designed and illustrated their title pages and arranged personal bookings for song recitals as the quickest and surest way of introducing them to the public. They were immediately and enormously popular, selling in the millions of copies and privately mortifying the publishers who believed that a high-class lady writer of high-class songs had no place in the music business.

It was increasingly evident that popular songs would not permit themselves to be limited by subject matter, rhythm or style. Songs of all kinds found ready listeners and purchasers, and more and more publishers entered the field, bringing out sentimental ballads, hymns, dialect songs, lengthy song-stories and shorter, coarser ditties with undertones of slapstick humor. Folks continued to wipe misty eyes as they contemplated the sad burden in the baggage coach ahead, but they brightened considerably at the prospect of a hot time in the old town tonight.

Making determined forays into music-publishing ventures were young men who were drawn to a glamorous way to make a living, with colorful entertainers as their companions and the glittering world of show business their territory. Their names have been left as a shining legacy to many firms still active on the modern scene—Marks, Feist, Shapiro, Bernstein, Von Tilzer, Remick, Harms, Mills.

But among the reasons for going into the business of music publishing was the rather unique one motivating the House of Witmark.

The Witmark brothers launched their now celebrated firm because one of its principals, age eleven, won a toy printing press as a school prize for arithmetic. This auspicious event occurred on the same day that an older brother, age fourteen, got fired from a detested job.

"Witmark Brothers, Printers" specialized at first in odd-job printing, and the work they turned out was not always handsome —or paid for.

There were five Witmark boys. Isidore was the eldest. His name was really Isidor, but he added the "e" when someone pointed out that there were an unlucky thirteen letters in Isidor Witmark.

Isidore wrote many of the firm's successful songs in later years, and was always its guiding spirit. Julius was next in age, and he was to become famous on the stage as "The Wonderful Boy Soprano." It was Brother Jay whose mathematical proficiency had earned the boys their initial publishing equipment. Finally, there were Ed (Adolph) and Frank, both of whom also sang professionally and shared in the firm's activities. The "M." of the corporation's "M. Witmark and Sons" of its later naming, stands for Marcus, the boys' proud father whose signature was required on the corporation documents because his sons were legally underage.

The idea of publishing music in addition to advertising cards and announcements was born as the result of a music publisher's refusal to share with Julius the profits from a song he popularized as the Wonderful Boy Soprano.

In his reminiscences, *From Ragtime to Swingtime* (published 1939; now out of print), Isidore wrote:

"For [Julius Witmark] to sing a song was to start the song on the road to possible fortune. . . . Julie had been promised by

[Willis] Woodward an interest in the song, 'Always Take Mother's Advice.' At the end of the season, however, he found it as hard to collect this promise from the publisher as he had found it to collect his ten-dollar weekly salary from Mike Leavitt." *

Such omission of payoff so enraged Isidore that he decided, "If a song-publisher tried to take advantage of Julie's personal magnetism as vocalist and living advertisement for sheet music, he and his brothers could retaliate by going into the publishing of music on their own."

The few publishers who specialized in popular songs were then located in downtown New York—on the Bowery, and in what is now Greenwich Village, whose northern boundary was and still is Fourteenth Street.

This old street, with its bargain specialty shops and cheap eating places, bears little resemblance now to its exciting past. Down its broad thoroughfare once pranced sleek horses drawing the shiny carriages of New York's elite. Buildings on both sides of the street housed the city's finest theaters, music halls, restaurants and cafés.

On Fourteenth Street, then, the Witmark boys prepared to invade music-publishing circles in protest against the powerful Woodward outfit.

Willis Woodward was outraged by the boys' move and prophesied that the firm whose executives were little more than children would last no more than six months. It was with a certain degree of smugness, therefore, that Isidore later wrote: "A half-century later the Witmark firm was still flourishing. Woodward's had long been a reminiscence of old-time publishers."

With Julius as a vigorous singer of the firm's songs and developing into a picker of hits; Isidore as a keen businessman as well as a "show-doctor"; Jay as a general assistant, and the other boys as performers and enthusiastic boosters, the House of Witmark soon became a titan in the popular-music field. Word got around that the boys had an unbeatable combination going to build suc-

* "Leavitt's Gigantic Minstrels" at Tony Pastor's Theater.

cess for a song, and thousands of original manuscripts of varying merit poured in from eager songwriters all over the country.

As the business prospered and more and more Witmark songs were introduced in New York's theaters by top entertainers of the day, the boys' delighted father became a self-appointed clacque of one. He devised the habit of appearing at theaters with a heavy cane with which he pounded noisily after each rendition of a Witmark publication.

Dispossessed from their Fourteenth Street office by a landlord who found the necessary demonstration of songs a nuisance, and forced out of their second office when the building that contained it was condemned, the Witmarks finally arrived at West Twenty-eighth Street, a location which was soon to give the business they were part of a new and immortal name.

After five active and progressive years on the street later called Tin Pan Alley, the boys found it desirable to move into larger quarters. The move was necessitated not only because of increasing business traffic, but also to make room for a growing bulk of manuscripts and printed music.

Ambitiously, the Witmarks leased an entire converted brownstone house in West Twenty-ninth Street, proceeding to decorate its façade with a fancy name shield and a scroll proclaiming the family motto: "Success Is Work." The motto later became the title of a march composed in its honor by Victor Herbert when his publishers—the Witmarks—erected their own building.

Up the ten stone steps which led to the main office of M. Witmark and Sons were to tread the feet of George M. Cohan, Gus Edwards, Willie and Eugene Howard, Victor Herbert and almost every other luminary of the day who had anything at all to do with music.

The first-floor windows of the brownstone were crowded with the Witmarks' burgeoning display of the popular song sheets they published, but it was in the building's basement that the five brothers took greatest pride. Here was housed the symbol of their vaulting ambitions—The Witmark music library.

Advertising in the vaudeville section of the *New York Dra-*

matic Mirror of September 17, 1898, the firm announced the library as "A New Departure—a New Department." In bold type the Witmarks announced that they had constantly on hand, for sale and to hire, "the *largest* collection of Vocal Concert Numbers and Excerpts in America."

Contemporary publishing firms raised their eyebrows at the exaggeration of the Witmark ad, knowing that the boys were far from having on hand the superlative collection they boasted. Such a collection did exist, however, in the stock of Arthur W. Tams who had a monumental reserve library of classical and semi-classical music, cantatas, oratorios and masses. The Tams Music Library, in the Witmarks' view, was the one to beat. They set out to make good their boast, concentrating for the time being on their "popular" department by signing contracts with as many of the current stage musical writers as they could persuade —among them Victor Herbert, Rudolf Friml, Karl Hoschna and Otto Harbach.

In their zeal to surpass the Tams firm, the Witmarks were frequently accused of encroaching on the older organization's copyright domain. The music-publishing scene was enlivened by a number of hotly contested legal battles over the rental rights of productions both firms had simultaneously and unaccountably acquired.

One such conflict, involving American rights to several German operas, cost the two litigants a total of $50,000. Isidore Witmark does not say in his book who came out ahead in this legal tangle, but he does comment that he and Mr. Tams were not on speaking terms for years following the suit. It may be presumed that the long silence was broken when two million dollars changed hands in 1925 as the Witmarks bought out their long-time rival and finally added to their shelves the coveted collection which justified their earlier claims.

From a toy printing press and the fumbling efforts of boyish enthusiasm, the Witmarks built a musical empire out of the popular music of their day. Time's passage has a way of burnishing homely names until they radiate grandeur. We are likely to forget that many of the names we point to as awesome belonged by simple birthright to humble human beings. We say "Macy's" and think of the world's largest department store, not of the retired sea captain with some pots and pans to sell.

In the music business, the grandiose names of today were the family names of vigorous young men who entered the battle of tune-touting at a time when the fight was joyously joined in Bowery beer halls and side-street saloons. We hear the name of Witmark and visualize a dignified old establishment firmly rooted in respectable tradition, not seeing the five energetic youngsters and their beaming papa who, as the boys grew old enough to shave, held morning conferences while squabbling over razors and soap in the family bathroom.

No Witmark sits behind a desk today in the chrome, glass and wall-to-wall carpeted offices on Madison Avenue. No Harms or Remick either, although all three names are lettered on a single door. The once-competitive firms are now amiably gathered in the embrace of a motion picture studio's holding corporation.

The names of other men who made a thriving American business out of American popular music are still around, too. Some of them represent as much activity as they ever did, some of them represent a residue of royalties for their estates.

Edward B. Marks, whose offices were never very far away from the Witmarks' in the old days, left a son to carry on for him in music-publishing offices now located in New York's Radio City. So did Maurice Shapiro whose son, Elliott, is now a partner in the firm of Shapiro-Bernstein, Inc., as his father was. But these three venerable firms which started out in the '80s and '90s with a common purpose despite their friendly rivalry, now represent three entirely different approaches to today's music business.

In the old days of publishers' nostalgic reminiscences, before music was put into cans, on magnetic wire or vinyl and emitted electronically from mechanical contraptions, the nation's song publishers had a mutual cause and a mutual address. Their cause was living music for live performance, and their address was Tin Pan Alley.

3. *The Alley*

THERE WAS A TIME when you could take a walk along Tin Pan Alley without getting tired. You would get off a horse car at the corner of Twenty-eighth Street and Broadway and start walking toward Fifth Avenue. By the time you reached Number 24 West and the cool, dim recesses of Everard's Café your trip would be over and you could join a gathering of publishers, song-pluggers and songwriters relaxing over five-cent pints of beer.

In the early 1900s as the music industry scrambled for identity most music publishers huddled together along Twenty-eighth Street, occupying offices hastily partitioned off within rows of once-dignified old brownstone houses. These had been the fashionable residences of substantial New York families who never dreamed that the commercial district of the city would ever extend so far uptown.

Abandoned as useless for dwelling purposes, the brownstones were permitted to grow shabby. Silent, reproachful, bereft of warmth and care, they gathered dust and vermin until enterprising realtors stopped trying to sell or rent them as homes and offered them instead to business concerns, at cheap rentals.

Men struggling to establish themselves in the music business doted on cheap rentals. Their trek to Twenty-eighth Street began, attracted by the sounds already emanating from rehearsal rooms and practice studios set up by dancing, vocal and instrumental teachers. Up the steep steps trudged children whose parents had been told of their promising voices, musical talent and natural grace. With them came eager lungs, a variety of stringed, brass, wind and percussion instruments and shiny tap shoes.

Then the music publishers came, making four small cubicles out of every small room and placing in each a secondhand piano, untuned.

On hot summer days, windows were thrown open to catch whatever breezes blew in from the Hudson and East rivers. To the blare of instruments, screech of vocalizing and stamp of dancing feet were added the sounds of composers and song demonstrators perspiringly at work.

Many of the songwriters had a habit of muting their pianos by placing folded newspapers between the strings. This was not done out of consideration for the sensitive ears of the colleagues with whom they shared their warrens, but in order to make it a little more difficult for competitive songwriters loitering outside to steal melodies in the making.

There are three contradictory legends about the formal christening of Tin Pan Alley, but all three have in common the name of Monroe Rosenfeld. One version insists that he coined the name himself. The others admit that he had something to do with it, but that the three little words were first uttered by two other guys.

Rosenfeld was a songwriter. If he had actually written all of the songs he claimed he did, he would hardly have had time to devote to his consuming hobbies—horses, girls and the filling of inside straights. Even his publisher (Edward B. Marks) called him a "melodic kleptomaniac" but kept him around because he was amusing, had a kind of extrasensory perception about hit songs (his own or an unwitting contributor's) and excelled in getting his own tunes performed at the popular downtown bistros.

Rosenfeld did not confine his money-making activities to songwriting, poker playing and horse betting. He also had a literary career. Whenever he was unable to persuade Marks to advance him some money to quiet the demands of his bookie, a poker debt or a current flame, he wrote and sold newspaper articles about the antics of his song-writing cronies.

On a summer day, Rosenfeld was on the prowl for salable copy to include in one of his potboiler articles, his extrasensory perception having recently failed him dramatically at the race track. Scenting a story possibility behind the tremendously popular "Down Where the Wurzburger Flows," he dropped in on its composer and publisher, Harry Von Tilzer, whom he found picking out a tune on a paper-muted piano.

In one version of the legend, Rosenfeld is supposed to have said to Von Tilzer: "That piano sounds like a tin pan. Matter of fact, this whole street sounds like a tin pan alley."

Another version insists that it was Von Tilzer who made the remark, with Rosenfeld quoting it. Variations of the Rosenfeld-Von Tilzer story allow that Rosenfeld *really* said it first, but put it in Von Tilzer's mouth to provide colorful copy for his article.

But according to a small, esoteric group of present-day publishers, neither version is correct. The description of 28th Street as "Tin Pan Alley," they say, was originally given by O. Henry to a lyricist, Stanley Murphy, who sometimes collaborated with Von Tilzer who was visited frequently by Rosenfeld.

O. Henry, Von Tilzer or Rosenfeld, the man who casually gave Tin Pan Alley its indestructible name provided the world with an apt handle that was immediately grasped by the press and public alike and has forever since been attached to the brawling, sputtering cauldron in which America's popular music is brewed.

Tin Pan Alley is no longer a place, and you could not stroll along it unless you were willing to embark on an ambitious walking tour.

If you insist on an itinerary, chart your course by starting in New York. Visit a dozen or so office buildings within a ten-block radius of Fiftieth Street and Broadway, going west to Eighth Avenue and east to Madison. In this area of approximately one square mile you can drop in on a thousand music publishers, give or take a few.

Now go to Chicago's Loop section to see another few hundred publishers.

Your next major stop is Los Angeles. In downtown L.A. and from Hollywood and Vine to a few buildings along the Sunset Strip you can chat with about three hundred publishers, although most of these represent the West Coast branches of firms you've already visited in New York and Chicago. Don't skip the movie studios, where high-salaried songwriters are applying their art to sound track which will be published in New York.

Nashville, Tennessee, and Springfield, Missouri, are interesting excursions to take, especially if you are seeking the major sources of country, Western and mountain music.

Philadelphia, these days, is an important music-publishing center, and so is Boston. In recent years, a few large Texas cities have also made contributions to the music business, most of them supplying the nation with what the trade calls "Bible Belt" songs.

From its early beginnings on a single New York street less than sixty years ago, Tin Pan Alley has become a national highway. There is, however, a way of seeing a representative cross-section of the thoroughfare without ever going outside the main entrance of one Broadway building.

Halfway between Forty-ninth and Fiftieth Streets on the west side of Broadway there is an eleven-story structure whose pediment proclaims it to be the Brill Building. There are three elevators to carry you to the floors above street level, but if you want to feel akin to the music business you'll take an elevator to the top and then use the stairs.

On each floor of the Brill Building there are about twenty doors facing the corridors. This does not mean that there are a mere twenty music publishing firms per floor. There are well over three hundred music publishers listed on the Brill Building's directory, which means that many of the rental suites are subdivided to accommodate more than one business. Not all of the subdivided offices contain competitive firms, although some do.

For purposes of taxation and classification and because of a tense situation created by the existence of two mutually hostile performance-rights societies (ASCAP and BMI) it is expedient for many publishers to split their business log into affiliated splinters. Also, the catalogs of publishing firms acquired over the years are usually preserved intact under the names of the original copyright owners. At the last count, a single firm of publishers in the building lists twenty-five ASCAP and ten BMI affiliates.

The public telephone booths on the street floor near the cigar and newspaper stand accommodate several more "firms," for the Brill Building is claimed as an address by many more people than are paying rent. "Meet you in front of my office, the Brill Building" is a bit of self-deception practiced by hundreds of daydreamers, including swarms of amateur songwriters who yearn to breathe the same air as the publishers they can't get in to see.

Aside from its bulging tenantry of music-publishing firms, the Brill Building also leases space to a variety of allied concerns. Artists' representatives have offices there, as do concert managers, publicists, dance bands and booking agents.

Because of its strategic location in the heart of New York's theater district, the Brill Building has attracted to its ground floor space two high-class eating places. One of these—Jack Dempsey's—is a favorite of fight fans and tourists. The other, The Turf, is where a number of professional songwriters and their publishers gather to eat, drink, swallow tranquilizers, complain and swap lies.

Further up the street, near Fiftieth, is a branch of Hector's cafeteria chain. Here, not in The Turf, is where you will find the peripatetic and unrecognized would-be songwriters who seem to spend their lifetimes in the Brill Building, seldom seeing the light of day and *never* seeing a publisher. They start on the top floor and work their way down to street level, collecting rebuffs. They pass The Turf slowly, looking hungrily through the large windows before slouching wearily along to Hector's. A lot of coffee is sold in that cafeteria, which does not exactly discourage the clientele of nomadic amateur songwriters but does charge a nickel extra for a cup unless it is ordered with food. The amateur hordes apparently do their eating elsewhere, but Hector's profits on coffee must be enormous.

If long-time tenants of the Brill Building will examine their old leases they will find, in Paragraph 10, the following stipulation:

"No tenant shall make, or permit to be made, any unseemingly [sic] or disturbing noises or interfere with occupants of this or neighboring buildings or premises or those having business with them whether by the use of any musical instrument, radio, talking machine, unmusical noise, whistling, singing or in any other way."

Obviously, the injunction is not enforced. If someone decided to make a test case of it, the Brill Building might find itself empty overnight.

There was no Brill Building when Tin Pan Alley earned its title, and remarkably few of the three-hundred-odd firms who occupy it were in existence when the music business was in resounding residence on West 28th Street and invented the phenomenon known as "song-plugging."

4. *The Big Plug*

WHEN TIN PAN ALLEY was the hub-bub of the music business,
its publishers were hardly recognizable as belonging to the honorable estate of publishing. They had none of the traditions and
few of the dignities associated with book, magazine or even
newspaper publishers. Their offices were dingy, unappetizing
rooms in which the chief furnishings were battered pianos,
scarred counters and poker tables. When a music publisher
wanted to talk to one of his writers, he usually had to hunt him
down in a saloon and sober him up.

But the greatest difference between music and any other kind
of publishing was in the method used to attract sales. The music
publishers had to expose their products entirely, and free of
charge, before anyone was willing to buy them. They could not
entice customers with provocative descriptions of a song's message. They had to give away the whole plot. Even then, no
amount of persuasive advertising could convince anyone that—
for example—Joseph W. Stern's "You're Not the Only Pebble on
the Beach," was a better or more desirable song than Witmarks'
"My Gal Is a High Born Lady" or Shapiro, Bernstein & Von
Tilzer's "A Bird in a Gilded Cage."

While a book had a certain intrinsic value and a magazine or newspaper was usually not printed at all unless it represented calculable advertising and circulation revenue, a published song was only a piece of paper until it was performed. Then it became its own advertisement, either justifying or disavowing its publisher's faith in his ability to please a fickle public.

With what would seem to be an unfriendly attitude on the part of businessmen who shared a title if nothing else, the publishers of magazines and newspapers of the early 1900s took advantage of music publishers' peculiarly inarticulate and helpless position. The music publishers could not successfully use general magazines or newspapers to advertise their songs, but the magazines and newspapers could and did capitalize on songs' popularity to build their own circulations at no profit to the music firms. Many periodicals and newspapers harking back to the century's beginning have in their files the early works of George M. Cohan, Harry Von Tilzer, Max Dreyfus and others, bought for a few dollars each and printed as circulation come-ons in special music sections.

Department stores and wholesale industries pounced on the appeal of sheet music for their own advertising purposes. Stores bought songwriters' unpublished manuscripts for five dollars apiece and printed them on advertising giveaways extolling the features of corsets, patent medicines and chamber pots. The manufacturer of Bromo Seltzer, along with a brewery and the producer of a widely distributed fruit syrup, printed songs purchased for a few dollars from struggling songwriters. They advertised their wares boldly on the back and sometimes across the face of the sheets and gave them away to dealers to pass out to customers.

With no ordinary means of effective advertising available, the music publishers had to devise an extraordinary method of creating a demand for their merchandise. They concentrated on getting their songs performed in places where a large number of people could hear them.

No public place was overlooked by the men who were Tin Pan Alley's song salesmen in search of captive audiences. Beer parlors, music halls, brothels, theaters, bicycle races, parades, election campaign stump-meetings and amusement parks were the natural showcases for songs, and to them the publishers plodded with dogged persistence.

It soon became evident that a man with even one or two songs to exploit could not cover all of New York's gay, garish or respectable places of entertainment and retain either his health or his wife. It became necessary to look for additional salesmen—men capable of persuading performers to sing their firms' songs and, when necessary, to sing the songs themselves—loudly.

The indomitable, die-hard way in which these hirelings pursued their jobs gave them their name. They were song-pluggers.

The song-plugger has always been one of the insufficiently publicized heroes of a business which makes it a habit of singing the praises of almost everything and everyone connected with a hit song except the one man who, more often than not, gave it the first all-important push toward success. In the time of Tin Pan Alley's beginnings, the music business could not have survived without the conscientious employees who, for small salaries, worked long hours and performed exceptional services to put over their firms' songs.

The music publisher who did not know his way around the night spots, from bawdy Bowery beer joints and the infamous downtown red-light districts, to the champagne elegance of uptown cafés, or couldn't afford to hire someone who did, was not a successful publisher for long.

The song-plugger covered a beat that made sissies out of reporters and policemen. On a typical evening, he might start at the Atlantic Gardens on the Bowery where an all-girl orchestra would, for a round of drinks, play several of his tunes. They would, that is, if the plugger got there early enough to treat the ladies before rival publishers' men managed to buy up all the time the evening contained.

The song-plugger carried with him a set of parts for the orchestra and a quantity of "chorus slips" on which were printed the lyrics of the tune's refrain. The slips were distributed by his own hand among the guests seated at tables or standing at the long, well-worn bar.

When the orchestra struck up the first notes, the plugger jumped up and beckoned the revelers to join in the chorus.

"Take back your gold," he would warble,

"For gold can never buy me."

Catching the eye of one of his earlier drinking companions he gestured violently at her until, with downcast eyes and virtuously folded hands, she lifted her sudsy soprano:

"Take back your bribe,

"And promise you'll be tru-hue."

At a time when New York was a hotbed of political corruption and vicious prostitution, the songs most likely to succeed as sheet music to be brought home to wife and mother were the ones which went overboard in tribute to maidenly virtue. "Take Back Your Gold," had been a smashing hit since 1879. It ran neck-and-neck with "Mother Was a Lady" which celebrated a virginal maneuver to thwart a presumed rapist by reminding him, in several choruses, that his sister could very easily be in the same fix. These and a dozen other similar ballads nightly brought tears to the eyes of New York's pleasure-seekers. The era found it fashionable to conceal its debauchery with decorum.

With a tea-jerker like "Take Back Your Gold" to peddle, the song-plugger knew he had a ready audience wherever he went. New York's vice and hypocrisy were not limited to a few neighborhoods.

Leaving the Atlantic Gardens while people were still wiping their eyes, the plugger would visit in turn several variety houses which lined the Bowery. Variety was the name attached to what in later years and in somewhat different guise would be called vaudeville—that excitingly nostalgic word whose derivation is so dull. In its original French (*Vau-de-Vire*—"valley of Vire") it merely signified the locality where lighthearted love songs were performed, notably by one Olivier Basselin who popularized them. As so often happens in the semantic grab-bag, the place became the name of the songs themselves just as, for example, the place-names Cognac, Champagne and Burgundy have become the names of potables. The later rechristening of vaudeville was in keeping with moralistic attempts to remove from "variety" the smudged reputation which rubbed off on it in the Bowery "museums" and city-wide sex palaces which were an inevitable part of the song-plugger's itinerary.

After banter with specialty acts at the variety houses and some ribald repartee with the girls in back rooms, the song-plugger would hustle over to the more dignified and prophylactic Tony Pastor's on Fourteenth Street in time to catch one of the era's great singing stars before she left her dressing room. A plug at Tony's meant a lot, for Pastor toured America and Europe with his respectable entertainment and a song in an act's repertoire could build up nationwide and international popularity.

Across the street from Pastor's was another music hall, Theiss' Alhambra, where a round of drinks for the orchestra might buy a rendition or two. A silver dollar pressed into the hand of a singing waiter would bring an additional plug. The waiters worked for "throw-money," which is to say they waited on table without salary, singing as they handed out mugs of beer. At intervals, one stepped onto a clear spot in the middle of the room and, bar-rag draped over his arm, lifted his voice above the din. When the patrons were in a good mood, they threw loose change in his general direction. Their aim was somewhat better when they were surly, and a waiter soon learned to duck flying bottles, dishes and chairs.

Also on Fourteenth Street were Huber's Prospect Garden Music Hall, Haub's Saloon and Cunningham & O'Keefe's, where professionals of the entertainment world gathered after work to exchange backstage gossip and brag about the number of encores they received.

From the Fourteenth Street theater and night spot district the now defunct Third Avenue El, then steam-driven, would carry the wearying song-plugger to within walking distance of Koster & Bial's on Twenty-third Street. Here, as at Tony Pastor's, a plug could lead rapidly to widespread exposure of a song, for Koster & Bial's was famous for importing European talent of superb quality. A song "adopted" by a European artist and added to the repertoire which he carried back to his own country could, another season, return to the United States as a fresh Continental hit. Although European sheet music sales did not mean much before the international copyright situation was ironed out, the stamp of English, French or German approval on an American song intensified its sales when it returned home with a European accent.

On and on the song-plugger plodded, meeting his colleagues wherever he went. Unlike rival Park Row newspaper publishers of the times, who waged circulation "wars" which often resulted in violent bloodshed, Tin Pan Alley's rival music publishers were not antagonistic to each other. There was fierce competition to get songs performed, but the pluggers were a chummy lot. The boys had to get along with each other good-naturedly, if only because it was inevitable for several firms to be represented at the same time in the same place, and too much valuable time could be lost in brawling. They devised a workable back-scratching compromise: "You get the crowd singing *my* song, and I'll pitch in when you put yours on the tables."

New York was studded from the Battery to Harlem with saloons, cafés, restaurants, music halls, hotels, dance halls and sporting arenas—athletic and erotic—where songs could be exposed to large numbers of pleasure-seekers. Not every plugger could make every stop every night, but every stop had to be covered with every song.

Hoarse, footsore, eyes streaming and nose smarting from too much smoke, belching sourly from too much beer, the plugger ended his nightly rounds after the last late spot closed. To go home for well-earned sleep in a quiet room where no music pounded at him? Well, no. After working so hard all evening, he considered that he deserved a little relaxation. His final stop, therefore, was more likely to be Everard's on Twenty-eighth Street, or a similar saloon, where he could strain his vocal chords further in shop-talk with other pluggers, breathe in some more smoke, drink a few rounds of beer with the boys.

Active in the music business today there is a handful of perennially young-at-heart publishers and top publishing executives in their sixties and seventies who were song-pluggers during this century's youth and their own. A familiar thread of continuity weaves in and out of the reminiscent tales they spin.

"I started in this crazy business as a plugger for Irving Berlin," more than one will say.

"Well, let's be honest," they add. "That came a little later. Berlin was still a singing waiter when I first met him. I *really* got my start by singing in a boys' choir down on Delancey Street."

A frequent observation about show business in general is that it seems to be dominated by the Irish, Negroes, Jews and Italians. This is not necessarily true—generalizations usually aren't—but certainly most of our great performing artists of past and present belong to these cultural groups, and certainly a large percentage of those who grew up in the publishing end of the music business were born to the Jewish faith.

In a way, it was the faith itself that played an important part in the future careers of many men now prominent in the music industry, for as sweet-voiced youngsters they sang for the Friday evening and Saturday morning services conducted in the New York synagogues.

In the search for the song-pluggers so vital to the exploitation of their songs, Tin Pan Alley publishers shrewdly led frequent raids on the Lower East Side synagogues. Boys raising devout eyes from the pages of their hymnals were often astonished to see in the congregation a flashily dressed uptowner who obviously was not present to pay homage to Jehovah. The boys who chanted the old Hebrew refrains had what today's musicians call a "schmaltzy" delivery, a style eminently suitable for the soddenly tearful songs of the early 1900s.

On one Saturday, a stranger hurried back to the choir room and cornered a boy who sang the solo part in the religious service.

"Hey, kid, how would like a singing job?" the stranger asked. "Here—take my card. I represent Remick—the music publisher. Come to my office Monday."

Round-eyed, nervous, dressed in his best Sabbath suit, the

young man traveled far uptown to Twenty-eighth Street at the appointed time to see the man who offered to *pay* him for singing.

He entered an office in one of the brownstone houses and saw that along three sides of the room there was a continuous counter. Standing in front of it was a milling throng of well-dressed people and behind it stood two men in gartered shirtsleeves and derby hats, smoking cigars. They were busily reaching under the counter for copies of music and putting them in the outstretched hands across from them.

The boy handed one of the men a card.

"I'm Benny. Mr. Gumble said for me to see him today."

The counterman glanced at him briefly and appraisingly.

"Singer?"

"Yessir."

"Choir?"

"Yessir."

"Got working papers?"

"Yessir."

"This way, bub."

Benny ducked under an open space in the counter and followed the man to a long corridor lined with doors. As he passed them he heard pianos playing and voices singing. None of them seemed to be playing the same thing.

After opening several doors, saying a quick "Sorry!" and backing out, the counterman finally found an unoccupied cubicle. Its only furniture was a piano with yellowed, broken keys and a straight chair. He handed Benny a sheet of music and said, "Here. Sing this."

Benny stared down at the meaningless notes.

"How can I sing it?" he asked. "I don't know how it goes."

The counter man shifted the cigar to the other side of his mouth and smiled without warmth.

"One of these days," he remarked to the ceiling, "they'll send me someone who can read."

"I can read!" Benny protested.

"Yeah. But not music."

The man poked his head out of the door and yelled, "Hey, Joe! Come back to Seven, will you?"

A man appeared at the door, carrying a sheaf of music sheets.

"Run through 'On the 5:15' for Caruso here, will you? We got ourselves another plugger."

Joe ran through the number, with Benny listening carefully. On the third time through, he joined his voice with the piano, reading the words from the music copy.

The counterman seemed anxious to leave.

"That's it," he said. "Now, take these slips and stay here with Joe until you learn all the songs. I want you to memorize them. I want you to know them so well you can sing them even if somebody else is singing a different song louder than you."

The cigar-smoker left, and Benny was alone with Joe and the piano. For the next hour or so, they went over the songs together. Occasionally Joe would be called away for a few minutes, and while he was gone the boy studied the words on the cards.

After several hours, Benny's voice was getting hoarse but he knew the songs of the Remick catalog. He was a song-plugger.

Song-pluggers usually worked in teams composed of vocalist and piano, and after he had been with Remick for a while Benny found a young man named George Gershwin whose piano-playing thrilled him. He decided that the two of them would make a good team and was pleased to learn that George was looking for a job. Proud of his new young friend, Benny informed Remick's professional manager, Jules Von Tilzer, that Georgie also *wrote* songs. Mr. Von Tilzer was less impressed by this intelligence than he was by the fact that young Gershwin could sight-read and transpose keys when necessary. He said, kindly, "We've got all the songwriters we need around here. Believe me, Georgie, Remick doesn't need songwriters. But if you want a job as a piano-player, that's fine. Forget about writing songs and go out with Benny and plug Remick tunes."

As one of Remick's teams, Benny Bloom and George Gershwin

THE BIG PLUG 53

spent their days demonstrating songs for vaudeville acts and their evenings paying calls on the growing number of "picture houses." Here the duo were part of the entertainment between showings of the feature films and short subjects. Benny would hand the man in the projection booth a handful of colored slides, plus a 25-cent tip. Between films, he jumped up on the stage brandishing a schoolmaster's pointed stick and, cueing Georgie below at the pit piano, started to sing the words printed under the illustrations which the projectionist flashed on the screen. The audience joined in, singing with the gusto and off-key harmonies that usually characterize amateur group vocalizing.

The idea of illustrated song slides had been conceived by George H. Thomas around 1892, when he was chief electrician at a Brooklyn theater. In the tearful production of *The Old Homestead*, a morality song entitled, "Where Is My Wand'ring Boy Tonight?" was rendered by one of the principals. During the rendition, the house lights dimmed and a drawing was flashed on a curtain. It illustrated a saloon in which a young man was seated at the bar. The song (written as a hymn in 1877 by the Reverend Robert Lowry) made it very plain that the wand'ring boy, curs'd by the evils of Drink and fallen among low companions, was not happy. Few eyes were dry when the song ended, the lights brightened and the play resumed.

Thomas thought that a song's message could be dramatized more effectively by a lot of pictures instead of just one, and further decided that a series of actual photographs would have greater impact than lifeless drawings. He tinkered with the idea for two years.

In 1894, the new partnership of Edward B. Marks and Joseph W. Stern, traveling salesmen turned music publishers, had as its plug song a tear-jerker the two men had written in collaboration. It was called "The Little Lost Child." When Thomas presented his idea for illustrative continuity to the publishers, they saw in the technique a vehicle for their song.

In keeping with the sorrowful narrative ballads of the day, "The Little Lost Child" told the tale of a waif astray in the streets who was picked up by a passing policeman and brought to the station house. There the kindly cop, a sad and lonesome man, discovered that the little lost child was his own, his very own daughter! How did he discover this? Why, he was entertaining the waif with the story of his life. Once, long ago, he said, he had a little girl who would be just her age now. But his wife had left him after a domestic quarrel, taking the baby with her and leaving him all alone. As tiny hands patted the unhappy policeman's face consolingly, the little girl's mother came into the police station to claim her. Guess who she was!

With a zeal born of showmanship and audacity, the publishers had Thomas set up his camera in a Brooklyn police station. A real minion of the law was induced to pose with a child actress and the mother was played by Mrs. Thomas.

The song slide was born, antedating by several years the first motion picture story.

The first performance of "The Little Lost Child" with its illustrated text of ten photographs took place during the intermisison of a Primrose and West minstrel show—over West's objections to an entr'acte not in keeping with the spirit of minstrelsy. Primrose had okayed it, however, and a favorite tenor of the times (Allen May) was engaged to sing the pathetic stanzas as the stills were flashed on a screen. Thomas, Marks and Stern paced nervously in the wings, unsure of how the audience would respond to such a new and unfamiliar offering. They need not have worried. The idea was an immediate success, once the projectionist got the hang of it and stopped putting the slides in upside down.

A brand-new outlet was added to the limited channels of music exploitation as song slides became a national craze. Slide manufacturers sprang up overnight. Songwriters began composing special musical material with pictorial treatment in mind. Entertainment teams became headliners as "slide-singers," with one of the pair handling the projector while the other did the vocalizing. Publishers put entire catalogs onto slides, increasing their orders for sets as the songs mounted in popularity. Automation had arrived in the music business, and many a song-plugger feared for his job.

The song slides, however, did not put the pluggers out of business. These men worked almost exclusively in the New York area, where they were still needed, while the song slides could be shipped all over the country. At first, the sets were given free of charge to theaters because of their plugging value to songs. Audiences liked to sing the words as a pit pianist or organist played the music. But it soon dawned on the publishers that their slides were part of the show in the theaters which used them, so they started charging an average of five dollars apiece for the sets. This not only brought in a nice profit on favorite songs, it also represented one of the first by-product uses of popular music in America.

Twenty years after they were introduced, song slides were still going strong when Benny Bloom and George Gershwin were a song-plugging team. By then, New York theaters and picture houses were not charged for the slides. Their large audiences made them worth-while plugging spots for new songs the Remick firm wanted to put over.

On Saturday afternoons, Benny's plug spot was the music department of the great Siegel-Cooper department store on the corner of Eighteenth Street and Sixth Avenue. Many adults today can remember this magical store to which their mothers brought them, as children, for a Saturday treat. The store's slogan—"Meet Me at the Fountain"—was nationally famous and, in many memories, a phrase to evoke the image of tall stone columns, a sensation of sliding joyously on cool marble floors, and the mingled smells of chocolate and dyed cloth.

Benny would bring along bottles of Woolworth perfume for the salesgirls who attended the famous store's tremendous music counters surrounding a piano on a raised platform. With two or three Remick pianists spelling each other at the keyboard, Benny sang his firm's songs for the crowd of shoppers who always gathered happily at the music department. Such sessions were a featured part of the department store's activity. The store got free acts. People came in droves to be amused, and after the entertainment they turned into customers.

When a large enough crowd had gathered, Benny handed out the ever-ready chorus slips. People bought sheet music in large quantities in those days, for few homes were without their parlor pianos. New tunes, especially, were in great demand. When it was Remick demonstration time, Benny sold as many as a thousand copies of assorted Remick tunes in a single afternoon. (The other publishers had their allotted demonstration times, also, and did as well.)

The perfume Benny brought to the salesgirls was always a good investment, for a customer frequently tossed a half dollar on the counter and said, "Give me six of the latest." Sheet music was ten cents a copy, or six for fifty cents. Gratefully remembering Benny's little gift, the salesgirls would push six Remick tunes toward the customer. When Benny wasn't there, they'd do the same for Witmark tunes, or Harms, or Marks, or Shapiro-Bernstein. All the pluggers knew the Woolworth perfume bit.

Like all his other colleagues, Benny's routine was not confined to picture houses and department stores. With the majority of publishers' offices located as they were near Broadway and Fifth Avenue, and with windows open during nice weather, someone could always hear the approach of a parading band. Then as now, New Yorkers loved a parade. When the shout went up from the front office that a band was coming, Benny would gather up band arrangements of Remick's songs and run into the street to distribute the parts to the marching musicians. Sometimes the ink was not yet dry on printed copies of new tunes, but "get there *first*" was a music business motto.

The weeks preceding local, state or national elections were busy ones for all of Tin Pan Alley's song-pluggers. Before radio and television made it possible for candidates to reach masses of their constituents via microphone and camera, they had to get out and stump for votes. Many of the candidates for local elections were too poor to hire Irving Hall or a similar political meeting place where the prospect of free refreshments could be counted on to draw a crowd. They hired, instead, a large wagon or truck outfitted with a three-piece orchestra. Trumpet, banjo and drums were considered an effective combination; they were easily portable, fairly inexpensive and sufficiently noisy.

Song-pluggers, rushing out of their offices along Twenty-eighth Street with chorus slips and sheet music in their hands, went into a frenzy of activity. They were like barkers for a medicine man or a carnival freak show. Tipping the three-piece outfit to play their firms' music, the pluggers sang at the tops of their voices until a crowd gathered, then handed out the chorus slips. When the crowd was big enough, the candidate for public office stepped up on the truck's platform and launched into his campaign speech. Very often his voice was drowned out by the clink of money as his potential constituents bought copies of the songs to take home.

With cunning forethought, the plug songs selected by each publisher's employee varied with the neighborhood. The lucky pluggers were the ones whose firms had catalogs with international flavors. On Mulberry Street, "My Mariuccia Take a Steamboat" was plugged by Shapiro-Bernstein. Von Tilzer's own "Down Where the Wurzburger Flows" put the Yorkville residents in a good mood, and Witmark's "Where the River Shannon Flows" was received with broguish shouts of approval in mid-town New York.

When the six-day bicycle races took New York by storm at Madison Square Garden, then on Twenty-sixth Street, the song-pluggers joyfully invaded it. Their main target was not the bands hired by management. The idea was to be on hand to fill in the gaps *between* band selections; and after midnight, when the bands closed their instrument cases and went home, to "entertain" the crowd.

The friendly song-pluggers from rival publishing firms chipped in to hire a piano. Rental rates were by the hour, and no piano-movers worked after midnight. Having tipped a piano-warehouse driver to drop the piano on the sidewalk outside the Garden, several of the pluggers pushed it into the sports arena. Brandishing megaphones and of course passing out the ubiquitous chorus slips, they took turns singing their firms' songs.

The bicycle races provided a double exposure for songs, for they were heard not only by the race fans gathered in the Garden by the thousands, but also by the vaudeville and night-spot entertainers who were in the habit of showing up there after they finished their acts.

Baseball fields, public parks, picnic grounds, river excursion boats and sidewalks in front of theaters where people queued up for tickets were magnets for the song-pluggers. So was Coney Island, where boardwalk strollers, Midway cavorters, Luna Park visitors and customers for Feltman's newfangled "red-hots" and old-fashioned foaming schooners were regaled with the popular tunes of the day by the hard-working young men who plied their wares like London's buskers.

The indefatigable pluggers with songs to sell undertook their exhausting duties cheerfully, even enthusiastically. They accepted without question the fact that personal and persistent song-hawking, which neither sleet nor snow nor dark of night could stay, was the only way open to them. Occasionally, some heavy thinkers in the music business tried something else. Their noble attempts to put over a song by ignoring completely the customary *modus operandi* usually had chastening results.

The late Harry Link, a determined nonconformist, once wagered that he could make a hit song by using bona fide advertising techniques. He had a number of friends who were in the advertising business, and he admired greatly their ability to create product demand via the written word. At the time of his venture, around 1918, he was a member of the old firm of Waterson, Berlin and Snyder. (If you try very hard, you may find someone over the age of fifty in the music-publishing business today who will not insist that he worked, one time or another, with this famous—almost legendary—house, whose principals were songwriters Irving Berlin and Ted Snyder, and Henry Waterson who has been called a creator of writers second only to Max Dreyfus, the venerated Dean of Popular Music.)

Link, who came from Philadelphia, picked that city for his great experiment. He selected for the test a sprightly new Irving Berlin song called "Smile and Show Your Dimple," and got to work. He flooded Philadelphia newspapers with ads which, in best copywriter fashion, eulogized the delightful cadences of the new Berlin melody. He plastered every window of every Five and Ten cent store with big, beautiful posters. He ordered enough campaign buttons to grace the lapels of all Philadelphians. He hired newsboys by the dozens to hand out circulars, and sandwich men to parade up and down the shopping centers. There was hardly a street corner, trolley car or building in Philadelphia which did not herald a printed message to the population that "Smile and Show Your Dimple"—the *great* new Berlin tune—could be purchased at any music counter.

Confident of success, Link had ordered twenty-five thousand copies of the song to be placed in stores on consignment. At the end of the test period he counted the returns and discovered, wryly, that a total of twenty-five hundred copies had managed to be sold by his carefully planned advertising campaign. End of experiment, but not end of story.

Mr. Berlin is a man who never wastes a song. His files, it is said, are full of possible hits that he hasn't gotten around to publishing yet. In 1933, he undertook to write the score of the stage musical, "As Thousands Cheer." He went to his files and dusted off an old copy of "Smile and Show Your Dimple," rewrote the lyric and handed it in to the show's producer. This time, with regulation song-plugging techniques employed by its publisher (Irving Berlin, Inc.) the song didn't do too badly under its new title—"Easter Parade."

In the Tin Pan Alley that was, when the only effective organ for song exposure was the lungs of the song-plugger, his effort not only sold songs in great quantities, it also frequently improved their quality. More than once after a song was introduced the audience's cool response would indicate that something was not quite right with either the melody or the lyrics. When this happened, there was still time to work over the song before it was printed in large quantities.

Those were the "good old days" sighed about now by successful music firm executives who were song-pluggers in their early years. They did not know it at the time, those earnest and perspiring boys with chorus slips clutched in their hands, but they were molding the future of American popular music. For, as most of them discovered, intimacy with the nation's favorite songs developed in them a sixth sense. Song-pluggers became hit-pickers by a natural process of association with the public's taste. In time, the men who were valued as song-pluggers realized that if they could pick hits for their bosses, they could do it for themselves. Many a successful music publisher in or near the Brill Building today started out as a song-plugger for a Twenty-eighth Street firm, and many a former song-plugger soon outdistanced his erstwhile employer.

Before radio shortened the active life of a new song, a hit could count on steady mass sales for periods lasting up to three years. When, through the efforts of a song-plugger, a new song was adopted by one of vaudeville's beloved performers, it became a big success in New York and all over the eastern circuit. The performer would make the song part of his act and carry it with him to the Middle West. Publishers would know, without consulting the itineraries listed in *Variety*, where the performer was appearing by the orders that started coming in for sheet music, from dealers in the South, the Southwest and on the West Coast. Orders from these successive regions might slacken off, but the publishers knew the song had only started. By now it was identified with the singer and, on his return trip across the country, he would find audiences yelling for him to sing the song they remembered hearing before. When he arrived back in New York, eastern sales would skyrocket again. This pattern continued as long as the vaudeville star kept the song in his repertoire.

The "long plug" is gone forever, replaced by the hit-and-run methods of the modern music business, which was wrenched from its horse-car pace and thrown into rocket propulsion almost before it had a chance to grow accustomed to automobiles.

5. *The Big Change . . . the Wire . . . and Haywire*

THE FIRST FLICKERS of domesticated electricity were welcomed with as much joy and wonderment in Tin Pan Alley as anywhere else, but they kindled a spark that smoldered ominously for the popular-music business. The powerful publishers were blissfully unaware that the man-made marvels of the nineteenth century's last decade were advance scouts for electronic monsters which were lying in wait to wrest control from their hands.

By 1900, Thomas Alva Edison's crude phonograph was completed. Guglielmo Marconi's apparatus for wireless telegraphy was assembled and demonstrated. The telephone was a new toy. The magic of electricity lighted dreams inside the minds of men like England's Sir John A. Fleming and America's Lee deForest, in whose laboratories were incubating cocoons of glass and wire that would grow up to be radio and television.

Song slides were entrenched in public favor and player pianos in many homes provided additional revenue for the copyright owners of the nation's songs. The appearance of a new contraption had been enthusiastically welcomed by crowds who visited penny arcades and fairground midways. This, a forerunner of motion pictures and animated cartoons, was Mr. Edison's Kineto-scope.

Stated simply, a motion picture is only a series of instantane-ously photographed still pictures run off in succession. The camera does not photograph motion itself, but captures each action of an object or body as it moves through space. Although the images seen on a motion picture screen are photographs of bodies at successive instants of motion, they are projected so rapidly that the human eye perceives them in continuous action.

Using this principle of visual illusion, Mr. Edison invented his Kinetograph, a camera using rolls of film instead of individual plates, and the Kinetoscope, an apparatus for peep-show viewing of the continuous film.

Eagerly pounced upon by game-and-vending machine opera-tors, the Kinetoscope (and its inevitable rival, the Mutoscope) was placed in penny arcades and rigged up with a crude sound-box. Garish placards above the devices—hundreds of them were lined up along the walls and center aisles—enticed amusement seekers with invitations to *"SEE BEAUTIFUL GIRLS TAKE A BATH! REAL LIFE ACTION PICTURES! WATCH EVERY MOVEMENT!"*

The intrigued customer put a coin in a slot and peered through the private viewer whereupon he saw, moving indeed, buxom beauties in ankle-length bathing dresses strolling along a beach and sporting playfully in the surf. Other peep-show attractions reeled off an assortment of pie-in-the-face comedy, dusty melo-drama or mildly suggestive farce.

Connected to the machine's sound-box was a wire running to an outside earphone. This, placed to the ear of the entranced au-dience of one, gave forth a tinny rendition of a popular tune.

Penny arcades also featured mechanical pianos which, fed with the required penny or nickel, thumped out the favorite melodies of the day, the black and white keys moving eerily as though fin-gered by ghostly hands.

The newfangled gadgets clanked and groaned away, producing crazy new sounds that fell on astonished but fascinated ears.

The publishers were well pleased. New things were happening to open up previously unavailable channels of exploitation for popular music. New things were happening to the trends and tempos of the music itself, too.

Publishers, their writers and song-pluggers were first bewildered, then enchanted, by a national mania for dancing. Up to 1910 the waltz had been supreme in the ballroom, for the slow ballads that were popular music's main fare lent themselves easily to three-quarter tempo. But suddenly people stopped rotating and started to glide, hop and dip.

The trend had been brewing for some time. As long ago as 1897 a young concert violinist and university professor whose name was Frederick Allen (Kerry) Mills composed a lively two-step march which he called "At a Georgia Camp Meeting." The song was written primarily to express his distaste for the contrived cadences and insulting dialect of bogus race ballads which followed in the wake of "Jim Crow." He chose to describe the way couples at southern camp meetings strutted competitively for a prize of a big chocolate cake after religious services were over.

The famous contemporary song-and-dance team of Dave Genaro and Ray Bailey had themselves choreographed a stage routine built around the camp-meeting ritual. They called it, not inappropriately, "the cakewalk." Closely associated with the Kerry Mills tune, the cakewalk was plugged vigorously by Genaro for years as a popular dance, and several publishers brought out their own cakewalk songs to compete with Kerry Mills, who issued his tune as both a march and a song. Most people, however, seemed to prefer remaining spectators instead of performers of the somewhat difficult steps. (In 1915, when the public was a little more accustomed to derring-do on the dance floor, Genaro finally succeeded in making his origination a national craze through a series of cakewalk contests.)

But if people resisted the cakewalk, they found other stage-born dances irresistible.

Vernon and Irene Castle were idolized by the American public as living proof that romance and marriage need not cancel each other out. Women, especially, yearned to follow in Irene's footsteps—on and off the dance floor. They needed partners for both locales. When husbands refused to emulate their darling Vernon, the ladies' demands were met by an outcropping of resplendent young men who danced very nicely and offered romantic services as well. When husbands learned what their wives were doing in the afternoons to make them so tired in the evenings, they hit the ceiling. But the dance craze was epidemic. Restaurants, hotels, cabarets and chow mein palaces were places to dance. Unemployed musicians found themselves being offered more jobs than they could handle.

It wasn't long before the censors took over.

The howls of outraged decency centered around the tango. Newspapers devoted front-page headlines to the controversy. From the Vatican in Rome came severe admonishments accompanied by a papal suggestion that, if grown men and women must dance vigorously, they should dance the tarantelle. Yale University loftily declared the tango taboo at its 1914 junior prom. With equal loftiness Harvard University announced that at *its* prom the tango would be permitted. John D. Rockefeller, defiantly, hired a teacher to give him private tango lessons. Several prominent citizens broke their legs when rebellion against censorship led them too energetically into dips and sways on embattled dance floors.

The tango had company in its pillory. Also lamented as immoral were the turkey trot and its quadruped counterparts the grizzly bear and the bunny hug, as well as the marsupial kangaroo dip, all variants of the fox trot.

What was so all-fired shocking about these dances? Not their interrupted 4/4 tempo; not the fact that they were, in contrast to the approved but strenuous old-fashioned waltz or the back-bending cakewalk or the athletic polka, comparatively easy to perform. What bothered the censors was the fact that the newfangled dances permitted a gentleman to hold in close embrace a lady to whom he may not have been married or even affianced.

Despite the jeremiads of clergymen, the press and offended blue-nosed socialites, the dances were enthusiastically hailed by the nimble-footed swains and sweethearts of the day. Possibly simplicity and tempo had something to do with their popularity. More probably, the censors were quite accurate. The dances certainly offered the "nice people" a forbidden sweetness of physical contact in the comparative safety of a crowd.

The mania for dancing to tempos livelier than the waltz caught the music publishers temporarily short of material. The publishers had spent long years patiently explaining to their songwriters that they were interested in investing only in "songs"—pleasant ballads that people could sing and whistle. The publishers were the bosses. Songwriters schooled themselves to put together one sentimental ballad after another, with happy thoughts tucked into the lyrics like prizes in popcorn boxes.

Now singers took second billing to dance orchestras, and "society" orchestras with their multitudes of strings so apt for waltzes gave way to bands whose instrumentation of brasses, woodwinds and percussion were more capable of emphasizing a beat.

Another new sound was being heard, too—a foot-tapping, blood-warming, ear-tickling echo from the lower Mississippi River basin. New York publishers tried hard to understand it, this insinuating music that nobody wrote down. They couldn't. They hastily thumbed through their inactive files for the almost-forgotten names of Negro piano players whose submitted songs had previously been snubbed as unsingable, therefore outlandish. If anyone could, the publishers thought, these fellows ought to be able to get that beat into sensible shape—a shape for printing.

Ironically, while jazz has made incalculable contributions to the popular-music business, the popular-music publishers seldom returned the courtesy. Tin Pan Alley's writers and publishers distorted, refined or synthesized jazz more often than they offered it up to the public in its primitive purity.

Perhaps the music publishers should not be blamed for their misuse, for jazz music was not easily printable and the publishers had to have material they could print and sell. People were spending more time turning the corners of dance floors than they were turning the pages of songs on parlor piano racks.

The decline in piano-copy sales challenged the publishers to come up with something they could merchandise. Along with the Negro piano players, they hired orchestrators to pore through catalogs and extract titles suitable for dance arrangements which were called "stocks." At the same time, they became suddenly indifferent to previously successful songwriters whose forte, at the publishers' own former insistence, was ballads. Even the best and most prolific songwriters were stymied. Unless a song could be danced to, it was not a good publishing risk. The ballad was knuckling under to novelty tunes, many of them—unthinkably— wordless. "My Melancholy Baby," published in 1912 and today a timeless standard, was hardly noticed during the jazz two-beat reign. Its smooth, unbreakable rhythm gave insufficient prompting to dancing feet.

The songwriters were furious. They maintained to a man that they were writers of melody and lyric, not perpetrators of crazy sounds. They accused the publishers of lowering the standards of American popular music.

The publishers sympathized with their long-time faithful writers, agreed that the business was certainly going to pot, and got out stock dance arrangements as fast as the presses could print them.

Along with the dance-craze dilemma, the music industry had other problems in the years between 1914 and 1917. There was a war going on in Europe, and Tin Pan Alley didn't quite know what to do about it.

As always, topical incidents were put through the popular-music mill. Someone did write a song about the German torpedoing of the *Lusitania* and someone published it, but nobody paid much attention. The public mood in the years immediately preceding our entry into World War I was not only unmilitant, it was decidedly anti-military. People didn't want to think about war, hear about war or talk about war. Certainly they had no inclination whatsoever to sing about war.

Following a human trait which approaches a nasty problem

obliquely or ignores it altogether in the hope that it will go away quietly, songwriters and publishers turned their attention to a variety of escapist subjects. When they mentioned war at all, they sneered at it. The attitude was "Well, something or other unpleasant is happening, and we know about it, but it sure as hell has nothing to do with *us*."

Besides, at the time we had a couple of annoyances closer to home, looming larger in the American public's thoughts than the quarrel across the Atlantic. The Mexican political situation threatened American boundaries, and even more alarming was the threat to American wallets in the terms of the new income tax amendment.

Thus it was that, looking away from the European conflict, American popular music "discovered" in 1914 a new and insinuating rhythm which its creator called "the blues." Neither the word nor the tempo was really new, for William Christopher Handy had composed "Memphis Blues" several years earlier, without creating too much excitement. It was his "St. Louis Blues" which electrified the country and set the forty-year-old cornetist, bandleader and composer among the immortals of American music.

Thus it was, too, that in 1915 American popular music "discovered" the Hawaiian Islands, which had been annexed to the United States since 1899. A little tardily, but with a great whooshing of grass skirts, Tin Pan Alley staked a claim on the territory in one of its typical song-cycles. A number of Hawaiian-type songs were hurried into print as soon as it became apparent that the first one was successful. Tin Pan Alley has never been reluctant to milk its sacred cows.

Although Americans were willing to sing England's war songs ("Keep the Home Fires Burning," "Pack Up Your Troubles in Your Old Kit Bag and Smile, Smile, Smile" and "It's a Long Way to Tipperary"), our personal sentiments, according to publishers of American popular music, were "I Didn't Raise My Boy to Be a Soldier" and "Don't Take My Darling Boy Away," along with "I Hate Like Hell to Go."

By 1916, still straddling a wobbly fence, the United States had loaned Great Britain and France five hundred million dollars to help fight the Germans while at the same time we continued to sell supplies to Germany. Our songwriters, still bemused by coconut palms and ukuleles, wrote more Hawaiian songs that year, a few flouted public sentiment by writing ditties encouraging enlistment, but the really popular songs were looking in another direction—"I Ain't Got Nobody," "Mississippi," "Pretty Baby" and—the smash hit—"What Do You Want to Make Those Eyes at Me For?" When the songsmiths explored foreign shores for subject matter, they carefully avoided controversial countries and stuck to jolly Ireland, which was neutral in the war.

The music industry had not yet recognized or assumed responsibility toward the world. It regarded itself narrowly as a medium for entertainment. In 1916, music seldom editorialized, except amorously. It commented, it burlesqued, it mocked and it reflected the temper of the customers, who wanted no part of Europe's hassle.

Good salesmanship frowns on forcing an unwanted or distasteful product down an unwilling throat, and the music business prided itself on super-salesmanship. Publishers gave out the word that war songs were not only uncommercial, they were taboo. If songwriters wanted their stuff published they would do well to keep turning out nice, comfortable, nonbelligerent ditties. Backstage in vaudeville theaters notices on call-boards warned performers to kill their war jokes and songs, by order of the management.

But American attitudes were fermenting with change. As the nation drifted toward preparedness, publishers drifted toward more patriotic sentiments. By the time the United States formally declared a state of war with Germany in April of 1917, the music business was ready to run up the American flag without reservations and decorate its offices with Liberty Bond and Uncle Sam Wants YOU posters. War songs became the ones to plug.

It dawned on the music industry gradually that songs were much more than melodic merchandise. Faced with a serious national crisis for the first time in its career as an organized American industry, Tin Pan Alley learned that popular music was a vital force for military and civilian morale. To publishers and song-pluggers, people stopped being anonymous customers. They emerged as mothers and wives and sweethearts of young men preparing to meet the enemy, needing music for faith and hope and reassurance.

One of the first inklings of popular music's importance as military matériel came when the United States government sternly banned two songs which the Federal authorities considered to be at cross-purposes with the national draft. The songs were "I Don't Want to Get Well (I'm in Love with a Beautiful Nurse")" and "There'll Be a Hot Time for the Old Men When the Young Men Go to War." In a move that came as a surprise to music men, the government ordered all copies of the songs recalled and destroyed, meanwhile issuing a ban against their performance in public places. In 1918, the same government agency requested music publishers not to issue any songs with a "peace" message. Such lyrics, it was pointed out, might comfort and assist the Germans who were snidely attempting to put our fighting men in a soft, surrendering mood.

During our brief but tense participation in World War I, show business slackened, with theaters and cabarets going dark and chilly as the result of wartime power and fuel restrictions. Moreover, the pleasure-seeking crowds were hard pressed by Liberty Loan drives and they spent their entertainment dollars for war stamps. The music business, however, flourished. People could afford the dime sheet music cost, and they flocked to buy new songs, not all of them related to the war.

In or out of uniform, people responded to a variety of music. They sang the "we'll lick 'em" tunes, of course, but they also liked the spate of nonsense songs Tin Pan Alley was turning out ("Lily of the Valley," "Ja-Da"). They were enthusiastic about the fine melodies written by Jerome Kern, Sigmund Romberg and Victor Herbert. They took to their hearts a collection of beautiful Negro spirituals which were given fresh impetus in the skillful arrangements of Henry Thacker Burleigh. They quickened to a contribution from the still-young and not thoroughly understood jazz style as it was expressed in an instrumental piece, "Tiger Rag," and they got an idea of what was imminent in the way of another social dance fad in "Shim-Me-Sha-Wabble."

As the war drew to a close, publishers settled down to adjust themselves to business as usual but soon found that nothing was usual any more. Europe was not alone in its shambles. France was digging itself out of war's rubbish, but the United States was creating its own.

Early in 1919, the Constitutional amendment prohibiting liquor was ratified and proclaimed, to become effective a year later. Side by side with sentimental ballads, musical comedy songs and an Oriental cycle which trailed the extraordinary success of "Dardanella," the prohibition theme appeared increasingly in songwriters' output. Harry Ruby asked "What'll We Do on a Saturday Night—When the Town Goes Dry?" Irving Berlin suggested a solution with "I'll See You in C-U-B-A," where it would still be possible to buy a legal drink.

By the early 1920s, the American public was accustomed to the idea of Federal prohibition, but it was not resigned. The government had passed a law, but could not control the lawlessness that accompanied it.

The effect upon songwriters and the music business in general was enormous. Prohibition led to smuggling and bootlegging, and the men who engaged in these lucrative enterprises became powerful in the entire entertainment world. The underworld liked consorting familiarly with show business personalities. The bootlegging set were big spenders, and night club proprietors were far from reluctant to take their money. Also, several of the tough but fun-loving types thought it would be nice to own their own clubs where they could not only reap all the profits, but also stand as boss-men to the entertainers who worked there.

Popular music had to get along with the gangsters who were at the controls or get out of the business, for song-plugging was still most effective when carried on in the night spots where rebellious, unconventional, high-stepping people gathered for pleasure.

Oddly enough, despite the hysterical abandon of the turbulent 20s, the period fostered some of America's greatest songwriters, who created for the stage, the movies and independent publication melodies and lyrics which are beloved standards today.

To many surviving publishers, song-pluggers and tunesmiths, these were the final, irretrievable golden years.

When the nationwide bravado that overextended itself in its frantic insistence on having a good time culminated in the market crash of 1929, the music business tightened its belt and got along somehow. But the depression was far less worrisome to Tin Pan Alley than a giant offspring of mechanical marvels which had been so warmly welcomed at the century's turn. This was radio. The men who had worked so hard to build an American repertoire of popular music heard in the mechanical monster's squawks the death-rattle of their industry. In their fury against the revenue-robbing menace, music publishers all but forgot any other troubles they were having.

Toward the end of his book of memoirs, *They All Sang*, written by publisher Edward B. Marks with A. J. Liebling (Viking Press, 1934), the author called radio "the most disastrous of all the mechanical developments which have so altered our Tin Pan Alley."

"Today," Marks wrote, "songs are made hits in a week, and killed off in sixty days. The public hears so many songs it has long ceased to distinguish among them. . . . More songs are produced than ever before, but nobody profits from them—except the broadcasters."

The publishers were in serious difficulty. People were listening to music, but they weren't buying much. Radio gobbled it up with a voracious gluttony, and the publishers became more and more frightened as it occupied the major portion of a fascinated public's attention.

Sheet music dropped to an alarming low as home pianos stood silent. Hand-cranked and even electrified phonographs became ghostly pieces of furniture and record sales came to grief. While publishers have always been bitter about the two-cents-per-side revenue they get from records and share with writers, they missed it sorely in the 1930s. Still another cross to bear was the emergence of "talkies" as a new national pastime. What time people spent away from their radio sets they spent going to the movies. Now, the publishers complained, the picture houses didn't even buy arrangements for pit piano or orchestra to play. Why should they? The music came from the same can the films did.

Vaudeville, that great mainstay of the music business, was mortally ill. There were no more programs of eight, ten or more acts of song and dance teams to plug songs. The vaudeville houses were showing pictures. Some acts were still booked into the presentation houses, but they became fewer and fewer. To show a profit at the box office, a film had to be performed continuously, emptying and refilling the theater several times a day. A picture could take up to two and a half hours to run. How much time was left for a stage show, for music?

Publishers and song-pluggers gladdened momentarily when big bands rose in popularity and "swing" was written into the musical lexicon. Bands were featured in the presentation houses and played for dancing in hotel ballrooms and college gymnasiums around the country. Here, at last, was some remnant of the "big plug," and it had a double advantage. Big bands introduced or familiarized a new song to large numbers of people (even, the publishers admitted reluctantly, via radio) and they also induced smaller bands to play the same songs favored by the headliners. One important source of revenue for publishers was the prepared band or orchestral arrangement. Instrumental parts for copyrighted melodies were written by publishers' staffs of orchestrators and printed up in quantity for sale to orchestra librarians. The "stock arrangements" could take up the slack in dwindling sheet music sales.

Now, however, the prominent bandleaders who set the pace for smaller combinations dealt the publishers a blow they found it hard to surmount or forgive. The big bands were willing to play the tunes, all right, but they got fussy about *arrangements*. They insisted on exclusive treatments. They were no longer interested in playing the publishers' pedestrian orchestrations suitable for "businessman's bounce" dancing. They wanted style. What's more, they wanted *personal* style, tailored by hand to their own inimitable artistry.

This was a new twist, and it was disaster. High-priced arrangers were added to staffs which could afford them. It was as though the publisher of a novel were told by Brentano's that the book would be ordered only if Brentano's could get—at the publisher's expense—specially printed and bound copies. Brentano's demand would be echoed by every leading bookseller in the country.

Thinking itself doomed by radio, talkies, the decline of vaudeville and sheet music sales and by the demands of bandleaders for expensive, individualized arrangements, the music business panicked. Following an earlier precedent set by M. Witmark & Sons, Harms, Inc. and Remick Music Corporation, several firms scuttled under the Hollywood wing. Others merged with former rivals to bolster their sapped strength, and some sold their catalogs of valuable copyrights for eating money.

Roughed up but resilient, and whether subsidized, merged or just struggling along, the publishers managed to survive the threats of the '30s. At the same time, they managed also to produce some of the best and most beloved American popular music to date. Songs of enduring quality and appeal came from independent writers, from the musical-comedy stage and from the sound track of movies. Little boys and girls of today recognize, after a few notes, dozens of the songs that made their appearance at a time the music industry was playing the third act of *Camille* —songs that made their appearance thirty years before they were born into this age of earth satellites and gossip about interplanetary travel.

Nowadays, when performing artists say with a sigh, "they don't write 'em like that any more" they are usually talking about the songs of the twelve years which preceded the Japanese attack on Pearl Harbor. Those were the years when the title pages of popular songs were studded with the names of songwriters whose works are, if not immortal, at least indestructible. In those dozen years, some of America's favorite lyrics and melodies were created by Irving Berlin, Ira and George Gershwin, Cole Porter, Mitchell Parish and Hoagy Carmichael, Johnny Mercer, Lorenz Hart and Richard Rodgers, Arthur Schwartz and Howard Dietz, Ted Koehler and Harold Arlen, Dorothy Fields and Jimmy McHugh, Walter Donaldson, DeSylva, Brown and Henderson, Edgar Leslie or Al Dubin with Harry Warren, E. Y. Harburg and Vernon Duke, Oscar Hammerstein II with Otto Harbach and Jerome Kern, Arthur Freed and Nacio Herb Brown, Johnny Burke and Jimmy Van Heusen, Harry, Charles and Henry Tobias. To name a few.

Nevertheless, the publishers complained that business was lousy until, toward 1940, a significant change in public response to music offered them a renewed toe-hold on income they had lost when sheet music sales dwindled and stock dance arrangements fell off. The change revived a staple item on publishers' shelves —one they had long since mourned as permanently defunct.

In former years, a lucrative by-product of popular songs had been the folio collection, an album-sized anthology of current and past favorites arranged either for the home piano or for other instruments played by amateur musicians. This business had all but disappeared during the radio-and-talkie-dominated '30s, with publishers left holding vast warehouse remainders of albums nobody wanted.

By the late '30s, the phenomenon of the idolized band vocalist or instrumental soloist gave new impetus to such collections. In hotels or at college proms, couples stopped dancing to cluster around the bandstand, raptly listening to a favorite singer, pianist, trumpet or saxaphone player, clarinetist.

People cleared their throats to sing again, but they insisted on singing like Frank Sinatra. At least, they wanted to sing the songs Frankie "chose" for them. Home musicians threw away their humdrum exercise books and courageously bought albums of "arrangements by" Coleman and Erskine Hawkins, Benny Goodman, Harry James, Artie Shaw. Parlor pianos were dusted off and on their racks were placed collections of melodies "as played by" Carmen Cavallaro, Cy Walter, Duke Ellington, "Father" Hines.

It sometimes happened that a relatively obscure but fan-favored instrumentalist didn't have the foggiest notion of how he arrived at his style. He just played the way he felt and, more often than not, could neither read nor write a note of music. Undaunted, the publishers had private recordings cut as the artist played his heart out. Paid hirelings with good ears and a knowledge of musical notation later played the records back in a quiet room, unscrambling the tricky styles and faithfully reproducing them note for note, break for break, take-off for take-off. Well, almost faithfully.

Publishers knew that an artist's name and photo on a cover could make an album walk off dealers' shelves. They filled the inside pages with a shrewdly assembled variety of songs, of which very few were the current hits or near-hits on which they were obliged to pay writers' royalties. Many of the titles were "dogs" on which they could recover some of their original investments; many were tunes whose copyrights had lapsed, in which case the proportionate profits were pure gravy. Very often a performer's name would be attached to songs he never heard of.

Old-timers in music publishing breathed a little more freely again as the depression years receded and the nation's economy was considerably improved by accelerated production of war materials "for defense." The music business tactfully refrained from commenting about the European situation in 1940 just as it had refrained in 1915 and 1916. Once again, it had irritating problems of a local nature to worry about, and one of the thorniest was its continuing struggle with radio. The accumulation of fifteen years of resentment and frustration found expression, finally, in the classic battle between radio broadcasters and the music industry's creature, the American Society of Composers, Authors and Publishers.

6. *"They're Playing Our Song"—ASCAP and BMI*

WE BROKE BREAD TONIGHT because they broke bread that night.

"We are singing in a full voice now because they sang in a small voice then.

"We gaze from the roof of a shining tower because they labored to build a firm foundation.

"We are because they were."

These impassioned words opened the Fortieth Anniversary Dinner (1954) of the American Society of Composers, Authors and Publishers. The speaker was the society's president, Stanley Adams. As one of the authors, he was and is one of ASCAP's beneficiaries, receiving a slice of its annual melon—now in excess of $20,000,000.

"They" were nine men variously active in America's music business who met at Luchow's East Fourteenth Street restaurant in New York one evening early in 1914. The table had been set and places laid for thirty-five, but only nine dinners were served. Invited but absent for a variety of reasons were a number of men who would be future ASCAP enthusiasts, among them Max Dreyfus, John Golden, Jerome Kern, Irving Berlin and Gene

Buck (later the yet unborn's society's brilliant second president). Those who were present—the eulogized Nine—had gathered at Luchow's to discuss what could be done about an irritating situation that had gotten under their skins.

One of the men was Victor Herbert. His operetta, *Sweethearts*, had been a smashing Broadway success for a year and its title song was one of the top hits of the 1913-14 season.

Herbert had a grievance, and it was this grievance which had prompted him to suggest the informal meeting, now historic, at a favorite eating place of music men.

One evening not long before, Herbert said, he had gone to Shanley's Times Square restaurant in the company of his good friend, Giacomo Puccini. As the men entered the restaurant the orchestra was in the midst of playing the entire score of *Sweethearts*. The leader bowed in recognition to Herbert, and the composer graciously inclined his head in acknowledgment.

Puccini smiled at his friend and remarked, pleasantly, "That's nice. More money for you. I hear this lovely music so much—everywhere I go. You must be getting very rich."

Herbert explained to Puccini that, in America, the only way composers made money, aside from box office receipts if they were connected with stage presentations, was from the royalties they got from the sale of published music. Therefore, he said ruefully, "Sweethearts" could be played every five minutes by every restaurant in New York without putting a penny extra in his pocket. Moreover, he added, the well-advertised Shanley performances of his score were cutting into box-office business at the theater.

Puccini, Herbert recalled, was outraged. This America! Had it no respect for its creative artists? Did it not protect the writers of beautiful music which brought pleasure and inspiration to so many people? Why, in Europe it would be unthinkable to play a composer's work without permission and, mind you, without compensation. Even the smallest bistro in Paris paid a fee for music into the treasury of a protective society which, in turn, divided the collected monies at year's end among the writers and publishers. Public places in Europe were obliged to obtain licenses from the society if they wished to entertain their clientele with music. If a composer should happen to stroll past an eating or drinking place and hear his music played, he had the right to demand to see the license. If the proprietor had none to show, the composer could summon the nearest gendarme, have the scoundrel arrested and actually impound the cash register.

This, of course, was as it should be. In Europe, the composer of *La Boheme* pronounced, the creative artist was appreciated.

Herbert's voice rose angrily as he recounted the Shanley episode to his companions in Luchow's private dining room. A man who ordinarily discouraged conversation at meals, he hardly noticed the food on his plate.

It was high time, he said, for something to be done in America to prevent restaurateurs, the worst offenders, from using American music without payment to the copyright owners.

Eight heads nodded vigorously in agreement.

Another of the men seated at the table spoke up. This was George Maxwell, a Scottish-born, harp-playing bachelor who was the American branch manager of the Milan publishing company of G. Ricordi & Company, which controlled the bulk of Italian opera, including Puccini's. Maxwell, who had traveled extensively in Europe, was also familiar with the manner in which foreign performance-rights societies functioned. They were great, he said, and they certainly gave the composers and publishers a well-deserved break. But, he added, he did not know exactly how their principles could be applied to the American situation. Copyright laws of the United States granted control to the copyright owners of music only if it was performed *for profit*. Restaurant owners, as both he and Herbert knew, smugly argued that inasmuch as they did not charge admission to their premises, the Copyright Act did not affect them.

Listening attentively to Herbert and Maxwell as they enlarged on the injustices suffered by American composers, authors and publishers were: Jay Witmark, of the publishing firm M. Witmark & Sons; Glen MacDonough, author and librettist, and composers Raymond Hubbell, Silvio Hein, Gustave A. Kerker and Louis A. Hirsch.

So far, we have met eight of the Nine.

Also seated at the table was a man who not only listened, but also contributed sage advice. This was Nathan Burkan, Herbert's (and others') brilliant attorney who had previously distinguished himself during congressional hearings which led to revisions, in 1909, of the outmoded Copyright Act.

While Luchow's string ensemble played—without payment to anyone except the musicians—the melodies whose status was being discussed, Burkan agreed to work up a test case against Shanley's in the name of his client, Victor Herbert, basing his argument on the premise that the performances of the composer's work were in fact for profit, thereby constituting an infringement of the United States Copyright Act.

Before the party disbanded, it was decided that the nine men would call themselves an organization. They promised to canvass the field of prominent authors, composers and publishers and induce them to join.

Within a few days, the same men met again at Luchow's. Burkan produced a copy of his complaint against Shanley's and passed around a proposed set of Articles for the new organization, as yet unnamed.

By February 13, a sufficient number of songwriters and publishers had expressed interest in the project to warrant a more formal meeting at the Claridge Hotel, where the American Society of Composers, Authors and Publishers was named, a board of directors selected and officers voted in. George Maxwell became ASCAP's first president, with Victor Herbert as vice president, Glen MacDonough as secretary. Playwright-producer John Golden was named treasurer and Nathan Burkan was unanimously chosen to represent the infant society as its legal counsel.

With high hopes and unwavering belief in the justice of ASCAP's cause, Burkan quickly brought the Herbert-Shanley case into the United States District Court. Just as quickly, he lost. The court agreed with the restaurant owner, decreeing that since no admission was charged at the entrance, there was no public performance for profit.

It began to look as though ASCAP had been merely a fanciful idea, but Burkan was neither ready nor willing to admit defeat. Still pounding the Shanley grievance, the lawyer doggedly brought his case to successively higher courts, successively losing each round.

In 1914, the membership of ASCAP boasted 192 hopeful, dues-paying members, of which 170 were composers and authors and 22 publishers. The membership shrank to a handful of die-hards during the next few years as the test-case litigation was dragged through unsympathetic courts. The music men, apparently, had been initially willing to declare themselves in so long as quick success was a possibility, but they wearied under discouragement and wilted away under pressures that were soon brought to bear against them. In the light of ASCAP's current dignity and power, it seems incredible that only six publishers remained staunch supporters of their own organization continuously from its inception in 1914. These were Max Dreyfus' firm of Harms, Inc.; Leo Feist, Inc.; M. Witmark & Sons; Shapiro-Bernstein & Company; Charles K. Harris, and ASCAP president Maxwell's firm of G. Ricordi & Sons.

Under John Golden's able stewardship as treasurer, however, ASCAP slowly built a bankroll to start its campaign in earnest. Still-faithful ASCAP believers stormed into restaurants, hotels and cafés brandishing the society's "Articles" and insisting on license fees. The first license issued (at $15 per month) was to Luchow's, whose proprietor could hardly refuse. For one thing, Burkan was August Luchow's lawyer and Herbert was a close friend and influential patron. For another, Tin Pan Alley's songwriters and publishers did a lot of their eating and drinking at the restaurant's tables and bar.

From 1914 to 1917, ASCAP was popular music's mouth, but it was without teeth.

In 1917, Burkan boarded the Congressional Limited out of Pennsylvania Station and hugged his briefcase all the way to

Washington. He was on his way to plead the aging Herbert-Shanley case before the highest court in the land. This was as far as he could go, and on the outcome would stand or fall the fate of ASCAP.

It would be nice to report that all of America's music business waited breathlessly to hear the decision of the land's most exalted tribunal on a matter which vitally affected every songwriter and every publisher. But only a few of the faithful were present to hear Justice Oliver Wendell Holmes read the unanimous decision of the United States Supreme Court in the case of Victor Herbert, *plaintiff*, versus Shanley's Restaurant, *defendant:*

". . . . If the rights under the copyright are infringed only by a performance where money is taken at the door they are very imperfectly protected. Performances not different in kind from those of the defendants could be given that might compete with and even destroy the success of the monopoly that the law intends the plaintiff to have. It is enough to say that there is no need to construe the statute so narrowly. The defendants' performances are not eleemosynary. They are part of a total for which the public pays, and the fact that the price of the whole is attributed to a particular item which those present are expected to order, is not important. It is true that the music is not the sole subject, but neither is the food, which probably could be got cheaper elsewhere. The object is a repast in surroundings that to people having limited powers of conversation or disliking the rival noise give a luxurious pleasure not to be had from eating a silent meal.

"If music did not pay it would be given up. If it pays it pays out of the public's pocket. Whether it pays or not the purpose of employing it is to profit and that is enough."

Victory! ASCAP was transformed from a dream to a reality by an eleventh-hour legal decision. Now all it had to do was make the decision stick.

Proving its point was to be costly. In the process, the perpetual neurotic conflicts at work within the body of the music business were to become painfully evident.

Even with the Supreme Court ruling in their favor, the music publishers and songwriters were reluctant to join the fight for their own protection. Loud-voiced opposition to ASCAP was so effective that in fright a number of publishers withdrew their support. Officials of the Hotel and Restaurant Association, for example, gave an ultimatum to Joe Weber (of Weber & Fields), then president of the Musicians' Federation. Restaurants, hotels and cafés, he was told, would cut down the size of their orchestras if they had to pay the ASCAP license fees. This threatened to throw thousands of musicians out of work. Weber's panicky reaction was to order union members to boycott ASCAP songs.

The union edict threw a scare into several of ASCAP's publisher members, who promptly disclaimed their association with the society by running music trade paper advertisements cravenly announcing that *their* copyrights were "tax free."

The next few years were a shambles. In and out of court with infringement cases which concentrated on the songs of two loyal members—Harms and Shapiro-Bernstein—Burkan and his supporters watched the membership vacillate and dwindle as publishers and writers alike chose certain sheet music sales and royalties over the uncertain and still nonexistent "performance" income promised by the new and unproved society.

With World War I intervening, ASCAP limped along weakly until 1921, when a dynamic young leader was pulled out of the author-member ranks to lead the society into a new strength. Gene Buck, a charter member of ASCAP and librettist-producer for at least thirty of the *Ziegfeld Follies*, threw his considerable energies and forceful personality into the ASCAP cause. Under Buck's leadership, the society's membership pyramided until it embraced most of Tin Pan Alley's recognized composers and authors. He also gathered into the ASCAP fold America's top "standard" (classical) publishers. Side by side with Buck, another persuasive gentleman was busily recruiting the popular-music publishers. This was E. C. Mills, then the guiding light of the Music Publishers Protective Association.

Although it was developing noticeable muscles, ASCAP was

given neither admiration nor respect by the users of music. Each hard-won ASCAP battle gave rise to bitter recriminations and counterplots. Seven years after the famous Supreme Court decision was handed down, a single word in Justice Holmes' address from the bench became the first dart hurled at ASCAP in a series of attempts to puncture its balloon. The word was "monopoly," and it was shouted loudest by the motion picture industry.

Motion picture theater owners had refused outright to honor the 1917 Supreme Court decision on the claim that music did not constitute part of what they sold to the public. Pit pianos and orchestras, they argued, were only incidental to the action on the silver screen. People paid to see moving pictures, not to hear music. Besides, the publishers had a colossal nerve. They found theaters useful for song-plugging, didn't they? Why should they penalize theater owners who magnanimously gave them a showcase they were only too happy to get?

The theater owners had a point. Realizing, however, that exceptions of any kind could invalidate or weaken ASCAP's purpose (songs were plugged in restaurants, too, after all) Burkan persisted until, in 1918, he brought back a court decision that motion picture theaters were subject to licensing under the Copyright Act.

The entire motion picture industry rallied to theater owners' support and retaliated by accusing ASCAP of being a monopoly in restraint of trade.

After a long legal hassle ASCAP was given a clean bill of health on the monopoly charge in 1924, and motion picture theater proprietors snarlingly joined the ranks of licensees. Their Hollywood connections, seething with resentment, continued to mutter "monopoly" *sotto voce* until they sidled into the music business themselves by buying out publishing firms when the movies began to sing.

Court battles for vindication of its license demands and in defense of its altruistic purposes were not the only problems besetting ASCAP. For the first seven years of its existence, composer-author-publisher members kept asking, "Where is the money?" It was not until 1921 that the society was able to justify its promises in that department, dividing then a total of $81,833 among its members, who wondered if all the fuss and furor were really worth while.

Under the courtroom shouting and members' complaints, ASCAP's patient, far-seeing legal counsel heard a distant rumble that seemed to be getting closer. It was radio static. Burkan prepared his associates for the biggest battle of all.

From an experimental crystal-set and earphone gadget, radio in 1924 began to show signs that in time it would emerge as a great commercial medium. If Burkan anticipated trouble, so did the broadcasters. They were using vast quantities of copyright music for free public entertainment but, they knew, it was only a question of time before the tab would be picked up by advertisers. When that time came, they predicted, the ASCAP troublemakers would try to snatch away the profits.

Consequently, in the spring of 1924, radio management persuaded Senator Clarence Dill, from the state of Washington, to introduce a measure which would have nullified the 1917 Supreme Court decision by giving to radio the privilege of using music without cost on the grounds that music so used was a public service. Besides, the implication was, authors, composers and publishers should be grateful to radio for "free advertising" of their work.

Radio's future importance as a tool for propaganda was prophesied in the months which followed the measure's introduction. Radio audiences were regaled with strong messages imploring them to support the Dill Bill by wiring their Senators and Congressmen. The hint was planted that ASCAP was a confidence game played by greedy music sharks who, if they had their way, would deprive the American home of the solace and pleasure of music. Although radio audiences were small in those days, owners of home sets told their friends and neighbors. For a time during and following the congressional hearings on the Dill measure, the public regarded ASCAP bitterly, picturing it as the illegal racket it was said to be.

With Burkan at the legal helm, ASCAP succeeded in killing the 1924 proposal in Congress, but it was a stormy battle. The vanquished broadcasters did not take their defeat gracefully, but continued to introduce more bills at the rate of one a year, aimed at removing from radio the necessity of paying for the music it used.

In the early days of radio, while stations were improving techniques and building programs, ASCAP's demands for fees—when they were made at all—were nominal. As radio began to make money, the fees increased and each increase enraged the broadcasters.

In 1932 ASCAP arrived at its expedient of charging stations a percentage of gross time sales. This enraged the broadcasters still further. They looked on the demand for fees with the same loathing that prompted a group of rebellious and indignant American colonists to dump Britain's tea in Boston Harbor. The only difference was that radio could not dump music. Its management tried, nevertheless, to convince everybody that the ASCAP demand was a feudal extortion system, thoroughly un-American, a trumped-up "protection" racket run by gangsters.

There was, the broadcasters insisted, no connection whatsoever between the playing of music and the receiving of profits. Some went so far as to deny that they broadcast *music* at all. "All we do," they asserted piously, "is emanate electrical energy." If music, which is air-borne, happened to get transmitted by way of electrical impulses, it was just a remarkable phenomenon of the marvelous age we were living in.

Mr. Burkan and associates soon put an end to that kind of fantasy and, radio's outcries notwithstanding, ASCAP annually harvested its fees in a manner not unlike a skip-trace collector with his foot in a truculent debtor's door.

In 1936, another congressional to-do threatened to pull ASCAP's teeth. This was the controversy over the Duffy Bill, actually passed through the United States Senate a year previously, before the music business could rally its forces.

With the approval of President Roosevelt and the State Department, the Duffy Bill was primarily intended at the time as a piece of legislation which would bring the United States into the Berne Convention, joining this country with the more than fifty foreign nations then honoring a world-copyright regulation.

In the absence of any real international law, the Berne Convention had become effective in 1887. It provided that literary material copyrighted in a signatory country automatically enjoyed copyright protection in *all* the signatory countries. The entire copyright situation—domestic, foreign and international—is so complex that legal entanglements here and abroad are in continual ferment. Not until 1954 was some semblance of order and stability injected, when President Eisenhower signed the Universal Copyright Convention agreement which gives reciprocal copyright protection in all of the signing countries.

But in 1936 the United States was not a member of the Berne Convention. For a published American work to be protected in foreign countries, it had to be copyrighted individually in each of the countries where it was likely to be sold. This led to a confusion of rates and a hopeless tangle of red tape. The government's position was that affiliation with the Berne Convention would be a good thing.

The music business, however, saw in the Duffy Bill a purely local danger. The measure proposed the elimination of the $250 penalty for infringement of the existing copyright laws. Duffy insisted that his bill carried within its framework all the protection necessary for the creators of music. If passed, it would have had the effect of nullifying the Supreme Court decision of 1917 by permitting local courts to decide on infringement cases without reference to the mandatory decree of the Constitution.

Radio lurked behind the scenes during the Capitol Hill conversations about "literary copyright," but its interests were apparent in some of the arguments presented by the Senator from Wisconsin. To dramatize his points, Duffy had amassed a trunkful of letters from constituents who objected in principle to ASCAP's existence. He had also got his hands on some rather testy letters written by ASCAP representatives to prospective licensees demanding satisfaction for alleged infringements in language that was far from polite. Armed with these, the legislator protested to the Congressional committee that ASCAP was arrogant, unjust and uncouth and should be put in its place.

Luckily for the music business, there was one clause in the Duffy Bill which damned it. This was the "manufacturers' clause"—a necessary adjunct at that time to any enabling act designed to allow any nation to enter the Berne Convention. The clause permitted nationals of foreign nations to print up in its original language any literature and export it to other member countries for sale. Because of this one stipulation, the music business received—inadvertently—the support it required to kill the bill in committee. The opposition came, swiftly and hotly, from the nation's labor unions when it was pointed out to them that this type of legislation would have a harmful effect on American workers.

With the powerful union leaders raising a hue and cry in condemnation of the Duffy Bill, it languished and died in committee.

Hard on the heels of this external political fracas came an internal political conflict that piled up more black clouds for ASCAP.

Herman Starr, a vice president of Warner Brothers Corporation and president of Warner's Music Publishers Holding Corporation, picked up his copyrights and left ASCAP in a huff. Reason? Mr. Starr felt that inasmuch as MPHC's catalogs—Harms, Remick, Witmark, Advanced, New World—accounted for a hefty portion (20 per cent) of ASCAP-controlled music, MPHC should be paid a heftier portion of the license money. ASCAP didn't think so, even though MPHC's 40,000 copyrights included most of the work of Victor Herbert, Jerome Kern, Cole Porter, Noel Coward, George Gershwin, Sigmund Romberg and Rodgers and Hart.

Mr. Starr's gesture proved empty. At another time, perhaps, his withdrawal from ASCAP might have been an opening wedge for the radio networks to wangle a better deal for themselves with the performance-rights society. At this time, however, contracts between the broadcasters and ASCAP were in more or less peaceful force, and radio shrewdly felt that even without the Warner-affiliated music firms there would be enough music left over to feed the hungry microphones. This, as it turned out, was the case. Mr. Starr sat on his copyrights, comfortably certain that the sentimental listening public would miss all the *good* music it was accustomed to hearing and put up a holler. The public, either ungrateful or indifferent, hardly noticed that it was missing anything. Music was still played, and nobody bothered to question who wrote it or published it.

The only losers in the sit-down were Warner's own writers and publishing firms, who had to go entirely without performance earnings via radio plugs during the several months it took to convince Mr. Starr and his supporters that they had goofed. The boycott put the Hollywood studio on the horns of a dilemma. Warner Brothers controlled five prominent music publishing firms, but they had to choose between farming out movie tunes to rival publishers and remaining off the air, where every plug for a picture's song was a plug for the picture itself. Without advance radio plugs, the musicals were making a poor showing at box offices. With a shamefaced grin, the holding corporation returned to mama.

These two obstacles surmounted, ASCAP could now concentrate on its perpetual gadfly—the continuous buzzing and stinging of litigation in municipal, state and federal courts. The most active department in ASCAP was its legal staff, whose members spent the next four years of their lives in one courtroom after another, defending the society's very existence, as strike bills, tax measures and a steady stream of legislative proposals were introduced, calculated to void or at least modify the society's licensing powers.

Seven states passed laws to restrict ASCAP's activity within their boundaries. One of them—Nebraska—outlawed any organization which attempted to fix the amount of money to be paid for public performance of music. It was, the state law stipulated, up to each individual composer and/or author to collect the performance money due him. This, of course, was impossible.

Few of these internal struggles reached public awareness. But the greatest crisis in ASCAP's history was brewing, and when it erupted the public could not help paying attention. For almost the first time, music lovers tuned in to their favorite radio programs learned that a song was not a subjectively privileged intangible, inhabiting the air like friendly bacteria and absorbed into the bloodstream of private memory. People discovered, with a shock, that popular music is a unique combination of service and product, as much a commodity as toothpaste.

In 1938, ASCAP officials started preparations for renewals of radio broadcast licenses, due to expire at the end of 1940. In framing new contracts, ASCAP took into consideration the fact that radio had gained stature as a commercial medium during the years which followed the signing of the existing contracts. Moreover, suspecting that most of the costly litigations had been incubated by radio interests, ASCAP executives thought it would be only fair if new fees were sufficiently high to provide a cash cushion against such irritations in the future.

ASCAP's upcoming demands were learned by the broadcasters, who made it known in no uncertain terms that they would not submit to the "highway robbery" the society had in store for them. If ASCAP got out of hand, they hinted, radio would get along without ASCAP music. As a matter of fact, they threatened darkly, they would set up their own performance-rights society and get all the music they needed from "other sources."

The threat amused ASCAP no end. There were no other sources. The society smugly believed it had the upper hand because of its gigantic reservoir of copyrights. By this time, most of the music written and published in the United States since 1884 was sheltered under the ASCAP umbrella. The Copyright Act of 1909 had stretched the period of protection for published works from 28 to 56 years, and the songs all America sang belonged to ASCAP publisher and writer members with the exception of public-domain oldies and a scattering of titles held by a noncompetitive performance-rights society, SESAC.

Brushing aside the broadcasters' warnings as whistles in the dark, ASCAP forbore to comment and proceeded to juggle percentage figures around behind closed doors. Society officials suddenly became inaccessible for meetings with broadcast executives who were anxious to get things understood and settled prior to the expiration of contracts on December 31, 1940. At ASCAP's offices, switchboard operators sweetly informed broadcasting officials' secretaries that directors were out of town, in conference or otherwise unavailable.

Broadcasters got the message. It was evident that ASCAP had no intention of arbitrating the situation before the deadline. ASCAP's trump card, they agreed, would be the presentation of outrageous demands at the last possible moment, which would put radio at an extremely uncomfortable disadvantage. Radio would either have to pay up or be unable to broadcast the musical entertainment to which audiences were accustomed.

The National Association of Broadcasters held a series of worried meetings, starting as early as 1938. The groundwork was sketched for the formation of a rival performance-rights society in the likely event that ASCAP should pull its trump card at the crucial moment.

In September of 1939, a special convention of broadcasters was held in Chicago for the purpose of authorizing the creation of a source of music independent of ASCAP. A resolution introduced at this convention read, in part:

"Whereas, an adequate supply of music is essential to the public service rendered by the broadcasting industry, and

"Whereas, the American Society of Authors, Composers and Publishers has a practical monopoly of the music presently performed by the broadcasting industry, and

"Whereas, the representatives of the National Association of Broadcasters have since last May attempted in good faith to bargain with the ASCAP for the use of its music on a fair basis and a fair price, and

"Whereas, the officers of the ASCAP have refused despite repeated requests even to appoint a committee to consider the price and basis on which ASCAP is willing to bargain so that the broadcasters have not been informed to this day what demands ASCAP is prepared to impose, and

"Whereas, the action of ASCAP in refusing to indicate its demands and the threats of its officers to exact concessions in advance as a condition prerequisite even to sitting at a bargaining conference, render it imperative to the very existence of the broadcasting industry that it take practical steps to the defense of its rights to continue in business, and

"Whereas, in view of the foregoing, the creation of an independent source of music is a necessary measure, now, therefore, be it

"RESOLVED, that the NAB cause a corporation to be organized with broad powers to carry out the building of an alternate source of music suitable for broadcasting and to make such music available to broadcasters and others."

The resolution further stipulated that the license fees for such independent music would not exceed 50 per cent of the amount ASCAP had exacted from signatory broadcasters in 1937.

On October 14, 1939, Broadcast Music, Inc. (BMI), was organized under the laws of the State of New York, with authority to issue 100,000 shares of capital stock, all of one class, and each of the par value of $1.00. Of this total, however, 80,000 shares were offered to owners and operators of broadcasting stations at $5.00 per share. (By July 1, 1940, 51,813 shares of the capital stock had been so sold.)

BMI was in business.

ASCAP had been fortunate, in its birth struggles, to have the guidance of Nathan Burkan, its legal genius. BMI, in its beginnings, had Sidney Kaye, without whom the new performance-rights group would probably have collapsed out of feebleness.

Kaye, as brilliant a lawyer as Burkan, nursed BMI through its infant months, carefully planning and supervising the fledgling corporation's campaign but managing affairs so realistically that should the broadcasters and ASCAP come to an agreement before the deadline, BMI could be shelved and its costs marked off to business losses.

As time ticked away without any indication of a possible amicable treaty between the two antagonists, Kaye quit temporizing and began aggressive maneuvers to empower BMI to make good its bluff that broadcasters could get along without ASCAP music. BMI tackled the formidable task of collecting popular songs—from independent writers who had not yet managed to make the ASCAP grade; from publishers not affiliated with ASCAP, and from public-domain melodies dressed up in new arrangements which could be copyrighted.

With still some time to go before their licenses with ASCAP expired, radio stations began to intersperse their programs with these hastily constructed BMI tunes, none of them exceptional although one—"Practice Makes Perfect"—did manage to make the Hit Parade list in August of 1940.

The music business in general was not in the least impressed by BMI, and the new organization found it hard to attract experienced employees. Although the salaries and working conditions offered were tempting, seasoned musical personnel hesitated to take jobs. Writers, arrangers, copyists and other musically trained men and women doubted BMI's ability to last. They feared ASCAP's reprisals if they should join the new corporation and be thrown out of work when, inevitably, it folded.

Possibly no one can be blamed for not recognizing, in 1940, the future (some would say "fatal") influence on American popular music that BMI was going to be. A whole new aspect of song writing, publishing and musical trends was in the offing. Without BMI and the doors it opened beyond Tin Pan Alley's *cul de sac*, it is doubtful that the annals of American popular music would include such proliferations as the now familiar country and Western, syncopated gospel, rock 'n roll and so-called "calypso" music.

Although these classifications existed in various forms and by other names and were immensely popular in sections of the country where they originated, their writers and publishers had to struggle for a recognition that was difficult to achieve without ASCAP's backing. Before BMI proved itself, ASCAP took a dim view of Western, mountain, religious or what was then called "race" music, looking almost exclusively to Broadway and Hollywood publishers and their established writers to supply the nation's popular-music fare.

Until BMI came along, the only performance-rights society available to writers and publishers of offbeat music (by ASCAP standards) was a privately owned corporation known as SESAC. When it was founded in 1931 by Paul Heinecke, one-time president of a German music publishing firm, its initials stood for the Society of European Stage Authors and Composers. Its chief function then was to protect the interests of European copyright owners when their music was played for profit in the United States.

When Hitler's machinations threw the international copyright situation into more of a muddle than it normally was, rights became so confused that they were finally put into abeyance by the Alien Property Custodian. SESAC, under Heinecke's supervision, became the performance-rights clearing house for American publishers of the spiritual, country, race, authentic jazz, Latin-American and other music classifications spurned by ASCAP. Heinecke retained the initials, but re-interpreted the name—Selected Editions of Standard American Catalogues.

SESAC differs from ASCAP and BMI both in that it does not especially care about the one shining goal which spurs everybody else in the popular-music business. It does not seek, or even want to be identified with, "hits." When one happens, it is an accident—as, for example, when the classical melody "Intermezzo" became a popular hit in 1940 after its appearance in a motion picture of the same name, starring Leslie Howard.

When SESAC was ten American years old, and BMI opened the purse strings for the kind of music never previously considered commercial, SESAC could stop worrying about getting involved with even accidental hits. It then turned its major efforts toward supplying radio stations with libraries of transcribed musical programs in a dozen or so categories. Scripts and program notes accompany the transcriptions, making it easy for announcers at subscribing stations to "ad lib" authentic biographical notes and scholarly comments.

A catalog of transcribed "bridges, moods and themes" was also made available to production managers wishing to create appropriate musical illusions for their programs. If an announcer wanted to set a mood for a weather report predicting turbulence, he could flip through the SESAC files until he came to "Storm" and play all or part of C. Sodero's "Roman Chariots" or some similar blustering orchestral excerpt. Under "Strange," for background or introduction to mystery dramas and psychological thrillers, the program director could choose five seconds of "Angel's Garden" as sung by a quartet, or forty-five seconds of an organist's eerie rendition of "All Hallow's Eve."

SESAC's move into the transcription business was probably the only one it could take to insure survival in the performance-rights field after BMI came into the picture. In its eagerness to build up a backlog of music, BMI became a generous, paying patron for the kind of songwriters whom ASCAP had rejected for so many years. The folk tune, cowboy lament, barbershop ballad, polka and gospel chant of a scornful yesterday became, almost overnight, a potential popular hit. People liked this music. They would have liked it earlier, no doubt, if ASCAP publishers had considered it commercial.

By Autumn of 1940, with the contract deadline only weeks away, ASCAP was ready to announce its new rates. What the broadcasters would be required to pay if they wished to enjoy the privilege of playing music in the catalogs controlled by the performance-rights society was a 7½ per cent slice of the networks' gross time sales.

Stunned, NAB broke down the new terms and compared them with those of the contracts then in force. The 7½ per cent take, broadcasters figured, would amount to something in the neighborhood of $9,000,000 for the rental of ASCAP music in 1941—an increase of 100 per cent over the amount paid by radio in

1939. This, the station owners claimed, would mean economic destruction to important sections of the industry.

ASCAP officials countered by accusing NAB of weasel-wording its objections and making statistics lie. After all, ASCAP pointed out, the fee percentage represented the merest fraction of the increased profits accruing to radio from its own hiked rates to a greater number of advertisers. Moreover, ASCAP reminded, radio station program directors and advertising-agency-controlled shows and sponsors, too, leaned heavily on music—ASCAP music—to make their entertainment attractive, hence profitable. Many stations were on the air twenty-four hours a day, playing and re-playing ASCAP music. Why shouldn't the broadcasters be required to pay a fair portion of their profits to the source from which they derived so much of their program value?

The stalemate had been reached. Radio refused to pay, and beginning at midnight on December 31, 1940, it would become an infringement for any radio station to broadcast any ASCAP music over American air-waves.

Both sides anticipated that the decisive crux of the situation would be the American public. ASCAP was confident that radio dialers would be outraged to the point of action by the sudden blackout on their beloved music. BMI was only too afraid that ASCAP was right, for all it had to offer in replacement of the familiar popular melodies were about three hundred new and untried tunes, some SESAC catalog acquisitions and approximately four hundred new arrangements of public-domain compositions. Added to BMI's nervousness was uncertainty about how radio advertisers would react to the musical fare available to their programs. BMI's worry was ASCAP's hope.

BMI's Sidney Kaye, anticipating a barrage of inevitable ASCAP lawsuits should any commercial network show be guilty of using the soon-to-be taboo music, had prepared an efficient department geared with cash and legal brains to protect BMI's licensees against charges of infringement.

After the stroke of midnight in New York City on that New

Year's Eve, 1940, eastern networks scrupulously monitored their shows to prevent the playing of ASCAP tunes. But midnight in New York was only 11 p.m. in Chicago, 10 in Salt Lake City and 9 in San Francisco. Network pickups of remote broadcasts which traditionally took New Yorkers along on midnight revelries as they traveled across the time zones gave BMI its first three hours of jitters. Each separate infringement, under the Copyright Act provision, was liable to a minimum penalty of $250. Kaye's legal staffers hovered nervously near their telephones all night long.

Kaye had thought of everything, it appeared. On his instigation a brainwashing technique had been in effect since Spring of 1940, conditioning the listening public to the kind of non-ASCAP tunes it might be hearing from January 1 of the following year. Without being identified in any way, BMI songs were aired throughout each broadcast day, skipping in and out among new and old ASCAP tunes.

Bandleaders who had regular radio shows had long since been asked by the networks to discard their ASCAP theme songs and have new ones in readiness.

A special public relations department had been established by Kaye for the networks to handle promptly by mail and telephone any and all complaints which might be forthcoming from the listening public when BMI music replaced ASCAP music entirely.

So, on January 1, 1941 and for weeks thereafter, BMI officials, the networks and Mr. Kaye held their collective breaths as they waited defensively for public outcry, sponsor exodus and the sheriff.

What happened?

Nothing.

The American public, despite its fondness for popular music and also despite the passionate propaganda issued by both sides in the controversy, proved to be remarkably indifferent. It got music, mostly "Jeannie with the Light Brown Hair," and it couldn't have cared less.

The elaborate public-relations setup so carefully prepared by Sidney Kaye had to cope with fewer than a dozen written complaints. BMI officials privately suspected that even these few protests were either dictated or influenced by ASCAP members or their families.

BMI could relax on one elbow. The public accepted its music.

In a little while, BMI discovered it could relax still more. Radio station and network advertisers, taking the public's temperature, noted that show ratings were not dropping off. Sponsors stayed put.

To Kaye, BMI officials and the networks, the most anticlimatic fact of the cold war months, during which they had tensed themselves warily to fight to bloody death, was that the anticipated ASCAP counterattack simply did not happen. Not one infringement suit was entered to keep Kaye's organization of battle-ready legal talent occupied.

Congratulating itself on its strategy now that the strategy seemed to be working, BMI concentrated on improving and augmenting its supply of popular music to fill the breach opened by the ASCAP embargo.

Up to the feared deadline, BMI's greatest single coup had been the acquisition of the Edward B. Marks Company's catalogs—for a rental price in excess of a million dollars. Marks, one of several big-time publishers approached by BMI, threw in his lot with the newly formed performance-rights society after weighty deliberation and for mixed reasons, only one of which was the considerable money involved.

A pioneer among early Tin Pan Alley's influential publishers and one of the first members of ASCAP, Marks had felt for a long time that he was not sufficiently appreciated by his colleagues. Not overly conceited, he was an ambitious man with a personal need for recognition. He wanted to be reckoned as a big man in his field. He felt he deserved more attention and better billing in the industry he had helped formulate and expand.

BMI's bid put him in the position of being the biggest boy on the block in a new neighborhood. While he didn't exactly jump at the offer, his shrewd trading gave him in one swoop a great deal of money and publicity (not all of it favorable) and a new-felt, invigorating sense of power.

The Edward B. Marks Company's bulging catalogs of new and old favorites, including their priceless copyrights of Ernesto Lecuona's excellent Latin-American music, were a good investment and provided a valuable ad for BMI. Attracted by the company they'd be keeping—and by the more than generous financial arrangements forthcoming from BMI—lesser publishers joined the fold.

To publishers, BMI offered what amounted almost to subsidy on a pay-as-you-go basis. In effect, the society said: "You fellows know your business. We'll guarantee you $20,000—or $30,000—or $10,000 the first year, *in advance*, for you to use in building up your catalogs with songs we can play." At the year's end, a bookkeeping system calculated which publishers earned their keep and which did not on the basis of tabulations of song performances. Another incentive to publishers was BMI's promise to pay for *each performance* of any given song. This was in favorable contrast to ASCAP's prevailing method of payment based on an intricate system of intangible values such as: How long had the publisher been a member of ASCAP? How valuable was his catalog? How recently did he have a substantial hit?

Small publishing firms which never in their wildest enthusiasm dreamed of so much money or such ready acceptance rushed to jump on the broadcasters' bandwagon. So did a number of enterprising fringe-dwellers who had always longed to be real music publishers but had never quite managed to raise enough money to begin.

Established songwriters, too, found the per-performance pay-off dangled before them by BMI much easier to take than ASCAP's unwieldy and confusing nine-point payment gauge which determined shares to writers according to the nature of their contribution to American music, their seniority in the society, their "availability" over the years and the number and popularity of their hits. Moreover, a songwriter was not then eligible for ASCAP membership until he had published a minimum of five songs. BMI paid off on the first one.

Hitherto unsuccessful songwriters, including many amateurs, saw in BMI the open-sesame for recognition at last. Their hopes were frequently realized, for the new performance-rights society was desperate for solid American songs which did not mention Jeannie's hair-do or require maracas and gourds for performance.

As BMI's position strengthened, ASCAP began to feel a weakening of its bank account. Ten months were to pass before total truce was declared, and meantime ASCAP suffered still another blow. A Justice Department suit, instituted in 1934, was revived by Thurman Arnold under the Sherman Anti-Trust Act. In this action, ASCAP was accused of illegally pooling copyrights in order to monopolize (there's that word again) the supply of music; discriminating against non-ASCAP composers and authors; restraining composers and authors in their right to bargain for the sale of their own music.

No stranger to the courts, ASCAP again faced the notoriety of public investigation if the suit were prosecuted. Still in the midst of negotiations with radio networks in an attempt to get itself out of its air-wave exile, ASCAP engaged Charles Poletti, then lieutenant governor of New York State, to represent it in conference with the United States Justice Department chiefs. By an ironic twist, the case came before the Honorable Ryan Duffy, federal judge in the Wisconsin District, who, as a Senator five years previously, had been the cause of so much ASCAP grief.

The only out, it appeared, was for ASCAP to sign a Consent Decree with the Justice Department and shake itself free (at least momentarily) from the stigma of "monopoly."

Under the terms of the decree, ASCAP unbent from its former rigid policies, agreeing that it would no longer insist on acting as the exclusive agent for its members. They could henceforth deal individually with users of music if they wanted to. The document also removed from the society's autocratic board of directors its self-perpetuating powers. And—from now on, a

LIBRARY
OKALOOSA - WALTON JUNIOR COLLEGE

songwriter would be eligible for ASCAP membership *and earnings* upon the publication of one song.

Humbled by court scoldings and softened by the drain on its income, ASCAP made its peace with the networks in November of 1941. On New Year's Eve it had asked for 7½ per cent of major networks' gross time sales. It settled for 2¾ per cent.

Who won? It's hard to say. Certainly, with radio's growth as a tremendous user of music, ASCAP's yearly dividends increased year by year, leaping higher when television appeared. Even at 2¾ per cent, publisher, author and composer members have shared in excess of $20,000,000 a year since 1955, with some songwriters above the $50,000 bracket. ASCAP money, it must be remembered, is for commercial performances only. Songwriters' and publishers' earnings also include publication royalties and a number of other revenue sources.

BMI has not done too badly for its members, either. There are no songwriter members, but publishers share their BMI license revenues with their tunesmiths on individually determined arrangements. BMI, which got into performance rights twenty-seven years after ASCAP was founded, pays out annually about half as much as the original society.

The music-publishing field, which counted around six hundred ASCAP and SESAC firms in 1940, swelled to three thousand in 1957. The majority of the increased numbers were affiliated with BMI. Even old, well-established publishing firms solidly entrenched in ASCAP before 1941 found it feasible and profitable to add BMI firms to their office space and letterheads.

Along with the multitudes of popular songwriters who joyfully welcomed BMI as a source of performance income never before open to them, composers of serious music—for almost the first time—found it possible to earn a livelihood from their work. BMI paid for performances of classical works to member publishers. Under the Consent Decree, ASCAP also opened its portals to modern young composers of fine music.

Starting in 1941, when BMI was hard pressed for new popular titles, old manuscript files were dusted off and opened. Millions of people heard, many for the first time, revivals of charming public-domain melodies and strains of (popularized) classical themes they might have missed if ASCAP's commercial Broadway standards had remained the yardstick for radio music.

Adherents to the two performance-rights societies continuously bait each other. BMI followers accuse ASCAP of being snooty. ASCAP champions look down their noses at BMI and condemn it for being corny, phony and cheap. Rock 'n roll and other crazy music would never have emerged to sully American ears, say some ASCAP writers (who specialize in ballads) if BMI hadn't pried open the manhole.

In 1954, several top ASCAP songwriters banded together in an attempt to prove conspiracy on the part of network broadcasters who have a financial interest in BMI. The conspiracy alleged was that station program directors and disk jockeys were pressured into favoring BMI-licensed songs over those licensed by ASCAP. This, the songwriters said, is in violation of the anti-trust laws. It discriminated against non-BMI songwriters who, they claimed, found it difficult in consequence to maintain their reputations— and incomes—as hit-writers. If their songs weren't heard, they protested, they couldn't very well become hits. The ASCAP group demanded $150,000,000 in "damages."

ASCAP songwriters, with ASCAP incomes well over $50,000 a year pleaded that they were being impoverished by all those unfair tactics on the part of network broadcasters. BMI, on its part, contended that its very existence was a spur to healthy competition in popular music. It was suggested that ASCAP writers were sore because the competition may have become too rough for them to handle. "Maybe," said a BMI spokesman, "those sophisticated, drawing-room, nice-Nelly, 'moon-June' type composers and authors just couldn't produce the kind of music the kids like. Tough."

Either implied or outspoken, also, was ASCAP's sometimes sorrowful, sometimes irascible prediction that BMI was inevitably downgrading the standards of American popular music. ASCAP took the attitude that it is the responsibility of the music industry as a whole to shape public taste in music. If the public were to hear nothing but claptrap cadences and idiotic babbling, then the public couldn't help having lousy taste in music.

Vivid charges and counter-charges were hurled by both sides in pre-trial hearings that dragged on until 1956, when the issue was placed before the House Anti-Trust Subcommittee chaired by (pro-ASCAP) Representative Emanuel Cellar (D., N.Y.) ASCAP was in strange territory. Itself the target for many previous charges of monopoly, ASCAP—through its songwriter members—was righteously charging someone else with the same horrid word.

In 1957, a measure was introduced by Representative George Smathers. (D., Fla.) This was a bill of divorcement. Radio broadcasters, the measure demanded, should be forced to divest themselves of their music holdings.

When—or if—the inter-organizational squawks are quieted, either through understanding or compromise or by the President's signature on an Act of Congress, a merciful calm will settle over popular music in the United States. Maybe.

ASCAP and BMI serve the music business and the public alike. It is generally agreed, even among those whose financial interests force them to take sides, that there is as much need in a democratic country for not one, but two major performance-rights societies as there is for a two-party political system. That the existence of BMI prevents ASCAP from becoming a smug and restricted club has already been demonstrated by the revisions in ASCAP policy and membership requirements, as well as in its ratings and payment arrangements.

Operating strictly as a nonprofit organization, ASCAP uses the annual dues (not fees) it collects—$10 from writers, $50 from publishers—for a number of worth-while causes. It contributes money, time and talent to deserving national and community enterprises, participates in research projects concerning the use of music in industry and for therapy and fosters musical talent in schools and colleges.

Although it is jealous and demanding where commercial performances of member-owned music are concerned, ASCAP is generous to noncommercial users of its music, granting free licenses to religious, educational or veterans' organizations, to the Armed Forces and to government- and college-owned radio stations operating on a noncommercial basis.

ASCAP has quietly performed many acts of kindness and charity above and beyond the literal interpretation of its bylaws. It has sought out indigent heirs of composers and authors whose creative lifetimes ended before ASCAP was born and has in many instances created trust funds or annuities for them out of respect for a musical heritage for which no money could legally be collected.

In 1939, ASCAP searched outlying Philadelphia cemeteries until it found the weed-choked, unmarked grave of James A. Bland, who died impoverished in 1911. Grass, flowers and a carved headstone now dignify the final resting place of the man who wrote "Carry Me Back to Ol' Virginny," "Golden Slippers," "Hand Me Down My Walking Cane" and "De Golden Wedding."

The society also sponsors the Annual Nathan Burkan Memorial Competition, awarding cash prizes to law students who submit winning essays on the subject of copyright. The contest is a calculated investment in good public relations. ASCAP, long heckled by litigation, feels that the more lawyers and judges become familiar with the complicated copyright laws of America as they relate to music, the less trouble it is likely to encounter when cases are brought to trial.

From its beginnings in 1914 as an idea in the minds of a few foresighted men of music, ASCAP has grown to formidable dimensions. It was the first American organization to take into account the songwriters' and publishers' rights to compensation for commercial performance of their copyrights.

But *how* ASCAP works is frequently a mystery even to its own members, especially the composers and authors, many of whom grumble constantly about inequities inherent in the society's complex system of allocating, as quarterly royalties, the annual collections of fees from users of the music in its repertory. Although admitting that its formula is far from perfect, ASCAP nevertheless feels that its present distribution setup is the fairest that songwriters have had in the history of the society.

Writer members are reclassified every year and the royalty checks they receive every three months reflect ASCAP's discretionary evaluations of their ratings in importance to American music as a whole.

ASCAP's annual collections from licensees are divided into four separate treasuries: the Sustained Performance Fund, representing thirty per cent of total income; the Accumulated Earnings Fund (twenty per cent); the Availability Fund (thirty per cent), and the Current Performance Fund (twenty per cent). Of these four funds, the last named is the only one which is a yardstick of a songwriter's present popularity with disk jockeys and performers, for it is based on the compilation of performance credits amassed during the preceding calendar year.

A songwriter's share in the Current Performance Fund is arrived at by a complicated system. Major radio and television networks operating out of New York submit to ASCAP title lists of all music used throughout each broadcast day, and the lists are broken down at ASCAP's offices as to their composer, author and publisher. The society also maintains a coast-to-coast monitoring system which spot-checks unaffiliated stations. These geographical listening posts are changed several times a year and they operate in much the same manner as a market or political survey poll which analyzes a whole nation's population by counting heads in representative areas. What ASCAP does is to multiply the aggregate of monitored performances by a mean-average constant to yield an estimated total of performances on all radio and television broadcasts.

ASCAP takes into consideration that some performances may be weighted. Songs used as jingles or background cues, for example, or new copyrights on public domain material, receive less credit than original works regularly programed. On the other hand, symphonic, concert and choral works receive special consideration based upon the length of their performance time.

Once the total performances of all ASCAP music have been estimated, the next step is to determine how much each member will be paid from the Current Performance Fund. To do this, ASCAP figures out how much a single current performance credit is worth by dividing the entire amount of money in the Current Performance Fund by the grand total of the preceding year's performances. Then, to learn each writer's share, *his* total of individual current performances is multiplied by the value of a single performance credit.

A publisher always receives fifty per cent of performance credit, but a writer's portion depends on the extent of his contribution to a song. If the work is exclusively an instrumental piece, the other half of the performance credit goes to the composer. If it is a song with words and music, the writers' half-credit is divided equally between the author and composer unless, of course, the song was created by more than two songwriters. One composer and two lyric writers on the same title page split the fifty per cent royalty credit accordingly—twenty-five per cent to the composer, twenty-five divided between the two lyricists. Credit for a song with "words and music by" several collaborators can present some interesting problems in arithmetic—and human relations. ASCAP maintains a large staff of accountants and skilled operators of automatic tabulating machines, but squabbles among the song-writing teams are beyond its jurisdiction.

But current performances, remember, represent only twenty per cent of the songwriter's royalty. The remaining eighty per cent of his check is translated from those other funds—Sustained Performance, Accumulated Earnings and Availability. This is what is meant by a songwriter's ASCAP rating. It is decided, also on a credit formula, by weighing his length of membership in ASCAP and appraising his year-after-year contributions to the ASCAP repertory. Writer members have the option of deciding for themselves whether they wish their contributions to American music evaluated over a five- or a ten-year period. Over ten years, royalties are smaller annually than they would be if the writer elects the five-year plan—but, then, so are the taxes.

ASCAP royalties have been respectfully and gratefully hailed as "annuities" by writer-members happily in the higher rating brackets, but they have also been damned as "measly pittances" by members who are not so happy about their ratings.

BMI claims that by paying publishers on a per-performance basis it compensates more fairly than ASCAP. Although this society has no writer members, it assumes that the authors' and composers' contracts with their publishers give them a better— certainly a more cash-in-hand—deal than ASCAP.

Toward which of the two performance-rights societies— ASCAP or BMI—should a new or aspiring songwriter look? One publisher with firms affiliated with both groups had this to say:

"If I were a songwriter, whether I joined ASCAP or brought my stuff to BMI publishers would depend on my personal character. If I wanted to set up an estate for my family to live on after I'm dead, I'd choose ASCAP. But if I were a guy who got lucky with one song and didn't know if I could repeat, I'd take BMI. Let's face it—ASCAP represents the more solid type of writer, like the novelist who can be counted on to turn out one good book a year, year in and year out. BMI gets more of the one-shots, maybe. But it pays off the whole amount of earned income right away for a fellow to spend while he can enjoy it, instead of spreading it out like dividends on a life insurance policy."

7. Tempo Fidgets

ITS OWN PRIVATE WAR having reached an uneasy truce in November of 1941, the music industry licked its battle wounds and looked nervously at the mess the world had got itself into.

Tin Pan Alley reprised the attitudes of 1916. Publishers didn't exactly turn down war songs, but they didn't publish them either. For the most part, songwriters found it expedient to avoid taking up cudgels, lyrically, for or against anybody.

There were two exceptions to the love ballads, stage and movie tunes served up on the musical menu late in 1941, after the ASCAP embargo was lifted from radio. They ventured to remind Americans that France and England were having a rough time, but they did it without mentioning why. One was Nat Burton and Walter Kent's "The White Cliffs of Dover" with a message of honest sympathy for the courageous British civilians under their nightmarish ordeal of savage Nazi bombings. The second, left over from 1940, was "The Last Time I Saw Paris," with words by Oscar Hammerstein II and a haunting melody by Jerome Kern.

Meantime, another cycle was in the making—as one always seems to be in popular music, whenever the air gets heavy with issues the industry deems it discreet to avoid. Songwriters did

107

not, as in 1916, escape into musical travelogs about Hawaii. Instead, they intensified a recently acquired habit of rewriting Tchaikowsky, with whom they had been having a one-sided love-affair for some time.

With an assist from an assortment of lyricists and arrangers, the great Russian classical composer became one of Tin Pan Alley's hottest tunesmiths almost fifty years after his death. Maestro Music Company published "Tonight We Love," with words by Bobby Worth and "music by" Ray Austin and Freddy Martin based on the first movement of the First Piano Concerto. Plucked from the same movement was "Concerto for Two." This is listed in *Variety's* "Music Cavalcade" as having "words and music by Jack Lawrence and P. I. Tchaikowsky," arranged by Robert C. Haring and published by Shapiro-Bernstein & Company.

Demonstrating that the composer of some of the world's greatest symphonies could write popular standards, too, the 1939 song called "Moon Love" (Fifth Symphony) continued in favor with its words by David and Davis Mack and musical embellishments by André Kostelanetz. Another posthumous hit enjoying a long run was "Our Love," also published in 1939 with words *and music* credited to Larry Clinton, Buddy Bernier and Bob Emmerich.

Classical themes become so indelibly identified with the Tin Pan Alley songwriters who rearrange them that, occasionally, their origins escape notice. One of the writers of "Our Love," Buddy (Daniel) Bernier, is the son of the late "Pop" Bernier, who also proudly fathered singers Peggy and Christine ("Daisy") of the Fred Waring organization. Whenever "Our Love" was played, Pop announced that "my boy Danny wrote that tune." One evening, Peggy and Daisy were on stage at the Forty-eighth Street Theater in New York from which the Fred Waring nightly radio broadcasts originated. Daisy had just finished her act and Peggy was getting ready to go into hers when a stage hand beckoned to them from the wings, making pantomime motions that there was an important telephone call for them.

Neither girl could leave the stage and frantically signaled back. Nervously getting through the rest of the show, the Bernier girls rushed backstage when the broadcast signed off.

"What's the matter?" they chorused.

The stage hand pointed to the wall telephone, whose earpiece was swinging loose.

Terrified that something catastrophic had happened at home, where "Pop" was baby-sitting for her little daughter, Peggy retrieved the phone and quavered into it.

Her father's voice shouted, "Peggy—Daisy—turn on a radio quick and listen to WABC! A heluva big band has been playing Danny's song off and on for damn near an hour. And guess who the bandleader is? *Toscanini!*"

With Russia's Tchaikowsky, Cuba's Ernesto Lecuona and America's Stephen Foster and a handful of unproved songwriters supplying the bulk of America's popular music throughout most of 1941, the industry—waiting for settlement of the ASCAP strike—was very nearly as unprepared for the suddenness of war as were the battleships riding at anchor in Pearl Harbor.

As soon as their first stunned surprise and outrage gave way to resolution, the heads of music-publishing firms held conferences with their best and most reliable songwriters, pleading for war songs that would surpass or at least equal the success of "Over There!" There may be a manuscript of such a song gathering dust in some publisher's file, but it was never released.

The best that Tin Pan Alley could do, in 1942, were "Praise the Lord and Pass the Ammunition!" "When the Lights Go on Again," "Johnny Doughboy Found a Rose in Ireland," "There's a Star-Spangled Banner Waving Somewhere" and "Der Feuhrer's Face." England supplied "He Wears a Pair of Silver Wings." From Irving Berlin's soldier show, *This Is the Army,* came the title song and "I Left My Heart at the Stage Door Canteen." Mr. Berlin was easily the year's—and the war's—most significant songwriter, sentimentally and patriotically. His "White Christmas" was introduced via the film *Holiday Inn;* and his "God Bless America," published in 1939 but actually written for and discarded from his 1917 *Yip, Yip, Yaphank* army show, has become the country's alternate national anthem.

During the war years, the music industry's perpetual perplexity about what constitutes a hit song remained unwavering, with publishers often misjudging their own products. In 1943, Warner Brothers released a musical film, *Thank Your Lucky Stars*, with music largely composed and written by the team of Arthur Schwartz and Frank Loesser. From this film Warner's music-publishing affiliate, M. Witmark & Sons, published the songs which, according to the best thinking in Hollywood and the R.C.A. Building, had the best merchandising potentials.

The title song, of course, was favored by executives on both coasts, but it ran into radio censorship difficulties because the first line of its lyric inquired, "How's your love life?" The plug tune, therefore, was scheduled to be "The Dreamer," sung in the film by Dinah Shore. In second place on the plug list was a sentimental little ballad called "How Sweet You Are."

But, it turned out, "The Dreamer" was almost unsingable except by someone with a voice whose quality and range equaled Miss Shore's. And although "How Sweet You Are" showed up nicely on the daily sales sheets, it was in no danger of being a smashing hit.

In the film there was a song which, in the vernacular of the music business, is called "special material." This usually means a song that's longer than the customary thirty-two bars—or shorter —or one that tells a story germane to the plot (in a picture or play)—or written specifically for a stage or night club singer—or otherwise not general enough to be commercially feasible as sheet music.

"They're Either Too Young or Too Old" was not considered suitable for exploitation as a popular song. The publisher had no intention of setting the (objectionable) lyrics and (overlong) melody in expensive type and printing copies which, the firm's sales manager insisted, would have extremely limited appeal. The song was just a bit of formless business interpolated in the film to provide guest star Bette Davis with an amusing and unexpected scene—unexpected, because Miss Davis did not usually burst into song. Positively, definitely, absolutely, the song was not salable.

The song was special material, it was too long and it did have lyrics that were somewhat suggestive. But Witmark and its sales manager (the late Bill Wiemann) failed to reckon with the mood of young men going off to war, who wholeheartedly approved the song's idea that the men left behind to date their girls were either too juvenile or too senile to be a romantic threat. "They're Either Too Young or Too Old" was the one song in the film that showed animation. The title kept turning up on salesmen's request slips. Where were the copies? Witmark rushed the song into print and it became one of the top hits of 1943.

The music industry boomed during the war. Songs were essential for military and civilian morale, and they were also consumed in great quantities by U.S.O. camp shows, at officers' and enlisted men's canteens, by celebrities on visits to hospitals, frontline barracks and bond rallies. Dimmed bright lights and liquor shortages closed the night clubs early, as they had in 1917 and 1918, but the night spots were no longer the "big plug." Wartime skyrocketed the sales of sheet music and records via millions of radios tuned in to catch the latest war news between programs of entertainment.

The busy air-waves vibrated with audible omens that new trends in popular music were gathering themselves. Vocal soloists, not bands, were the star performers. The demand for swingy, dance-geared music was replaced by a revival of interest in sweet, singable ballads. The songwriters were delighted. Now they could write real songs again, and the technical improvements in radio since its infancy in the '30s meant that they could write songs with more flexible ranges. The early microphone artists, because of the imperfect medium, had performed best with simple songs constructed on a five-note scale. This limited songwriters and publishers alike, who found it necessary to keep their material within the scope of radio's mike-conscious performers and the technical problems of transmission.

As radio sending and receiving equipment improved, there began to emerge a group of singers whose tonal qualities could be more faithfully transmitted. Lyrics still had to be simple—a problem for the lyricists—but melodies could and did begin to roam further away from middle C in both directions.

Up to the war years, too, the majority of the celebrated vocalists singing with broadcast bands or starring on their own programs were what the business calls "boy singers." "Boys" like Al Jolson, George Jessel, Eddie Cantor, Gene Austin, Morton Downey, Rudy Vallee, Bing Crosby and the younger Tony Martin, Frank Sinatra and Perry Como were the sought-after plugs for new songs and records.

Now, however, with many of the up-and-coming boy singers off to the wars and the established boy singers spending much of their time entertaining the armed forces at home and overseas, "the girls" had their inning. This is not to say that feminine vocalists had never been popular. There were great stage and club singers like Sophie Tucker, Helen Morgan, Ruth Etting and Hildegarde. There were recording favorites in the "collector's item" category ... Bessie Smith, Ella Mae Morse, Mildred Bailey, Ella Fitzgerald, Lee Wiley, Ethel Waters. But with the exception of hello-folksy Kate Smith and "novelties" like the sweet-singing Boswell Sisters who brought a new kind of syncopated harmony to the sister act, the girls had never reached the record-selling ability of the boys.

The war years changed all that. Attractive, hard-working, likable Dinah Shore stepped out of the anonymous ranks of band vocalists and became a beloved radio, movie and recording artist. Star-maker Tommy Dorsey proved that what he had done for Sinatra he could do for Connie Haines and Jo Stafford. Bea Wain, Margaret Whiting, Mary Small and Ginny Simms found themselves in the coveted top echelon of radio and record demand. The girls had arrived. Their faces began to appear on sheet music title pages and record album covers. They had come to stay, too. After the war, they made room for Peggy Lee, Doris Day, Lena Horne, Theresa Brewer, Georgia Gibbs, Patti Page,

Pearl Bailey, Kay Starr, Joni James, Toni Arden, Sarah Vaughan, Eileen Barton, Rosemary Clooney, and others.

Happily turning out a variety of popular songs—bisexual, now that the girls were big plugs like the boys—the publishers were unaware, or seemed to be, that still another important trend was in the making.

The incoming trend was an entirely new note in modern popular music. It had the sound of folk music but it was *new*, not just the warmed-over revivals of songs of yesteryear.

"The Nashville Influence" is what Tin Pan Alley, for want of a better name, called songs with peculiar, noncommercial titles like "The Great Speckled Bird," "The Wabash Cannon Ball" and "Old Cold Tater." What were Brill Building publishers supposed to do with music calling for yodel-y voices, scraping fiddle strings and gee-tars?

They didn't know, but it occurred to them soon that it behooved them to find out. Down in Nashville, Tennessee, a corny show called *Grand Old Opry* was pulling in thousands of cheering fans every day. The music on this stage (and radio) program, almost all of it written by the men who performed it in front of their own bands, was published and recorded by a few Nashville firms. Since 1941, these firms had been accepting invitations to join up with BMI. They had been spurned for years by ASCAP publishers, who brushed off their musical specialties with contempt as "that hillbilly stuff."

Western songs, which bore a resemblance to the Nashville offerings in that they too were unsophisticated, had given broad hints for years that cowboys and corrals and simple, personal expressions about homely topics held charms for popular-music lovers who had never been west of Buffalo, New York. During the depression years of the '30s, Boston-born Billy Hill's "The Last Round-up," "Wagon Wheels," "Empty Saddles" and "Old Spinning Wheel" were received enthusiastically all over the country, including Manhattan, and so was Bob Nolan's "Tumbling Tumbleweed."

All hints notwithstanding, the Broadway music business paid

little attention to what was a dormant trend until, in 1944, Cole Porter's version of a Western song—"Don't Fence Me In"—became an overnight sensation. Mr. Porter had written his song several years earlier, but it lay a-moldering on a shelf at Harms, Inc., until it was planted in a Warner Brothers film (*Hollywood Canteen*) by one of Tin Pan Alley's most beloved song-pluggers, Mose Gumble.

But even the brilliant success of "Don't Fence Me In" failed to convince the industry that a significant new twang in popular music had sounded. The song was thought to be a hit because it was written by Cole Porter and given lavish production in a star-studded movie, followed by aggressive plugging as soon as its effect on sales was noticed.

But "Country and Western" music, as it came to be called, started invading Tin Pan Alley's profit sources—sheet music, radio performances and record sales. It made inroads into one of popular music's new plugging channels—the juke box. It brought to the listening public something of the freshness of mountain streams and wheat fields bending in the wind. It whispered of sagebrush and tablelands. It strolled along sophisticated city streets wearing overalls and high-heeled boots.

Radio's exposure of this new music disgusted ASCAP publishers, but they began to suspect that they would have to get into the act or lose money. The shifting population in the United States in wartime, with armed services and defense plants displacing millions of people from their native regions, introduced Southern, mountain and Middle-Western styles to large numbers who had never heard it before. They liked its warmth and simplicity, and they carried it back with them to their home towns and cities.

As in an earlier time, when publishers had to scramble to "discover" tunesmiths capable of writing commercially in the jazz idiom, they now had to find Tin Pan Alley songwriters able to capture the mood of gospel-heeding mountain folk and range-riding cattlemen and tailor it into "popular music"—that is, into songs that could be exploited with primary emphasis on the sale of sheet music and albums. A few publishers sent staff members down into Nashville to work in record stores there and try to find out just what it was that made country music tick. Somehow, they never quite learned. They satisfied themselves, finally, by doing what they had previously done to another type of folk music, the New Orleans and Chicago jazz out of which their popular songwriters had decanted their dilutions of blues, syncopation and swing. Because country and Western music (unlike jazz) could be balladized to an agreeable extent, some of these distillations were successful as popular songs. The ballad has always been the mainstay of the music-publishing business as interpreted by sheet music sales.

The music industry noted, not with any sense of impending danger, that the new kind of music seemed to find its most ardent fans among the nation's teen-agers. The publishers were not excessively alarmed. After all, they didn't publish music for children. But teen-agers were beginning to display their enormous influence on the music business. They were popular music's best customers, but they were not big sheet music buyers. They stormed theaters to hear and squeal at their current singing crushes. They listened to radio and *they bought records*.

The door was closing on sheet music as the publishers' main source of profit. Soon it would slam in their faces. The end of the war would mark the beginning of their defeat as arbiters of popular music in America. Although they did not yet have to face the fact that a record would eventually become the only profitable means for issuing a new song, they looked sorrowfully at dwindling sheet music sales.

To many, the answer seemed to lie in doubling their activities in educational music.

8. *"Pop" Goes to School*

"EDUCATIONAL MUSIC," in Tin Pan Alley's glossary, does not presume to teach anybody a darned thing. It's just music that is specifically intended to be sold to the nation's schools (also to institutions or industrial plants) for performances by sundry amateur musical groups.

Despite the somewhat austere dignity of its title, the "educational department" of a popular-music-publishing firm issues easygoing arrangements of popular copyrights that run the gamut of musical expression, including (sometimes emphasizing) such nonacademic examples as the latest sophistications or nonsense to froth out of juke boxes.

In surprisingly recent times, the only publishers considered eligible to supply music befitting students needs were the so-called "standard" publishers (Carl Fischer, G. Schirmer and the like) who issued solo and group arrangements of classical, semiclassical and "artistic" music deemed appropriate for youthful rendition.

Around the middle of the 1930s, some publishers of contemporary stage and popular music attempted to matriculate their lively titles but were confronted by an almost solid block of ascetic educators who were scandalized by the idea.

116

Conservatively dressed popular-music representatives were sent to educational conferences to find out what teachers would like in the way of popular music and what the popular-music publishers could do to help them brighten up school music curricula.

Although these gentlemen were careful to garb themselves in conservative suits (no checks or stripes), white shirts, plain ties and professorial hats (some wore eyeglasses they did not need) they were received as if they had descended in flying saucers wearing green scales and waving disintegrator guns. What did the educators, recoiling, want in the way of popular music? They wanted no part of it!

The teachers and superintendents soon had to accept, however, that their innocent young charges were growing up in the jazz age and jazz, with its emotional message, was much more appealing to youth than the "Fairy in the Dell" type of sentiment that nauseated them when they opened their prophylactic music books.

As the publishers continued to knock on school doors with well-arranged popular music for vocal, band and orchestral groups, a few educators began to equate their pupils' indifference to classroom music fare with the frequently trite and la-de-da pieces allowable for performance. They noticed that restlessness disappeared and children sat up with bright attention whenever popular music—the kind they were hearing at home, on radio—was discussed or played in class. Choral groups which dutifully intoned "Trees" arranged for part-singing began to sing their hearts out, eyes sparkling, when they were given a sprightly version of, for example, "Smoke Gets in Your Eyes" or "Stars Fell on Alabama."

By 1940, many enlightened educators were permitting their glee clubs and instrumental organizations broader leeway in the popular music category.

In 1947, the *Music Education Source Book* of the Music Educators National Conference said, choosing its words carefully, "It is recommended that high school music teachers become more tolerant and familiar with what is good in popular music and use it for constructive purposes as well as for enjoyment and relaxation. This music will surely influence the lives of our young people and we must do what we can to direct its influence to good ends."

The well-established music-publishing firms whose catalogs bulged with the cream of popular music spanning many decades set up special departments in their offices. These were figuratively—and sometimes actually—roped off from contamination with the more typically Tin Pan Alley cubicles of the "professional" departments from which emanated the Broadway miasma. To head up their educational departments, publishers enticed dignified ladies and gentlemen with academic or musicological backgrounds to act as editors and liaison personnel. Editors were necessary to take out the too-jazzy stuff, and staid liaison personnel were necessary to take out the teachers.

Without educators' ultimate open-mindedness, the publishers would probably have made much slower progress than they did with their zealous attempts to entrench popular music as a respectable part of school curricula. When they tip-toed discreetly into the hallowed halls of learning, they found themselves in a very strange world—a world without "payola," song-pluggers or publicity shenanigans. Their only means of "plugging" (a word *never* used in the educational department) was to exhibit their wares demurely at educators' conventions and to vie for acceptance of a copyright title on the programs of the hundreds of interscholastic contests and festivals conducted by the nation's primary, secondary and university glee clubs, bands and orchestras.

To succeed in getting a title on such a program was and is the educational department manager's dearest wish, and not for prestige alone. The interscholastic contest rules require all contestants to perform one selection in common on their programs, along with whatever pieces they choose to do on their own.

With everybody rendering the same composition, the judges can better compare each group's abilities. And—with everybody rendering the same composition, the one selected by the national contest committee is bought by each participating group in quantities that would make your head swim.

Until the end of 1940, decorum prescribed that all music geared for school use be printed with puritanical black-on-white covers innocent of illustration. To this day, many of the publishers who pioneered in the forbidding blackboard bailiwick wince perceptibly when a daring art director decides that color *and* illustrations are desirable for the title pages of songs or folios to be offered up to school authorities.

There were sound commercial and public relations motives behind the publishers' eagerness to identify popular music in the educational field. These more than justified their fearful willingness to surround themselves with "squares and longhairs" and invest a considerable amount of money in waging their long campaign. Diminishing sheet music sales as records began to take over was one reason. There were others.

After a song becomes a popular hit, whether it was written as a single piece or as part of a musical-comedy score on stage or film, it is the goal of the publisher to establish it in perpetuity. He calls it "building a standard." So many songs are ground out of the music mill that, a publisher realizes, it is best not to rely solely on people's memories.

Out of a thousand school children, publishers calculated, perhaps fifty may grow up to become teachers, some of them teachers of music. Teachers are, they agreed among themselves, a segment of the public. The public loves the songs of its childhood. *Ergo*: Indoctrinate embryonic schoolteachers with a popular song and they will, as full-fledged educators, sing or teach it to their pupils. Also, a teacher who might prefer to avoid strictly up-to-the-minute pop hits may be willing to reach back a few years for melodies past their frantic plug peak. Standards!

In the economy of the music business, too, educational departments are a force for stabilization as well as profit. To a large extent, sheet music and record sales depend upon the broader economy of the country itself. During times of war or prosperity, sales boom. During regressive or depression times, they slacken. This basic law of supply and demand does not, however, govern money spent on music in the educational field. Despite general cutbacks in spending on the part of the postgraduate public, schools get appropriations to purchase music even during bad times.

Consequently, one of the most important assets of a popular song copyright is its long-range ability to earn money by going to school. Another is the fact that educational-department earnings are derived from true and worthy *publishing* activities as opposed to the record-ravenous, performance-pushing activities of popular-music exploitation as it exists on the level of the professional department.

Here's how the educational department of a popular-music publishing firm works:

Take a song. Take "Begin the Beguine," for instance. It's a likely choice because, as a show tune automatically published in sheet music form late in 1935 by reason of its inclusion in the Cole Porter-Moss Hart stage musical, *Jubilee*, it was a dismal flop from Tin Pan Alley's viewpoint. It sold few copies and remained singularly unnoticed until bandleader Artie Shaw gave it a brilliant dance arrangement and recorded it for Victor in 1940.

From quiet beginnings and after four years of dust-gathering, the copyright—out of its stage context—suddenly became valuable. Major companies brought out dance records, music dealers and jobbers demanded sheet music. "Begin the Beguine" was a popular hit song. Could it be groomed as a standard? It could. Popular singers and pianists picked it up. Bands gave it elaborate arrangements and played it as a *tour de force*.

In the educational department of Harms, Inc., which owned the copyright, editor-in-chief Frank Watson realized that "Beguine" was that gladsome phenomenon, a hot hit on its way to becoming a standard and eminently suitable to arrangements for schools. He ordered the full treatment. This, in itself, is enough to make a song rich.

The older and larger publishers (Harms is both) maintain stables of staff and freelance copyists, transposers and arrangers whose tedious and exacting job it is to transform the simple melodic line and chords written for a popular "lead sheet" (piano copy) into as many of the hundreds of possible combinations the front office thinks it can sell to the educational and do-it-yourself markets.

For multiple voices alone, for example, there are at least seven salable arrangements, abbreviated in publishers' catalogs as: SA, SSA, SSAA, SAB, SATB, TTBB and SSCB. The S stands for soprano, A for alto, T for tenor, B for baritone and/or bass. The C represents a chastening euphemism in musical etymology. It once meant "castrati," those golden-voiced pre-pubescent boys whose angelic tones were preserved by music lovers of a cruel era by the act of castration. It now means "cambiata," or "boys' changing voices."

Aside from key transpositions for each one of the solo instruments, there are almost endless possible combinations of instruments—ranging from small string ensembles (with or without harp or piano) to full brass band and symphonic orchestra, including a part for the conductor.

When "Beguine" got the full treatment, it ended up in no fewer than fifty different publications. The Cole Porter song, a delayed hit, is one of the most valuable properties in popular music. It is an indestructible standard—it attends school regularly —it continues as a performance favorite on radio and television— it is one of the most requested numbers on the dance floor. Its original copyright will not expire until 1963, when it will be renewable until 1991.

The full-treatment system often results in some interesting bloopers in the ordinarily precise and humorless sanctuaries where educational music is tended.

The word was given out, once, that the songs from Sigmund Romberg's "New Moon" were to get the works when, some fifteen or sixteen years after its original Broadway success, a Jeanette MacDonald-Nelson Eddy film was in the offing. The publisher's arrangers and printers got busy. When final blueprints were placed on the editor's desk for a final check before going to press, his howls could be heard even far away in the professional department, where three pianos were demonstrating three different tunes.

What complete idiot, he demanded, ordered SA, SSA and SSAA arrangements of "Stout-Hearted Men"?

Well, the arranging staff chief said, nobody exactly ordered them, but the song was part of the score, wasn't it? What was so terrible?

The editor closed his eyes in pain.

"I can see it now," he said in a quiet voice. "The high school auditorium is crowded with proud parents who've come to hear their daughters sing in the glee club concert. And there the darlings are—a stageful of innocent young girls, dressed all in white and wearing gardenias. They open their pure young lips to sing, and what do mama and papa hear?"

He paused, losing the struggle to maintain control. Pounding the desk, he shouted: "They hear their daughters yelling—'Give us some men—some stout-hearted men'!"

On another occasion, a routine editorial decision to authorize the addition of a new folio to an existing series very nearly resulted in an international incident.

The series, as often happens, was identified by being printed with a cover of colored paper stock. This common practice enables shipping departments to fill orders quickly at the warehouses, where racks of printed music reserves resemble a labyrinthine maze. Dealers, jobbers and purchasing agents familiar with a publisher's catalog replenish their stock items by ordering, for example: "Blue Series (or Red, or Yellow)—6 Folk, 12 Christmas, 4 Western, 8 Polka." This time, the new folio was added to the Orange Series, a sizeable number of separate books with specialized musical subjects. The new folio was a discriminating selection of beloved Irish ballads.

Nobody gave much thought to such a routine print order until the Orange Series Irish Melodies Folio was noticed lying about by one of the firm's song-pluggers, name of McCoy. He noticed it, unfortunately, on St. Patrick's Day, having returned to the office briefly while on his annual rounds of celebration. He not only quit on the spot, he also broke several articles of heavy furniture and threatened to have the publisher's entire catalog boycotted in America and wherever good Irishmen breathed.

A new printing was hastily ordered. The Orange Series now includes one folio printed in bright Kelly green.

When Hollywood makes a film based on an old stage musical show, the original songs are reissued as sheet music by the publishers. The usual practice is to work up attractive new title pages with illustrations more in keeping with the new movie's advertising blurbs. That explains why a song called something like "I'll Walk with God" hit dealers' shelves and educators' conferences all over the country with a cover on which dancing girls in G-strings kicked their shapely legs toward the title.

9. *D. J. plus A. & R. equal V. I. P.*

WHILE THEY WERE busily building educational departments in an uneven race with diminishing sheet music sales, music publishers clutched eagerly at what they jubilantly hailed as a cheap and easy plug for new tunes—the emerging disk jockey show.

The disk jockey is a fairly new phenomenon of the music business. He could not have existed before the electronic age which spawned him, although he had ancestors of sorts among wandering minstrels, town criers and street hawkers. *Variety* claims to have originated the title in the late 1930s. The show business publication did not intend to be flattering when it reported on the activities of low-watt radio station announcers who were playing ("riding") phonograph records ("disks") during the hours when no live programs were being aired to carry advertising messages. The implication was that such goings-on were snide tactics on the part of weak-voiced radio stations whose managers were too poor—or too miserly—to pay for bona fide actors and musicians.

Recording companies, successful bandleaders and the nation's employable musicians as bespoken by their mentor, James Caesar Petrillo of the American Federation of Musicians, objected strenuously to radio stations' use of canned music as entertainment fare.

The record companies took a dim view of the way a single purchase of a single disk threatened to depreciate consumer sales because of its repetition. Their thinking—then—was that audiences would get sick of the thing and refuse to buy it for home playing.

Bandleaders resented the deception that they were making personal appearances in the small radio station studios as announcers held chatty, if one-sided, "conversations" with them.

Petrillo was loudest, bitterest and finally most effective with his denunciations of disk jockeys, insisting that they were putting his union members out of work by substituting records for living instrumentalists. He was not appeased even when the Federal Communications Commission put an end to the deception by ruling that all broadcast material on records or transcriptions be plainly identified.

The listening public didn't seem to care whether the shows they heard were performed in the flesh or on grooves. As a matter of fact, many people argued that the expert renditions by big-name bands and famous singers on records were preferable to the often mediocre live talent the smaller stations could afford to hire. The "Make Believe Ballroom" programs as conducted by Al Jarvis in Hollywood and Martin Block in New York became the favorite listening fare on both coasts, with long lists of advertisers eager to buy participation time.

As the all-record shows gained in popularity, Petrillo got madder and madder. He didn't much care one way or the other what the public liked or didn't like. His sole interest was in protecting "his boys." If a record which depended on the time and talents of musicians had a potential of perpetual profit, then somebody—the recording companies, for instance—should pay a royalty into the musicians' union coffers for every record released.

The recording companies didn't think so. After all, they pointed out, musicians were paid union rates or better when they were employed for recording sessions—just as, for example, type-setters were paid salaries for their part in printing books. Why should musicians have a perpetual interest in music they merely performed as part of their jobs?

Musicians were not typesetters, Petrillo stated with dignity, they were artists. Their talents were as important as the composer's to the value of a record. In 1942, he forbade his union members to hire out for records altogether, except for those used in the war effort and at home.

The allowable exceptions were of no value to the recording industry, for it obviously could not police the destiny of any record after it was released for quantity distribution. Consequently, until the dispute was arbitrated two years later, the records heard over radio or retailed in stores were either re-issues of earlier pressings or, if new, had musical backgrounds of *a capella* choruses in lieu of strings, brass, woodwinds and percussion.

(This issue was raised again in 1948, when a similar ban was imposed by Petrillo who lashed out anew at recording firms, disk jockey shows and juke box operators whose "mechanical music" was robbing his boys. Both conflicts had the effect of limiting musicians' incomes considerably for a while.)

The record companies, as Petrillo anticipated, finally had to come to terms with the powerful musicians' union. A royalty arrangement was agreed upon, with companies promising to pay a tax into a union "benefit fund" on every record sold. The settlement had two major effects, aside from lifting the ban: Musicians would presumably be better off in the future when they were out of jobs or sick; and the royalty paid out by the companies was tacked onto the price customers paid for records.

Music publishers, during the record famine, had a chance to evaluate the impact of records on their sheet music sales and performance royalties. The accounting was a revelation. Up to that time, the publishers controlled the songs America heard, and they had the last word as to which of their copyrighted titles they would allow record companies to wax. They gave permissions cannily and without an excess of cordiality.

Acting as liaison with the publishing firms were record company employees called, then, "mechanical men." A "mechanical man" would approach a publisher with ingratiating courtesy, respectfully asking for new songs appropriate for his company's artists. A publisher could sit in haughty command at his desk, mulling over recording companies' urgent requests for top-drawer material and magnanimously decide: "Well, we'll let Decca have this one—*if* they promise us Bing. Otherwise, we'll give it to Victor for Vaughn Monroe."

Record companies, on their part, knew that the songs given to them were the ones the publishers planned to "work on"—that is, plug vigorously. The publishers' efforts to sell sheet music would have a beneficial effect on record sales. "Mechanical man," therefore, were anxious to overcome publishers' somewhat luke-warm attitude toward record licenses because of the paltry recompense involved. Under the revised Copyright Act of 1909, publishers collected a maximum royalty of two cents per recorded song, the two pennies to be shared with the songwriters who were joint copyright owners. The Act could not possibly have taken into account the inventions and discoveries of the future. It could not anticipate radio, television and juke boxes or the mass production of multiple-speed hi-fi phonographic equipment leading to monumental sales of single records and albums. When it was written, the two-cent "mechanical reproduction" clause incorporated almost casually into the Act applied primarily to the existing player-piano rolls and to penny-arcade machines in which animated cartoons were accompanied by wheezing music box gadgets.

In addition, the clause had been calculated to forestall monopolistic tyranny, for it states that when a music publisher licenses a copyright for mechanical reproduction he automatically abandons his right to limit any other mechanical reproductions. As soon as one record company issued an interpretation of, for example, "Love," every other record company in the country was free to cover the song with releases of their own without having to apply for a license to the publisher.*

The two-cents-per-side royalty meant little to the publishers in the 1940s in comparison with the upwards of ten cents per copy earnable from sheet music, more on printed album collections, and they were not anxious to court trouble by abandoning their copyrights willy-nilly. Moreover, hampered by Petrillo and wartime restrictions on shellac, the recording industry was not in a position to produce records in large quantities.

Because piano copies and folios were still selling wildly, the publishers regarded the record-playing radio programs merely as additional exploitation media for their merchandise.

Then it began to dawn on them that records—especially when they were aired repeatedly by the disk jockeys—had an incredibly stimulating effect on sheet music sales. This was right down their Tin Pan Alley. They grew enchanted with disk

* *Note:* The two-cents-per-side maximum is still in effect, and so is the automatic abandonment of copyright on mechanically reproduced music. Although most of the music-publishing industry agrees that the outmoded Copyright Act badly needs revision, it is somewhat nervous about bringing the subject up in court. The older publishers, especially, with fat catalogs of everlastingly favorite standard songs, prefer to let sleeping dogs lie lest a probing look at the entire copyright situation disturb lucrative renewals with songwriters and their heirs.

Also resistant to change in the law are the juke box operators, many of them the same gentlemen who supply pin-ball machines to bars and coke parlors, as well as slot machines and other chancy devices to gambling houses. Under existing terms of the Copyright Act, they are under no obligation to pay music royalties. The two-cent fee earmarked for copyright owners is paid by the record company out of earnings. A juke box operator buys a record for considerably less than a dollar and, at a nickel or dime a play, can "earn" up to $100 or more on it before it is worn out and has to be discarded or replaced.

While newer publishers who entered the field after disk jockeys and record companies swept into power would very much like to get more than the divisible two cents per recorded copyright, their voices are drowned out by stronger factions. One of these, of course, is the recording industry itself, which has no desire to invite the necessity of paying more than the present law says it must.

jockeys and the free rides offered by hitch-hiking, via the radio plug, to the best-seller lists. This new plugging was quicker than vaudeville and far less wearing on shoe leather. Instead of maintaining large "professional" staffs of a dozen or more song-pluggers, they could hire fewer and, with solid "ins" with the disk jockeys, let automation do the rest.

So, publishers concentrated less and less on their traditional song-plugging methods and began relaxing their jealous custodianship of songs insofar as the record companies were concerned. The "mechanical men" found it easier to get publishers' authorization to record new and renewed copyrights.

The transition of popular music's control from publishing to recording may have been inevitable. This is still a hotly debated issue, with many objective authorities insisting that publishers' greed for cheap plugs tempted them to trade discriminating selection of songs for indiscriminate currying of disk jockey favor.

Never especially endowed with analytical perception about the public's moods and tastes, considering that these merely followed the prevailing song styles, the music-publishing industry failed to notice what was happening. Those nice, easygoing, plug-profligate disk jockeys were beginning to take over.

By the end of World War II Americans were displaying a new mood about popular music, and their new tastes had been developed as they sat in front of their radio sets listening to disk jockeys between news bulletins.

People still wanted popular music—in fact, they craved it. They wanted a lot of it. But, thanks to the disk jockeys, it was no longer the song itself which mattered to them. They were less interested in the melody or lyric than they were in *interpretation*—by a singer, an instrumental soloist, a vocal group or orchestral combination.

Presiding over their interminably revolving turntables in radio studios all over the country, the disk jockeys had steadily been giving people warm, intimate glimpses of performing artists—and, incidentally, of themselves. Publishers had been eagerly willing to keep them supplied with information about new records because of the plug songs they represented. But the disk jockeys were far more interested in the personalities of the recording artists, the new sounds cropping up in elaborate or novel arrangements, than they were in the quality of a song, its writers or its publisher. So was the public.

In those early disk jockey days, when the only people who liked the platter-and-patter programs were several million Americans, the stations or their announcers frequently had to spend their own money for the records they played, building libraries deliberately in the face of union disapproval and the recording industry's critical tolerance.

Among the disk jockeys themselves a lively competition sprang up which transcended their efforts to increase their own value as radio station employees by attracting advertisers. Some of the boys began to build highly specialized programs, fancying themselves as music critics, talent scouts and entertainers. They began to resent the publishers' and recording companies' habit of doling out records when and as they saw fit, affixing a rigid release date to each with stern injunctions that it was not to be played on the air until authorized.

In New York, such restraint on the disk jockeys' enterprise as entrepreneurs was effectively circumvented by Art Ford, who originated a series of "sneak previews" of unreleased recordings. Then master of a microphone in a tiny sending room at a 250-watt station in Long Island several years before he became one of the top men in his field, Ford considered it a matter of personal pride to get a new record on the air before any other disk jockey. In order to realize this burning ambition, he often managed somehow to persuade record manufacturers' technicians to get copies to him before even the record companies received their shipments. Once, as he attended a screening of a musical motion picture, a lucky short-circuit gave him the opportunity to make off, under cover of the dark, with an album of the film's sound track. He had the music on the air over Long Island several weeks before the music was scheduled for general release.

It should be pointed out here that there were—and are—two distinct classifications of disk jockey, each with a considerable membership. One plays records as a kind of "stage wait" until the next commercial is due. This man does not "sell" records, he sells products. The other has his quota of commercials to fit into the broadcast, and he does a bang-up job of selling sponsors' products, but he is also capable of generating sparks of excitement about music and the entertainers who perform it in records.

This is the group from which emerged such radio and television personalities as Arthur Godfrey, Steve Allen, Robert Q. Lewis and Tennessee Ernie Ford, all of them former disk jockeys on small radio stations and paid to sell merchandise. By injecting their own personalities into the chatter about products and the records they played, their talent as performers outdistanced their considerable ability as pitchmen. All over the country, as you read these words, in thousands of radio stations, thousands of young disk jockeys sit near their microphones and turntables practicing to be Arthur Godfrey.

With Petrillo appeased and wartime restrictions lifted on shellac and the materials from which phonographs themselves were made, the recording and recording machine manufacturers went into heavy production. Unbreakable, long-playing 33-⅓ r.p.m. disks were introduced by Columbia, side by side with its regular 78 r.p.m. issues. RCA Victor offered to fight with 45 r.p.m. records which, the company claimed, captured more faithfully the tones of instruments and voices.

Now the disk jockeys had plenty to choose from—in three speeds, no less—and they became choosy indeed. In mountain and country regions, they demanded more and more "hillbilly" music, and got it. In major cities all over the country, individual disk jockeys became haughtily selective about song styles, favorite vocalists and instrumental soloists or groups, touting this or another locally until familiarity bred not contempt, but favor.

The music publishers blithely continued to turn over masses

of copyrighted songs to recording companies. If one should happen to be waxed by a singer or combination which struck disk jockeys' favor, the *song* was "made."

A typical example of the kind of tumult the disk jockeys were capable of creating is the classic story of a song called "I'm Looking Over a Four-Leaf Clover," written in 1927 by Mort Dixon and Harry Woods as a happy-type ballad. In 1948, for some reason (possibly at the behest of Mr. Woods, who is a song-plugger of some magnitude and persuasion) bandleader Art Mooney revived it with a raucous, accelerated arrangement on a record, copies of which were sent out to leading disk jockeys.

One of the disk jockeys to receive the record was jazz enthusiast and expert Albert (Jazzbo) Collins, then employed by a Salt Lake City station. Along with the record Al received a personal note from Mooney which said, in effect, "Al, old boy, you'll be doing me a terrific favor if you play this on your fine program. I'll certainly appreciate it."

Because Al assumed that Mooney knew he played only jazz on his popular program, catering to the Salt Lake area's devotees of New Orleans and Chicago styles, he confided to his audience that he didn't know what the next record was all about—the title didn't exactly sound like jazz—but they'd listen to it together anyhow.

When the record began to spin, Al's astonished ears heard *banjos*, which are about as acceptable to jazz lovers as sirloin steaks are to vegetarians. The disk jockey was incredulous and more than a little outraged. When the record had played through once, he said over the microphone: "I don't really believe this, but maybe I'm wrong. Let's listen again."

After the second playing, telephone calls began coming into the radio station from the outside. To Al's amazement and disgust, as many people thanked him for the record as raged against it. He tried to keep track of the pros and cons, but gave up. Still smarting because he felt he had been tricked into playing the kind of music he personally despised and further goaded because so many of his supposedly sophisticated and discriminating listeners actually *liked* this cornball rendition, he said on the air: "Okay, you music lovers. You dig this? So listen to it all afternoon!"

Al sat back, flipped the "repeat" switch on the turntable and proceeded to read a book while banjos and voices in unison bellowed "I'm Looking Over a Four-Leaf Clover"—over and over. Infuriated listeners put through calls to the station, jamming its lines. When other infuriated listeners got nothing but busy signals, they began calling police headquarters.

The station's manager, driving to an appointment, heard what was going on over his car radio. He stopped the car near a telephone booth and tried to put a call through to his secretary—the assistant station manager—Al Collins—the office boy—anyone. Telephone operators informed him that every phone and extension in the station was occupied.

Enraged, he drove back to the station in order to get at Al, whom he planned to fire on the spot. When he stormed into the disk jockey's cubicle and found Al calmly reading in an atmosphere of four-leaf clovers, he turned purple. Al looked up through his heavily rimmed glasses and made a thumbing gesture toward the telephone. "Hi, Daddy-O," he said sweetly. "Ever think your little old station would flip like this?"

That afternoon made popular-music history. The story was carried by Salt Lake's newspapers, picked up by wire services and plunked down on the front pages of the nation's press as a human-interest yarn. Out of curiosity, people all over the country stormed record shops and bought the Art Mooney record. Sheet music had an upsurge of sales, a matter of intense gratification to Jerome H. Remick & Company, which promptly dusted off its reserve copies and printed a new edition with Art Mooney's picture on the title page.

If no one had proved it before, Albert (Jazzbo) Collins proved in 1948 that the disk jockey was a formidable force. How formidable, the entire popular music world would soon discover. The position of a song on a record is unique—not only in the arena of radio programing, but also in the broader category of the music industry as represented by songwriters, publishers and record companies. A record is a four-headed business freak.

On programs of recorded music as conducted by radio station disk jockeys, the records are played as attention-getters so that sponsors' sales arguments can be communicated to potential customers who are presumably lulled into a receptive frame of mind by melody. For this purpose, then, the records are both "acts" and sales promotion devices.

Even though they are intended to capture the public for advertised products, however, the records frequently capture the public for themselves instead. The participating sponsor of a disk jockey show is not in the least interested in selling records. Nevertheless, he does. It was no secret to the disk jockeys, the record companies and the publishers that radio sponsors were (unintentionally) selling more records than they were their own advertised products. Thus, the records represented two pieces of property—themselves, and the tangible values inherent in copyright ownership. Listeners might not rush out to buy Guppy Gasoline or Vigaro Vitamins, but they could be counted on to buy the latest Crosby, Como or Sinatra release they heard on a night-time record show.

By the early 1950s it was fully and indisputably established that the disk jockey was popular music's most effective "big plug" for a new tune, his activities reflected in juke box plays, over-the-counter record sales and, to a lesser degree, in demands for piano copies and instrumental arrangements. Television, at that time, contented itself primarily with refurbishing older, more familiar songs on the general run of programs, the exceptions being the "Hit Parade" and programs starring popular singers with fat recording contracts and, sometimes, personal financial interests in publishing firms.

The disk jockey who once had to buy, beg or steal records began to be ardently wooed by the recording industry, with most companies issuing specially processed disk jockey records in advance of or simultaneous with general distribution to retail outlets. Some even wait for early disk jockey reaction before going into major production.

The songwriters, the publisher and the recording artist also have a stake in any new release. It is not unusual for a powerful disk jockey to receive mail, telephone calls, telegrams and personal visits from every one of the interested participants or their representatives. Several topnotch singers have found it profitable to hire the services of special careerists who call themselves Disk Jockey Exploitation Representatives. These individuals do a job that is a combination of public relations, press-agentry and song-plugging, waging intensive campaigns aimed exclusively at the nation's disk jockeys on each successive record waxed by the employing artists.

At this writing (1957) there are approximately three thousand disk jockeys in the United States. Of this number, about three hundred are of great importance to artists, publishers and recording companies because of their regional "record sell," and thirty or forty of these are acknowledged as the Big Men.

Located in key spots from coast to coast, the powerful disk jockeys are capable of stimulating enormous popular demand and sales in their areas—an activity called "kicking off" a new release. Polled weekly by the music trade publications *Variety, Billboard* and *Cash Box,* their reports on most-played, most-requested records present a cross-section sampling of national response to new songs; or new arrangements of old songs; or new singers; or new performances by established singers. If a song has been recorded by more than one company and artist, the polls indicate which is the big one—the "money disk."

In the frantically competitive record business, trade publications' record reviewers and the nation's disk jockeys—at least, the most important ones—can receive as many as two hundred and fifty or three hundred new releases some weeks, with the average running around one hundred and fifty.

To a degree, the main body of the disk jockey fraternity takes its cues from the advance reviews and poll sheets. Not all disk jockeys are music critics or even sure of their own taste when it comes to programing their shows. Moreover, not all of them have time to preview the records privately before airing them publicly.

The recognized pace-setters are located in strategic cities like Philadelphia, Cleveland, Boston, Nashville, Atlanta, Chicago, Detroit, Milwaukee, Pittsburgh, Washington, St. Louis, Memphis and Cincinnati. New York and Los Angeles, the music business knows, cannot be regarded as accurate barometers of nationwide response, but a mean average of the strategic cities is likely to reflect general reactions accurately, to an extent not often enjoyed by national political surveys.

If, in the poll columns, the top men in key cities are quoted as saying that Riff-Raff's release of "Psychosomatic Love" as sung by Cos Cob is the most-requested tune of the week, a surprising number of the three thousand disk jockeys all over the country will start playing and replaying that particular disk until—in short order—the sheer weight of repetition, familiarity and nuisance value make it a nationwide best-seller. Intensive disk jockey exposure can move as many as a million copies of a record off dealers' shelves in a few weeks. Novelty songs burst quickly into (and out of) favor, with ballads building more slowly but lasting longer on the sales sheets.

About themselves and their influence in the music business, most disk jockeys are serious and contemplative. While some like to grind personal axes or broaden the concept of their jobs to include missionary work for talent, tunes or culture, most of them agree that the main thing is to play the records from which they get the heaviest audience reaction.

Realistically, most of them recognize that their chief function in life, lurking beneath microphone relationships with listeners, is to sell advertisers' products. Some do this directly, by voicing enthusiastic or wheedling messages from the sponsor. But there is an increasing tendency toward automation of commercials, with hard-sell copy and catchy jingles transcribed on records or tape and supplied to station production men for airing at specified times. In order to keep dial-twisters tuned in, the disk jockeys must build their programs with a pretty good idea of how to please their listeners. A record spinner on a midnight-to-dawn show is unlikely to play nursery tunes, and the early-morning man avoids dreamy mood melodies that might send his audience back to sleep.

A disk jockey is an entertaining fellow who can project a comfortable feeling of neighborliness. For the most part, he *is* a neighbor. The "neighborhood" may be a hundred square miles in an industrial metropolitan area, or it may be a few farm villages surrounding a 500-watt radio tower. His neighborhood can change in climate throughout the day, too, influencing his selection of records. He'll program peppy stuff for the early risers, a nice steady beat for housework hours, the latest new sounds for the after-school crowd, sentimental standards for after-dinner stay-at-homes.

Live network disk jockey shows are rare. The quality of neighborliness is hard to sustain on a coast-to-coast hookup. It can be done, of course—Godfrey and Tennessee Ernie managed. But for lesser personalities, it is easier to achieve the local touch by being local. Network shows preclude intimacy on the disk jockey level. A man broadcasting from a New York studio, for example, must be careful not to say, "What a gorgeous, sunny afternoon!" Somebody listening in Petaluma, California, may at that moment be looking out a window at a gray, drizzling morning.

Disk jockeys can grow up to be stars, and sometimes do, but it is not so easy for a star to be a disk jockey. From time to time, in recent years, all-record programs have been taped by "names" like Crosby, Sinatra, Waring, MacRae and many others and have been aired as "disk jockey programs" on local or network stations which make much of the celebrated personalities attached to the shows. The stars play records, make pleasant or witty conversation and speak the words which lead inevitably into commercials; but they are not disk jockeys.

Possibly, the stars lack the motivation of the real disk jockey, who feels an urgency to keep abreast of current popular music trends while he projects an empathic rapport with his audience.

With him it is not "you out there in radio-land" but a closer, more personal "you" he addresses. He knows that if he doesn't hold the attention of his listeners he'll find himself out of sponsors, then out of a job.

Holding listeners' attention is a feat accomplished so well by disk jockeys that they dominated the big plug for popular music from 1945 onward. Postwar America was buying less and less sheet music, and publishers were forced to make drastic changes in their thinking about records. They were not converted to a preference for recorded songs over printed songs, but they found it necessary to revise their merchandising approaches. They had to face the fact, finally, that printed music was no longer the mainstay of their business as publishers.

It was a bitter realization, still the cause of much grief and anger among the older firms, but in fact "publishing" was becoming a vague and inept word. Profits from popular music were to depend not on bona fide publishing effort, but on lateral and often peripheral activities. The previously disdained two-cents-per-song royalty began to look good. A smashing record success —a million-copy seller—meant $10,000 for the publisher (another $10,000 for the writers). But, the record royalties were not an end unto themselves. There were all those radio performance fees piling up at ASCAP or BMI every time a record was aired. And when a song became a hit on a record, then—and only then—sheet music sales livened. The cart was in front of the horse, but the horse was pushing it.

Tin Pan Alley was no longer the teeming, glamorous thoroughfare for the popular-music parade. Traffic was being diverted to Record Row. And where once the music business revolved around the songwriter and the publisher, its new pivot was our old friend the former "mechanical man" who used to ask publishers so sweetly for permissions to record their copyrights.

This gentleman was replaced by a less humble personality with a new title: Director of Popular Artists and Repertoire. The formidable A. & R. man had evolved, by way of the influential disk jockeys to whom music publishers had relinquished their husbandry of popular music.

After all, what do disk jockeys do? They play records. And where do the records come from? Recording companies. The chief ingredients of a record are a song, of course—but, also, something more in keeping with what the disk jockeys had educated the public to demand: interpretation by a personality. The personality is an artist, and he sings (or otherwise performs) a repertoire of songs. Hence the key department of popular artists and repertoire, requiring a very special kind of director capable of linking the one with the other in such a clever way that the result is a record which masses of people are willing to buy.

With several recording companies bringing out releases of the same song, under the monopoly-preventive "mechanical clause" of the Copyright Act, it is obvious that the one with an indefinable quality for compelling public attention is the one which outsells the others. When people buy Biscuit's recording of "Maytime on Mars" instead of Cupcake's or Piecrust's, it is because Biscuit's A. & R. man conceived an interpretation which may include an eerie Martian-type echo chamber—or four trick voices—or a minuet interpolated audaciously (but oh, so effectively) after the third refrain. Of course, if Cupcake's release offers an interpretation by the current teen-age crush, it can give the Biscuit disk lively competition.

If interpretation, the artist and the song—in that order—are a record's foundation and framework, and the disk jockeys its windows to the public, the A. & R. men are its architects. They are men of structural importance to the entire modern field of popular music—to those on all levels of the industry who earn their livelihoods from it, and to those who merely consume it.

A songwriter named Hoagy Cole Rodgers-Berlin could write the world's most perfect popular song and never hear it performed—except at his own parties—unless an A. & R. man decided to record it. A prominent publisher might believe with all his music-filled heart that this was truly the greatest melody and lyric ever penned by mortal man, yet refuse to do anything with it unless an A. & R. man decided to record it.

There are, perhaps, a dozen or so major record companies out of the several hundred doing business with whom the nation's top performing stars have contracts. The companies whose releases consistently show up most often on the "top record seller" lists are Columbia, (RCA) Victor, Decca, Mercury, Coral, Dot, Epic, MGM, Atlantic, Liberty, Kapp, Cadence and Capitol (all subject to dethronement at the public whim). It is no exaggeration to say that the popular music the nation will be hearing and buying tomorrow on records and in print will depend to an incredible extent upon decisions that were made, a few weeks ago, by the executives who are these companies' A. & R. men (also subject to dethronement).

Getting to be an A. & R. man is no trick. All you have to be is a genius. Not an ordinary genius like Leonardo Da Vinci, Thomas Edison, Henry Ford, the Wright Brothers or the man who invented the safety pin, but someone with a combination of all their talents plus an occult sixth sense for divining what goes on in the uncharted reaches of the adolescent mind. (It is generally agreed among all music-mongers that the mass market for "pop" records of currently idolized personalities, either single or long-play, is the nation's youth, with their sentimental elders more likely to be prospects for album collections as performed by familiar favorites.)

Please note that the foregoing list of requirements for becoming an A. & R. man does not include a degree in music. The men who hold down the nation's top directorships of artists and repertoire for record companies are frequently innocent of formal musical education. There are exceptions. One is the much-publicized bearded dynamo who is Columbia's ace artist and repertoire director, Mitch Miller. He plays an oboe. Among others who have been powerful A. & R. men, one was an amateur collector of jazz records; one was the proprietor of a record shop and sold behind its counter; one was a trade-paper reporter and advertising man, and one was once an office boy for the firm he later served as the final authority on what popular music would be recorded, and by whom.

Mitch (Mitchell William) Miller is credited with being more than the mere genius accounting for Columbia's phenomenal popular record sales and one of the world's greatest oboists. He is also gratefully acknowledged by singers Rosemary Clooney, Guy Mitchell, Tony Bennett—and others—as their star-maker, the creator of their careers. He discovered them as undeveloped performers and, as someone has said, "invented" them as top-bracket personalities, bringing out their best talents by main force until their brilliance and success dazzled even them.

It was largely through Miller's efforts, too, that television—once considered almost worthless for exposure of new tunes—has become the last remaining stronghold of the "live plug" and the most sought-after showcase for popular music.

Although it is a cliché along Tin Pan Alley and Record Row that there are no secrets in the music business, Columbia's A. & R. man once had a secret. Mitch Miller knew that at ten o'clock on the evening of November 15, 1954, something was going to happen which could set the music business on its sensitive ears. At the time, even he did not know the full import of his secret. All he was sure of was that a new idea, in a new guise, was about to make its appearance in what he himself calls the record rat-race.

Miller's well-guarded secret had had its origin almost a year earlier, when publishers (Hill and Range) brought him a demonstration record of a song submitted by a lady composer (Jenny Lou Carson). Its title was "Let Me Go, Devil" and the publishers excitedly opined that its curse-of-drink-and-gambling theme, a little hillbilly in style, was a natural for Columbia's swagger-voiced Frankie Laine. Miller liked the melody, but was disturbed by the lyric. To his mind the listening public accepts the offbeat only if it is attractive and palatable. He was put off by the sordidness of the song's message and advised the publishers to try him again when they could come up with a better lyric.

The song's writer, however, refused to make the change. During the next few months the publishers succeeded in getting a few recordings of the unchanged song from other companies, most of whom treated it as a lachrymose vocal with guitar accompaniment. These records were duly sent to the nation's disk jockeys, who confirmed Miller's distaste for the song by ignoring it. "Let Me Go, Devil" was a flop and no one (except its writer and publishers) gave it another thought.

Early in 1954, music publisher Eddie Joy, who combines his publishing activities with artist management, brought Miller a demonstration record of a song called "Marionette," sung by a rich-voiced contralto. Miller's reaction to the song was lukewarm. But, he asked, who was the singer? In a few days, the A. & R. man auditioned an eighteen-year-old brunette named Joan Weber, signed her immediately for Columbia and started searching for material for her to record.

One October morning, Miller received a telephone call from the director of the Westinghouse TV show, "Studio One." He was told that the program was rehearsing a script built around a disk jockey and was asked if he had a suitable song—a fresh one, preferably recorded by one of Columbia's most popular singing artists. Miller said he'd see.

While he was pondering this assignment, the publishers of "Let Me Go, Devil" brought Miller a new lyric, with a new title achieved by the changing of one word. The A. & R. man liked it and played it for "Studio One's" producer who also liked it well enough to request permission from the copyright owners to use the song title as the title of the drama itself. The producer asked Miller who was going to record the song, expecting to be assured that the vocalist would be a nationally favored star. He was, consequently, a little doubtful when the A. & R. man announced his intention of recording the song with his discovery, Joan Weber, an unknown. With singular complaisance for a producer, however, "Studio One's" executive agreed to abide by the music man's judgment.

Miller set up a recording date and coached his singing find for her first session. Two weeks before the scheduled "Studio One" performance, he sent special pressings of the record to a large list of disk jockeys from coast to coast, hoping he would get a hint to guide him on how many records to order from Columbia's manufacturing plant. The results were discouraging. The disk jockeys were apparently unwilling to back an unknown singer, especially as the song she sang was one which had been unpopular with them under its original title, so little changed.

At ten p.m. on November 15, the millions of people tuned in to CBS stations carrying "Studio One" saw a television drama called "Let Me Go, Lover," whose title song was performed only on a record, not by a visible actress. The following morning, record dealers all over the country were stormed by people asking for the song they had heard the night before, sung by "that girl with the wonderful voice." Disk jockeys received calls from their listeners, asking to hear "Let Me Go, Lover." They had it in their files, but most dealers did not have it on their shelves. Uncertain of its reception, Miller had ordered only 20,000 copies for regular distribution.

Before November 16 ended, Columbia's distributors had placed orders for 185,000 copies. The record company ran its manufacturing plant at high gear night and day, turning out pressings. Within twelve days, 700,000 copies had been sold over dealers' counters, and requests were still pouring in.

Mitch Miller's coup was more than a personal triumph, a send-off for a new recording personality and a nice flurry of activity on a Columbia disk. It proved beyond all existing doubts that television was a gigantic juke box—a terrific plugging medium for new songs, recapturing all the impact, and more, of the old vaudeville circuits. This should have been apparent before but wasn't, despite the success of an earlier TV theme, "Dragnet," the epidemic kid appeal of "Disneyland's" "Davy Crockett" (ten million records sold) and heavy demands for singer Jane Froman's TV-introduced inspirational theme song, "I Believe."

The remarkable difference between all previous TV musical exposures and the excitement created by "Let Me Go, Lover" was that the "Studio One" production cast a popular song as an integral part of a dramatic performance, making it as important to the action as the central characters. This made history—for television, and for popular music exploitation.

Before the Mitch Miller-"Studio One" eye-and-ear opener, the music industry as a whole had regarded television as only potentially effective for the plugging of new songs. Even after the medium emerged as the nation's number-one entertainment power, its program directors avoided new songs in their musical offerings, emphasizing instead a somewhat limited repertoire of familiar tunes which could immediately set a mood or identify the time of a play's action. If the television audience heard as background to the screened title and credits which preceded a play a muted phrase or two of "Over There!" it knew at once that the play would have something or other to do with America's participation in the First World War. "The Band Played On" was sure to introduce characters wearing the straw skimmers and bustles of 1895, or thereabouts, in New York. Dramas about the Old West were (and still are) profligate with their use of "Oh! Susanna," which was apparently the only song ever played on tinny pianos in frontier saloons during the gold-strike, honky-tonk era west of the Great Divide.

When television focused its lenses and tuned its audio equipment toward vocalists and bandleaders, the early showings continued to emphasize nostalgic melodies rather than new songs. "What we're aiming for," program directors told performers politely, "is identification. That's what keeps the ratings up. The viewers just don't identify with unfamiliar music."

In time, singing and baton-wielding *stars* with their own fifteen-, thirty- or sixty-minute shows demonstrated that familiarity with themselves was enough for viewers to identify with. This phenomenon became increasingly evident as the performers' channel ratings leaped to impressive heights even against strong (non-musical) opposition on rival channels. The popular singers and bandleaders, of course, were also recording artists. As stars, they were not obliged to yield to program directors' pleas for "song identification." They could build their own shows and they were more than willing to intersperse their programs with renditions of their latest record releases. This made a lot of people happy—the writers of new songs, their publishers and the recording companies. It also made the stars happy. Each television exposure of a new song boosted its record sales, and top recording artists' contracts with the record companies provide them with a percentage of the gross earnings of their records.

Another facet to new-song-plugging was added when popular television variety shows began to introduce established and upcoming recording artists who were anxious to feature *their* new record releases. In many instances, vocalists who commanded exorbitant prices for their own programs or for night club performances were willing to appear on a coast-to-coast variety show for a minimum check, provided they were allowed to "plug" their own new recordings.

Television proved itself as the undisputed number-one plug for new songs with "Let Me Go, Lover" on that night of November 15, 1954. Ever since, the medium has superseded all other plugging goals, giving birth to a number of new music publishing firms as sidelines of television film or spectacular production; making popular recording artists out of opera stars, television actors, comedians and even the clergy, and extending Broadway— the traditional street of musical-show first nights—across the length of the coaxial cable.

Not all the credit can or should be given to Mitch Miller, for his was only one of the minds at work behind a project which was actually an experiment. Nevertheless, the explosive success of the experiment confirmed the fact that effective dramatic presentation of popular music is thoroughly understood by the men who know best its impact on the public—the A. & R. men.

They are the men with stethoscopic sensitivity to the racing pulses of teen-agers who, hungry for new sounds and trigger-ready to adulate new personalities, part with their spending money for stacks of records of all kinds. They seem to know instinctively what will appeal also to other mass-buying groups—the young married couples building popular-music libraries, and the past-thirty-five adults who constitute America's biggest purchase-power group. They are impresarios with the uncanny ability of a Barnum or a Hurok when it comes to finding and grooming new talent. Their hardheaded competence to deal realistically with market facts and figures provides a rare, built-in safety valve for their artistic enthusiasms. Their almost unerring judgment seems to be based on clairvoyance, for nothing in the popular-music industry is stable, predictable or conclusive. They are unique in the world of business—and, make no mistake about it—what they are in *is* business.

Each is unique unto himself, as well. There is no such thing as a typical A. & R. man. Among the three leading majors, especially, there is as much determined effort toward nonconformity as there is among star performers who fight shy of type-casting. Each recording company presents individual problems—of policy as well as of method.

When Mitch Miller joined Columbia, having somewhat to his own surprise put in an A. & R. apprenticeship at Mercury Records (he was a Philharmonic oboist, remember), he did not face the same situation as did—for example—RCA Victor's one-time popular artists and repertoire director, Joe Carlton, also a Mercury alumnus. When Miller graduated to Columbia he came into a firm whose position in popular-record sales was near the bottom of the list. Carlton, on the other hand, stepped into a company which had long been a power in single popular disks along with classical albums. He inherited an imposing roster of "names" (Perry Como, Eddie Fisher, Tony Martin, Dinah Shore and many others). Miller had to create new names, and he did it by making vocalists sing as they never knew they could and by backing them up with odd instruments—a jazzy harpsichord for Rosemary Clooney's "Come On-a My House" and (while he was still with Mercury) wood blocks to simulate a snapping bull whip for Frankie Laine's "Mule Train."

Carlton was not equipped, either musically or adventurously, to orchestrate with insane instruments. He was backed up by Victor's longtime contracts with top talent, but because interpretations and syles were able to drown out the effectiveness of even highly regarded entertainment names on a label, he—no less than Miller—had to be able to recognize quality and salability in a song and fuse it with a performer.

Working as he did with Perry Como required the tact of a diplomat and the insight of a psychologist. Mr. Como is the least temperamental or difficult among performers of his stature, but his relaxed manner conceals a deeply felt concern over the impression he makes on his public. He has very definite ideas about the songs he considers appropriate and is one of the most self-demanding of recording artists. Once, his performance on a record dissatisfied him and he refused to permit its release in the United States after a quarter of a million pressings had been finished. Victor shipped them overseas, and the record became a sensational hit in England. It was never sold here.

When, therefore, Carlton brought the valuable star a song with a meaningless title and a jumble of silly words written in what was, then, called "rhythm and blues" style (since immortalized as rock 'n roll), Mr. Como turned it down flat.

"Not my style," he said.

But Carlton had an A. & R. hunch and pleaded with the singer to cut the song along with others at the next recording session.

"We'll put it on the flip side, if you insist," he said, "but I'll bet you it will sell a million copies."

It did. The song was "Kokomo" and no one was more surprised than Mr. Como when, after he introduced it on his television program, wild screams from the teen-agers in his audience ate up several thousand dollars' worth of the sponsor's time.

In contrast to both Columbia's man with the beard, bounce and ballyhoo, and also to Victor's succession of more dignified types, is Decca's Milton Gabler, now a vice-president of his firm. He is one of the least publicly known but intramurally most respected artists and repertoire directors in the recording industry, possibly because he holds fast to the belief that the lion's share of credit for a hit record is deserved by the *song*, not a trick arrangement, a trend-mimic or even a stellar performance. He cannot read music, but by Decca's many top artists Gabler is affectionately called "The Ear." During a recording session it is not unusual for his mild voice, made booming by the loudspeaker, to interrupt a thirty-piece orchestra from the control booth with: "Sorry, boys —the third sax came in just a half-beat too late on that B-flat after A-natural in the second bar. Watch it, please."

While all A. & R. men shoot for a common goal—a succession of hit records which, totted up at the end of any year represent more sales and higher profits for their employers than those of any previous year—Gabler, who consistently manages to achieve this goal, brings to his job a critical self-analysis and an uncommon sense of responsibility toward his artists.

Gabler was invited to Decca on a part-time basis in 1941 when the firm's then incumbent president, Jack Kapp, arranged to buy out his own former employers, Brunswick Records, inheriting six thousand jazz and pop recordings on the Brunswick, Melotone and Vocalion labels. Kapp, faced with evaluating and classifying what was to him a chaotic library, remembered the unprepossessing young man who ran the Commodore Music Shop on Forty-second Street and seemed to know more than most people about jazz and jazz musicians. Gabler has been Decca's guiding genius ever since.

Although there is an undercurrent of polite feuding among A. & R. men, who regard each other's methods and results with sardonic suspicion, Gabler is remarkably unruffled by the fierce competition. Like all the others, he makes it tacitly understood by publishers who approach him with new material that he expects an exclusive first recording of any song he finds promising. "Exclusives" are legally prohibited for mechanical reproduction of songs, but no A. & R. man will open his door amicably twice to a publisher who peddles a song from company to company, allowing two or more to have it "first."

But "first" is a word which has become relative when used to describe a hit record, and Gabler differentiates sharply among the three kinds of "first" applicable to his product. There is, he says, an "accidental first," a "cover first" and a "creative first."

An accidental first can happen when, forced by commitments

with stage producers or motion picture studios, a record company brings out an album of the show's music with the original cast. One of the songs in the production becomes a hit, whereupon the company either excerpts the sound track or records the number with another artist for a single "pop" success. Another accidental first occurs when a vocal star, against the A. & R. man's advice, insists on recording a song he likes and, despite the director's misgivings, it catches on. This happens rarely. Performers, for some reason they wish they could fathom, are notoriously inept at picking their own songs.

A cover first is what happens when a rival company has recorded a song with one of its artists but fails to make a hit of it. According to Gabler, it doesn't make him a genius when he figures out the pattern of the song, links it to a different artist and the new combination becomes the "money record."

A creative first, on the other hand, is what brings a glow to the A. & R. man's heart and makes him feel that all the arduous work which goes into his job has been worth while. When he hears a new song . . . perhaps doctors the lyrics a bit (with the author's permission) . . . supervises a deft arrangement for either an established or an obscure artist he believes in . . . selects the instrumentation and nurses it through a recording session until it is imprisoned, a flawless gem, on a flat vinyl disk—that, says Gabler, is a feeling money can't buy.

The A. & R. man's job is complicated and many-faceted. It is not limited to recognizing quality in songs brought to him by publishers, singers, songwriters and would-be songwriters and maintaining friendly relations with artists. Presiding over a recording session, despite what you occasionally see on television, is a grueling, demanding and often tedious affair at which he must be as alert as a bird dog. With temperaments at trigger readiness and each musician on his mettle, a blown line of lyric—a fluffed note on a horn—incorrect mixing of instruments and voices at the control panel—an automobile horn or police siren outside—can ruin a performance that has been polished after hours of rehearsal and dozens of discarded "takes."

The A. & R. man has final responsibility for the product, and also for the budget allowed for each session. The musicians' union permits three hours only for a recording session at scale rates. Overtime is expensive, and so is the studio rental. In the allotted three hours, an A. & R. man must try to cut a minimum of four sides (two complete records). The cost of overtime is not the only consideration. Most-in-demand recording musicians, as well as the star performers, have other engagements to fulfill. If the records aren't completed at one session, it may be weeks before the A. & R. man can arrange to have them all together again.

A recording session is only part of the A. & R. man's job. He travels with purposeful restlessness, visiting disk jockeys and looking over the titles of regional juke boxes to discover what trends may be in the making. He prowls night clubs, cabarets, resort hotels and sometimes even amateur theatricals for new recording talent. He watches the operations of rival A. & R. men with vulpine vigilance and he keeps a watchful eye on what is happening among the mushrooming phenomena known as "indie diskeries."

Increasingly, as the music business grew wilder and more unpredictable, with Record Row a street on which anything could happen so long as it met with adolescent approval, little independent record companies began to spring up like fungi all over the country. With perhaps hardly more than a tape or wire or acetate recorder and a playback machine, such a company would "find"—or write—something it called a song, "find" a singer or singing group to record it, get it played vigorously by local disk jockeys and wind up with a regional best-seller.

When this happened, one of several things took place. A local record dealer would pass the word along to a record distributor, who in turn would tip off a major record company, that out in Rising Gorge, Colorado, a little indie record was making a big noise; copy herewith. The major's A. & R. man, if he liked the song or performance or both, then made the best deal he could for the record.

If the tip-off reached a publisher instead of the recording com-

pany, via sheet music dealers, song-pluggers or a fan, the publisher would take over the song by persuading the little diskery to
give it up, and it would reach an A. & R. man via a song-plugger
with an enthusiastic story to tell about its success story out West.

It behooves an agile A. & R. man to gain knowledge of the little record directly, because a publisher might bring it to a rival
A. & R. man.

But more often than it is agreeable to report, the little record
company decides to become a big record company, with visions
of sudden and continuing riches. After all, look at the excitement
this little old outfit created with "Scram!" sung by the "company's" wife's quadruplet cousins, the Four Fractions, who accompanied themselves on washboard and musical saw. Why, the
jubilant independent disker asks himself, should he sell out to a
rich New York publisher or big record company? Why not
keep it in the family?

This is one of the many heartbreak highways along Tin Pan
Alley and Record Row.

From time to time, to be sure, a sporadic independent diskery
may make a killing on a freak hit record, but the money is usually
lost without much delay—the way a gambler wins, then loses, in
an all-night crap game. Without considerable capital behind it,
a small independent company—even one with a sensational hit
record—finds itself confronted by almost insurmountable odds.
The majors can afford to gamble. If one or more records prove
to be investment losses, there are hundreds of others in the making to balance the books at the end of the year. For the independent company with only one basket for its eggs, there is
seldom as much time as a year.

Spurred on by dreams of keeping company with Columbia,
Decca and Victor, the independent starts cutting more records—
in the same vein as its initial success, perhaps, or in a more ambitious style. Now it finds it must pay cash on the line for everything—labels, printing, musicians (at union rates), processing, new
equipment, rent. The songwriters are likely to demand a piece
of the business, and so are the performers.

It is too much to expect lightning to strike twice, the new company's principals agree. An exploitation setup is required, with salaries to pay. Most important, however, is distribution. Without distribution, a record company is dead. But the active distributors will not accept the unknown company's merchandise except on a consignment basis. They pay—usually at the end of ninety days (sixty more than the independent's creditors will allow)—only on the number of records sold. The rest are shipped back, at the independent's expense.

Without sufficient capitalization to carry it along in the event that the second release—or the third or fourth—does not equal the disk jockey play of the first, the little company finds itself pouring out money without return. Meantime, the majors are waiting to sign the Four Fractions (if they really had talent). And perhaps a New York publisher, sensing ability in "Scram's" songwriters, makes an offer for their next song—which he will demonstrate hastily to a New York A. & R. man.

Occasionally some of the more aggressive and well-heeled little firms give the bigger ones a bad time, by bearing down hard on flashy promotions in a key area. They reward regional disk jockeys for playing a plug record repetitively. They induce regional juke-box operators to stack the record in their machines, either by direct payment or by giving them free boxes of the disks. These investments pay off if the record breaks big locally and the rest of the nation takes it up. When the hit-and-run operations are successful—as they are, from time to time—the major companies find themselves temporarily outclassed. For the most part, however, the independents fold one after another and the music industry remains in the hands of the major recording companies' A. & R. men.

To the main body of music publishing, A. & R. men are feared, respected, hated, envied and fawned upon. While openly lavishing praise and presents on A. & R. men to whom he is trying to sell new songs, the publisher secretly regards them as music mongrels, tyrants and usurpers of powers which rightfully belong to him. This opinion is largely shared by the fraternity of long-established songwriters as well, who see their position as America's melody-makers being pre-empted by outlandish newcomers whose fractured lyrics, sickeningly repetitive notes, maniacal sounds and primitive beats are—they claim—favored by the powerful A. & R. men for quantity successes regardless of quality.

Because of their corroding discontent, publishers and songwriters who remember "the good old days" are likely to mention, not always in a whisper, a word that has plagued the music industry during the whole of its commercial lifetime. The word is *payola.*

10. *Payola!*

Payola is a compulsion neurosis of the music industry. It is characterized by anguished payments of tribute in the form of cash, checks or expensive presents to those in a position to increase the profits from popular music by recording it, performing it or exploiting it above and beyond the call of ordinary duty.

All remedial approaches to cure payola have proved ineffectual so far, mainly because the patient refuses to cooperate. The individual victim does not really want to be cured. He wants all the others who share his neurosis to submit to corrective therapy but considers that he, himself, is perfectly normal.

There are laws in the music industry's own framework which make payola a punishable act. The laws are circumvented, ignored or flagrantly disobeyed by the very people who made them.

One of payola's clinically interesting symptoms is the "don't-quote-me" reflex, accompanied by nervous twitches, the closing of doors and the lowering of voices.

"Don't quote me," a music business personality—usually a publisher—will say, "but payola is as much a part of our industry today as it ever was. The law? Don't make me laugh. Nobody will admit to paying off, and nobody will admit to getting paid. But

154

trying to plug a tune without putting your hand in your pocket would be like trying to bail out a leaky rowboat with a pair of chopsticks."

The word "payola" has been added as a colloquialism to the American language largely through its repetition in the theatrical world's great trade paper, *Variety*, a publication famous for the creation of a colorful occupational patois. When the word was coined, *Variety* was engaged in fighting a situation which not only threatened the music business generally, but also its own advertising revenue specifically.

In 1916, *Variety* realized it had been steadily losing music publishers' advertising accounts because the publishers found it more effective to pay vaudeville acts to perform their songs than to advertise them at space rates.

Publishers' custom of making payments to performing artists was hardly new when *Variety* began its crusade against what was then called "the direct-payment evil." It had existed and had been accepted as a matter of course since the beginnings of Tin Pan Alley, when it was expected of song-pluggers that they buy drinks and presents for the performers who sang their firms' songs, often cutting them in on royalties. Pluggers and sheet music salesmen made routine trips to stores where their publications were sold over the counter, dispensing largesse to the salesgirls who could influence customers' selections.

Interested bystanders are fascinated, but puzzled, by the hypocritical, name-calling antics undertaken by music personalities who practice payola but deny it. It is hard to say where legitimate business romancing stops and payola begins. The entire situation is so touchy that a music publisher's innocent gesture of sending Christmas or birthday gifts to people in show business is looked upon suspiciously and lumped in with illegal practices. What in other American businesses is regarded as seasonal tradition is, in the music business, labeled bribery.

The purchasing agent in almost any office or factory usually has to make several trips to carry home the loot he receives at Christmas from firms whose products or services he has ordered throughout the year. Business executives' secretaries and switchboard operators receive gallons of French perfume and other goodies during the Yuletide season. Even the housewife who sends her family's dirty clothes to the neighborhood Chinese laundry gets a box of lichee nuts or a package of Oriental tea as a holiday expression of appreciation.

But in the music business, so much fuss is made about questionable pressure on exploitation advantages that watchful competitors are likely to scream "payola!" every time a gentleman publisher pays for a lady singer's lunch.

Because of the spotlight on payola, a number of people with the ability to help transform a song into a hit have gone to drastic lengths to display the purity and emptiness of their hands. Bandleader Fred Waring, for example, made it a practice to hold open conferences with music publishers' representatives in the Automat, where he provided his own nickels. Guy Lombardo recoils with exaggerated horror when presented with any kind of a gift, however small, from any person even remotely connected with song exploitation.

A. & R. men, disk jockeys and performing artists have deliberately made known their absolutely rigid rules about not accepting tribute in any form from music publishers. Nevertheless, the legend persists that these people not only accept payola—they expect it.

The sad, ludicrous, ironical truth is that payola is a senseless practice. Why should a music publisher have to pay people for using a product without which they could not earn their living? The answer is that he does not have to. All he has to do to wipe out the payola blight forever is to stop paying. Unfortunately, there is no way to make *all* publishers stop; and until all of them do—simultaneously and unequivocally—not one of them will; as long as he can afford it.

Attempts have been made in the past to abolish or at least curb the evil. The first of these was the formation, in 1916, of a "voluntary" organization for trade protection whose motivation was the elimination of the bribery system.

Vaudeville was the major means of exposure for songs, and music publishers competed violently with each other in persuading vaudeville acts to plug their tunes. The persuasion took many forms, all of them negotiable. The rivalry and competition were so frantic that, in the end, the publisher with the largest bank account was the one whose songs got the most performances.

The music business became one big auction sale, with the plugs knocked down to the highest bidder. Then, not satisfied with the mere privilege of paying performers for their renditions of specific plug songs which would probably have been performed anyhow, the publishers further belittled their products by offering run-of-the-act contracts to the entertainers. In this way, a rich publisher could sew up vaudeville headliners who committed themselves to using only those songs that were in the subsidizing publisher's catalog.

Singing quartets, trios, duos and solo vocalists were placed under contract to whichever publisher got to them first with a generous offer. Acrobats, jugglers and animal trainers were similarly approached. A plug was a plug, and these acts used music as entrance and exit cues and as background to whatever they were doing on stage.

Ridiculously, even acts which needed no music at all were quick to find a way of boarding the gravy train. Monologists, melodramatic skit personnel, comedians and pantomimists discovered that publishers' gold could be panned if they hired a local boy to sit in a balcony box and, some time during the performance, burst into spontaneous song.

Touring dance bands, of course, were on publishers' payrolls, in return for which they limited their repertoires to their benefactors' stock arrangements.

The situation got wildly out of hand. A number of the less wealthy publishers gave up in disgust, salvaging what they could by selling their catalogs of copyrights to the richer firms. Many small publishers, unable to compete on the terms of the industry's ground rules, were forced into bankruptcy and their catalogs were bought at distress prices.

The large firms hurtled along in the momentum of their own impetus, some cheerfully paying out as much as $25,000 in a single month to professionals for vaudeville plugs. They remained more or less cheerful about it until *Variety* added up for them what this method of direct payment was costing them.

Prodded into sober thought by the trade paper, which hinted broadly that the road to bankruptcy was navigable by even the richest among them, the publishers began to squirm uncomfortably. The harder they squirmed, however, the faster they continued to pay for plugs. They realized with dismay that they were enslaved by the genie they had uncorked. If one publisher dropped out of the dispensing circle, another publisher's songs received the plugs. Some of them began to look around piteously for help.

Help was forthcoming in the person of one John J. O'Connor. Then a writer-turned-business manager for *Variety*, O'Connor was the one who drew to boss Sime Silverman's attention the parallel between the increasing bribery system and the decreasing advertising volume.

Given leave to attempt a rescue, O'Connor set about organizing the music publishers to prevent them, if possible, from destroying themselves. Visiting every publisher in the United States, O'Connor invited them to join an organization for trade protection whose main purpose would be the immediate elimination of the direct-payment practice. This group he named the Music Publishers Protective Association.

Because the battle had to be fought on the vaudeville front, leaders in that medium were told that the newly formed association would benefit them as well as help the publishers out of a bad spot. They were not completely convinced, although O'Connor did succeed in persuading vaudeville's Pat Casey to act as general manager and Maurice Goodman, Keith-Albee's counsel, as attorney.

The association was almost ready to fight when it elected O'Connor as chairman of the board and publisher Edward B. Marks as MPPA's first president.

Marks' willingness to head the group was not wholehearted for, like every other publisher of the day, he saw no way out of feeding the hands that were biting him. In *They All Sang*, his memoirs as told to A. J. Liebling, Marks summed up the situation as it appeared to him and his partner, Joe Stern:

"In the eighties performers had paid for their music, and extra for their orchestrations. In the nineties we had given them free music and orchestrations; we had cultivated their acquaintance; tried to fit them with songs to suit their personalities. Toward the end of the century publishers had begun to give Christmas presents to performers. But now, with the rise of vaudeville, a system of direct subsidy began. The newly created professional managers, high-salaried men, eager to make good, felt they had to show results. Competitive bidding began, and soon many acts were drawing more from music publishers than from the vaudeville circuits. At the height of the bidding, the industry paid a tribute of a million dollars a year. This expenditure brought no increase in the total number of plugs or the total sales of the industry. Publishers paid simply as a defensive measure against their competitors, who otherwise would have monopolized the plugs. The thing had a bad effect on total sales of songs in a short while, because acts used numbers utterly unsuited to their talents. By the same token it had a bad effect on vaudeville.

"Stern and I stood out against the thing, because we sensed that it would ruin the houses that spent the most money. It took will power to stay out of the procession—just a little more than I had. One day I authorized our professional manager, who had been straining at the leash—I should say at the rubber band on the bankroll—to go ahead and see to it that our numbers got a few breaks. In two days he came back disappointed. 'Boss,' he said, 'I can't give your money away. Every team worth a damn is signed up to sing for other publishers.' "

It was shortly after this experience that Marks was approached by O'Connor to head up the new trade association. The music industry, even then, was so convinced that payola was the best way to plug songs that of O'Connor's invitation Marks wrote:

"At first I demurred."

Beset by similar incentives and torn by similar misgivings, most of the publishers O'Connor visited were halfheartedly willing to cooperate in combating the payment menace. There were three important hold-outs, two of them formidable. The successful firms of Feist, Remick and T. B. Harms decided to decline membership. They intended to go on doing business their own way. Feist and Remick, as prominent publishers of popular songs, implied by their refusal that they would continue to pay for plugs. T. B. Harms' manager, Max Dreyfus, did not think it necessary to join the association because his firm's catalog consisted almost entirely of operetta and stage production music. For these, he said, he never found it necessary to participate in the payment system.

Feist's and Remick's refusal to discontinue their direct-payment practices could have negated the entire program of the new publishers' association, for the performers didn't care *who* paid for plugs so long as they got paid. The hold-out publishers, with enormous catalogs of popular songs past and present, were in a position to supply as much music as vaudeville acts needed—in quantity, at any rate, if not in diversity, quality or relevancy.

MPPA would have folded at its birth if O'Connor had not had a brilliant plan devised. He invited John J. Murdock to go to a show with him. As E. F. Albee's associate, Murdock was in a position of power in the Keith-Albee Orpheum circuit which booked acts for almost every theater in the United States and Canada.

Puzzled but amiable, Murdock accepted O'Connor's invitation and accompanied him to an evening performance at the Alhambra Theater in New York. As the two men settled into their seats, the curtain was raised on the opening animal act. While the dogs performed on stage, the pit orchestra played "I Didn't Raise My Boy to Be a Soldier," a 1915 copyright written by Alfred Bryan and Al Piantadosi in reflection of the nation's anti-war feeling. It was Feist's number-one plug song.

In the second act, a singing duo harmonized the melody.

In the third act, a tense dramatic sketch, softly played background music established the appropriate mood with muted violins playing—over and over—"I Didn't Raise My Boy to Be a Soldier."

On a well-balanced vaudeville bill, histrionic timing traditionally demanded that the blessed relief of laughter should follow the emotional tensions evoked by a dramatic playlet. This night was no exception, and Murdock listened incredulously as the comic made his entrance to cue music which was a pepped-up rendition of Feist's plug song.

The vaudeville executive's incredulity was transformed into glazed-eye fascination as the song was enthusiastically presented by an energetic male quartet (three choruses)—a boy soprano planted in the audience sang it throbbingly between scenery changes—the closing acrobats executed graceful somersaults and other muscular feats to a rapid waltz arrangement of the melody.

Murdock's first action the following morning was to issue rush orders to the managers of all theaters in the vaudeville circuit that no music could be played for any act unless the copyright owner of the music was a member of Music Publishers Protective Association.

The executive's official clamp-down was not motivated by sympathy for the music publishers. Murdock's own intelligence advised him that the direct-payment system would ultimately have a destructive effect on vaudeville and performers alike, for the subsidized singers were forced to sing many songs that were entirely inappropriate to their talents. Moreover, he felt that the constant repetition of a few songs would in time tend to antagonize audiences.

A few days after Murdock issued his orders, vaudeville headliners with repertoires almost exclusively confined to Feist and Remick songs were informed by the theater managers that they must henceforth omit from their acts any songs which were not from the catalogs of MPPA members. All others were restricted, the command added, and disregard of the order would mean cancellations of bookings.

As soon as the directive was understood and performers looked hastily at the publishers' names on their music, loud outcries of rage and pain were heard backstage in vaudeville theaters all over the country.

By this time, MPPA with its original enrollment of thirty-five publishers, had two—and only two—articles of agreement. One was the signed statement that payments to performers for plugging songs were henceforth eliminated. The other was the adoption of an initiation fee of $1,000 for all applicants who sought membership *in the future*.

Not many minutes after they heard the vaudeville circuit's new rule, two celebrated headliners of the day (one of them was Sophie Tucker, the other a Remick song-plugger's wife) made haste to relay news of the ban to the two publishing firms most affected. With equal haste, the managers of Feist and Remick appeared personally at the MPPA office and paid $1,000 apiece to enroll in the association they could have joined a few days previously for nothing. To make it unanimous, Max Dreyfus of T. B. Harms also signed up.

Within twenty-four hours, the overt payola to vaudeville performers stopped.

Within another twenty-four hours, payola was underground. The same publishers who swore earnestly to uphold MPPA's taboo against the practice found loopholes in their own rules through which they could crawl back to the confusion that was, for them, a comfortable solution to competition.

At a later meeting of MPPA, it was sanctimoniously decided by the membership that the organization should stop "crusading" and turn its attention to "other, more pertinent matters." This was a tactfully phrased admission that the publishers resigned themselves to a compromise. "We'll condemn payola publicly," the resolution implied, "but we'll camouflage it so we can practice it privately."

Johnny O'Connor gave up in disgust.

Grown dignified with the passage of years, MPPA now concerns itself with legislative problems affecting the industry and acts as a clearing house for publishing conflicts as they arise. It serves as liaison between its members and the various affiliated trade labor unions and protective societies. It studies court decisions pertaining to copyright and has a part in lobbying for (or against) those decisions. It conducts a title registration bureau to prevent overlapping of simultaneous publications with identical or too-similar names. It acts as publishers' agent in licensing the use of music for motion pictures and transcriptions. It audits and collects royalties for its publisher members from the performance-rights societies. It investigates copyright infringements.

MPPA no longer concerns itself with the payola that inspired its birth. It does not even admit that payola exists.

Since the twenty-four-hour hiatus in 1916, the practice of bribery as a means for popular-song exploitation has continued with no further major interruptions. Before radio, publishers resorted to various devices which they conveniently tucked under the deceptive heading of "public relations." It became an acceptable ruse to add the name of a popular bandleader or singer to the title page of sheet music as a co-writer, even though the credited entertainer had nothing to do with the creation of the song. Such a performer could be expected to plug the song vigorously, for as a "collaborator" he received more than the mere honor of co-authorship; he got what appeared to be—but wasn't—a legitimate cut of royalty earnings.

When radio replaced the vaudeville stage as the big plug, payola again reached outrageous proportions, with new pay-off plots staked out by music publishers. Program directors of radio stations—and their secretaries—found themselves agreeably showered with valuable gifts which were figuratively wrapped in printed lists of plug songs.

This time, it was not the publishers who attempted to put a stop to payola, but the song-pluggers. In 1934, these employees organized a society which they called Professional Music Men. Ostensibly founded to act as a social and welfare group, the Professional Music Men at first limited their activities to the running of benefits and raffles to raise money for sick and needy song-pluggers and their families. As payola practices increased, the professional men realized that their jobs might be in jeopardy if the bribery system were permitted to flourish unchecked. In time, they feared, a publisher would not need to maintain a staff of salaried contact men; his checkbook could accomplish more easily the results he sought. This fear was given substance when, in a few major publishing houses, talk got around that the professional (song-plugging) departments were going to be discontinued.

The Professional Music Men announced their intention of applying for a union charter, a move which infuriated music management executives as much as it worried them.

Emboldened by organization and a shared purpose, the contact men ignored threats of dismissal and established the first union local to invade the music-publishing field. As union members, the song-pluggers had protection they lacked as individuals. Their greatest strength was not in their own scant numbers, but in the support they could now count on from strong international and local unions in allied fields.

A music publisher with a fat wallet might not worry too much about reprisals from a single contact man or even from the whole group of contact men, but he was likely to think twice about firing one for union affiliation if in so doing he exposed his business to sympathetic boycott. Members of other brotherhoods could hamper a publisher's activities considerably, for he depended on truck drivers for deliveries, electricians for radio station transmission, printers for production and the members of the American Federation of Radio Artists and the American Federation of Musicians for performances.

Forced to accept the unionization of their contact men, the publishers reluctantly entered into wage, hour and benefit conditions and also into fair-trade agreements, one of which concerned payola. When the re-named Music Publishers' Contact Employees Union of Greater New York was formally accepted as an affiliate of the American Federation of Labor in 1939, it had already adopted in a section of one of its articles a penalty for "giving or offering a consideration of any kind for the purpose of inducing anyone to render or to permit the rendition of any musical composition."

The union ban on payola practices is still in effect, with offenders liable to fines up to $5,000 if proved guilty of bribery. Guilt is never proved, mainly because charges are rarely made—officially. Unofficially, there is hardly anyone connected in any way with the music business today who will not, when pressed, point accusingly at almost anyone else as a perpetrator or receiver of payola. As for himself, he confides, he is probably the only one in the music racket who is innocent.

How does it happen, a publisher asks, that a certain popular singer can afford alimony to several ex-wives and still shower his current flame with mink and diamonds? Payola. And what about that new girl singer—her manager takes credit for her success, as well as half her earnings, but there she goes in one of her two new foreign racing cars. How come? Payola. And if you really want the lowdown on the sensational success of the crazy new song that's making the publisher, record company and vocalist rich—well—ask the A. & R. man how he got his new swimming pool. Then ask a couple of d.j.'s how on their salaries they could afford trinkets like identical star-sapphire pinky rings.

Because records are the pivot for song successes today, it is the powerful A. & R. men who are most often branded by music publishers as receivers of payola bribes.

"Don't quote me," a publisher says, "because I depend on these vultures for a living. But—I can't get a record unless I'm willing to make a private deal. Private deal! That's double-talk for payola. For instance—take the time I brought a swell tune to this A. & R. man and he said it was pretty good but it needed a little doctoring. So naturally I said, 'You be the doctor.' That's what he wanted, and I knew it, and he knew I knew it, but God forbid he should come out and say so.

"What did the 'doctor' do? Well, he maybe changed a B-flat to a B-natural in the introduction, and he maybe changed the word 'scaddum' to 'scaddoom'—lyrics, yet! And he maybe changed an eighth note to two sixteenths. So now he's a co-writer on the song, see, and he's cut in for a piece of the royalties. This is a subtle operator, you understand. Everything's kosher and aboveboard. No money passes between my hands and his. But some of them aren't so dainty, believe me. For them, it saves time and conversation if I go with a pocketful of bills. No checks. Payola's illegal in our business. But who's going to know if I hand over a few pieces of green paper with pictures of dead presidents on them? And who's going to ask how come he lives like Rockefeller on his twenty-thirty thousand a year salary, before taxes?"

Still rankling in the breasts of several prominent music publishers is a situation they found themselves in a few years ago. As the story is told by one of them, they were approached separately by an A. & R. man in need of immediate funds. He did not ask any of them for a large sum, borrowing amounts under five hundred dollars from each of the men he visited. When he expressed his thanks for the loans, he said to them in turn: "You won't be sorry. I'll remember that you loaned me money like a good friend when I needed it. So—like a good friend—I'll see that your investment pays off for you when you bring me your new songs."

Individually, the publishers were well satisfied with this arrangement, considering the money they had "loaned" as part of operating business expenses under the heading of "good will." Each man believed that he had been the only one from whom the A. & R. man had borrowed money.

In subsequent months, it became apparent to each lender in turn that the A. & R. man was not living up to his friendly promises. When the publishers brought him their new songs, they found them being turned down without comment.

Ordinarily, a publisher would be inclined to shrug off this sort of disappointment as a hazard of his trade. But one of the disgruntled creditors happened to drop a hint to a publishing crony that apparently paying off to a certain diskery, which he named, was an investment of dubious value. The second publisher, recognizing a brother victim, suggested that the two of them conduct a discreet survey to find out if they had more company. Judicious sleuthing uncovered several others who had been touched for "loans" in the same manner by the same A. & R. man.

Instead of having a wry chuckle over their profitless generosity, the group decided to teach the man a lesson. While they were organizing their plans, one of the publishers dropped out of the plot because two of his songs had just been accepted. He considered his investment re-capitalized.

The remaining publishers, in an almost unprecedented move over the head of a man they relied on for records, took their grievance to the recording company's top executive. Among publishers, the feeling is that top management officials are not entirely unaware of the payola aspects of their business but that they generally choose to ignore it unless it is brought forcibly to their attention.

When he was presented with (oral) testimony about his employee's alleged privateering, the executive manfully refrained from inquiring into the accusers' willingness to participate in bribery so long as it might prove profitable. Instead, he called the accused A. & R. man into his office and sternly demanded an explanation.

The A. & R. man was stunned. Indignantly, he charged the publishers with manufacturing a slanderous assault on his integrity because he had turned down their worthless songs. Moreover, he maintained, they were unfit for the society of honorable gentlemen like himself.

He said: "Why, yes, I borrowed some money from people I *thought* were my friends. As a matter of fact, they practically forced the loans on me. So far as I knew, there were no strings attached or I wouldn't have touched the money. I *borrowed* it with every intention of paying it back. If you don't mind, sir, I'll write the checks here and now."

The company executive shrugged. His employee could clear himself of corruption. Could the publishers? Recording companies have rules which forbid the acceptance of bribes. Publishers have laws which forbid them to offer bribes.

A. & R. men's assistants, publishers say, get around the bribery system in a number of clever ways. One is to tell a publisher that his song is so great the boss sees it with a special arrangement calling for a brilliant, high-class production. Unfortunately, it's too bad that excessive operating costs and fees for extra musicians—a matter of several hundred dollars—are going to hold up a sure hit. The budget just won't stand it until next year, maybe. The publisher says he will be delighted to assume the additional "production cost" rather than wait, and the several hundred dollars pass into the assistant's pocket.

Publishers have found other ways to invoke the forbidden payola even when none is demanded, either openly or by innuendo. When he has a "hot" song, a publisher wants a fast decision from the A. & R. man who guides the recording career of a particular singer who, the publisher believes, will surely make the song a hit. However, if the song should be turned down by this particular A. & R. man with this particular singer, then the publisher wants an equally fast decision from another pair. Turned down by both, there are still other A. & R. men and other singers. If one of these should produce a record, the first choices may yet cover it and raise the song to the best-seller lists.

Because he knows that the A. & R. men insist on "exclusives" which are not strictly legal but are granted nevertheless, the publisher doesn't dare approach the second man until the song has been rejected by the first one. He wants action, and the best way to get it is in private audience with each A. & R. man in turn. He doesn't want to leave his precious manuscript or demonstration record on the pile.

Private audiences with A. & R. men are not difficult to get, for these gentlemen are always anxious to hear good new tunes. Their jobs depend on them. But publishers seem to have worked out a psychological slide rule by which they measure such intangibles as proper timing, emotional climate, receptivity and mood for each A. & R. man. A publisher may believe in his heart

that it is of optimum importance to see A. & R. man No. 1 between nine and ten o'clock in the morning, when he is fresh and
cheerful and sipping his second—not his first—cup of coffee. It
would be a mistake to see this man toward lunchtime, the publisher believes, or in the late afternoon hours. Nope—between
nine and ten, and halfway through the second cup of coffee is
the psychologically right time, all right. This cerebration may
be based on observation or hearsay, or it may be based on nu-
merology and a theory about cosmic rays; but that's the way
the publisher reads it.

Now, how can he get an appointment on short notice for the
precise time he requires? The simple way would be to call up
and ask for an interview at the specified time. This procedure,
to the publisher's mind, is fraught with dangers. The A. & R.
man might say he's sorry, he's busy at that hour, but has some
time around 11:45. (When he's hungry?) He might say "Couple
of the boys are coming in around four tomorrow. Why not join
them?" (Have the boys—whoever they are—put the jinx on the
song by looking bored? Or, worse, mention it later to *another*
A. & R. man, who will immediately know that the publisher
offered the song first to a detested rival?)

No. The best way to get the desired appointment is via the
young lady who occupies the desk outside the great man's private
door, his hard-working secretary.

"These gals act like bodyguards and they are treated like they
are queens," a publisher comments. "Well, let's face it. They *are*
queens in this business. A nod of their permanents can make or
break you when you've got a hot song to hustle.

"If the girl likes you, she'll give you an appointment for the
time you want. Then, when you're inside playing a demo record,
she'll see to it that he's not annoyed with phone calls or other
interruptions. Maybe she'll give you a little more time in there
than the next publisher.

"I've given this matter a lot of depth study, and I've found
there's one way of getting the girls to like me. It has nothing to
do with the Dale Carnegie technique or my charming personal-

ity. The psychology is, spend like a maharajah around Christmas-time and like a quiz-contest winner during the rest of the year. Find out when the girl's birthday is. Remember her cute on Mother's Day. Keep a list of her favorite little luxuries for Valentine's Day, Easter and so forth. Take her out for a glamour evening once in a while. It's a real good psychology, spelled p-a-y-o-l-a."

Bribery works both ways, the A. & R. men hint, and the publishers are equally guilty of pressing their advantage—when they have one. A publisher with the score of a new musical comedy featuring singers not under individual contracts to recording firms has such an advantage. An A. & R. man asks the publisher to release the copyrights first to his firm, which wishes to put out an album with the original cast. Knowing that he has a valuable property on which other record companies will bid, the publisher says, "Well, all right, because you're my friend. I'll release the score to you first if you'll give me records on six new ballads I got in the shop now, and also get out new arrangements of a few oldies that need a shot in the arm."

Next on the publishers' list of payola complaints are performers.

"It isn't bad enough," one grumbles, "that the big-time singers have gone into publishing setups of their own, which cut down on how many of my tunes they're willing to record. Some of them won't give me a break on a song—even if the A. & R. men want them to cut it—unless they make something on it that don't show up on income tax statements. So I keep them happy with notes of appreciation for past favors, and I tie the notes to packages.

"No, of course they don't ask for presents. How do I know they expect them? Doesn't everybody?"

Another publisher describes a payola practice he has encountered:

"Say there's a singer who's just beginning to break big. He's on records, naturally, and the juke-box crowd likes him, and he's starting to get guest shots on the big TV shows—with squeals. A few weeks ago, maybe, he was just a two-hundred-a-week crooner in a night spot. But now he's on the way up, and the way things go in this business he'll probably hit the top before long. He may last, or he may just be a flash-in-the-pan until the bobby-soxers go for someone else. It don't really matter for a pop tune, because either way he'll sell a lot of copies while he's hot.

"So he comes to me and he says he's got a lot of back bills piled up, and it would be bad publicity if it got out that he owed money. He says he won't get top pay for the TV shows because he's plugging his new records (not my songs, incidentally) and he'd like a little cash to get squared away. He promises on his mother's head he'll record my next novelty. So of course I advance him a couple of thousand.

"Now, I got to cover it somehow. Why would I be paying a singer two G's? It would smell to high heaven of payola. So I dig in the files and find a song I once paid maybe ten bucks for, because the guy who wrote it needed ten bucks. The song's a dog. I'll never do anything with it. But I write in the singer's name as a co-composer or co-author, and I mail a copy to Washington with four bucks for a copyright. Then I put the manuscript back in the files.

"A man from the Treasury Department happens to find out I gave the singer money and wants to know why. So I whip out the song. The snoop wants to know why I paid two thousand dollars for something I didn't publish, and I have the answer all ready. I say, 'Sir, in the music business songs have styles just like in the ladies' garment business. When I bought this song, it was in style. Before I had a chance to publish it, the fashion changed. Now I'm waiting for it to come back in style before I work on it.'

"How does the Treasury Department happen to find out? Well, of course, the two thousand dollars is a *business deduction*, see?"

Publishers say there are instances of hidden or sublimated payola with which they must contend in order to keep performers happy enough to give consideration to their songs.

One points to the bags under his bloodshot eyes and announces that they are payola-puffs. "I'm getting a little old to go pub-crawling night after night," he sighs, "but unless I do my songs are going nowhere. All the boys and girls are doing night club acts, these days. So what happens? So-and-So just gets into town from Vegas, where he's been a smash. Now he's booked into the Copa or Brooklyn. So he calls me up, or has his manager do it for him, and tells me when he's opening. That's my cue to get up a party and phone for a reservation.

"My wife's tired, too, but these openings are like command performances. We round up some social obligations and hit the night spot before So-and-So goes on for his first show. On the way in, I stop and chit-chat with the proprietor or the *maitre d'* just to let him know we're there to catch the fellow's act. It makes him look big in the eyes of the management, and that's what we're there for. Of course we clap our hands red when he does his bit, too. We're a high-class claque, only instead of being hired like the old-time claques I pay the bill, including cover charge. And if I do it Monday night for So-and-So, I got to do it Tuesday night for What's-His-Name—and so on.

"Sure—it's deductible. But how long can a guy my age go without sleep? It was all right years ago, when I was building the business and had enough moxie to stay up all night with the vaudeville crowd. I even enjoyed it, then. This is a personality business. I can't turn over the night work to a younger man in my outfit, because the stars would be insulted if I didn't show up in person. If I stay home with my pipe and slippers, like I'd like to, there are plenty of johnny-come-lately publishers just waiting to get in solid with the acts. You got to keep plugging."

Running neck and neck with A. & R. men and performers in publishers' exposé of payola-seekers are the nation's disk jockeys. When the outcries are loud enough investigations are sometimes made, quietly, by music trade journals or by the radio stations themselves. Bribery is seldom uncovered. Nevertheless, publishers insist that one or another of payola's many disguises is very much in the disk jockey picture. "How," they ask slyly, "can you figure the way some of them live? I know an insurance salesman who makes the same dough as a lot of them—around a hundred and fifty a week. *He* can't afford custom-tailored suits."

In any group of three thousand individuals—as, indeed, in any group of three hundred, thirty or three—there are variations in personal integrity. Like many performers and bandleaders, most of the top-rated disk jockeys have erected rigid barriers against bribery. They may accept a case of a new advertiser's product to "sample" but are likely to get nervous if a music publisher's or recording company's representative offers to treat them to so much as a bottle of pop.

The publishers maintain, however, that the smart disk jockeys have found ways to augment their incomes with payola money.

"Here's what happens," a disgruntled publisher says. "Couple of years ago one of the big-shot d.j.'s made himself some nice extra income from a few publishers for pushing their plug tunes. On the quiet, of course. But he got regular envelopes with green stuff in them. So he lived up to his end of the bargain—crammed the air with like three tunes, see, played them all day long and kept talking them up.

"Now it happens he's a pretty big wheel in his territory. He's got a good spot on a station and millions of people tune him in like clockwork. So what's next? They go out and buy the records he's plugging. Thousands of 'em every day go into the store and plank down like eighty-nine cents apiece, plus tax. This shows up like a thumb on the dealers' order sheets, and it makes a statistic on the survey tables in the trade papers.

"Next thing you know, the d.j.'s out West and down South figure that if this big wheel is behind the disks, they got to be good. So they dig through their stacks on the desk and *they* begin to plug, too, only they're not getting paid off.

"Pretty soon, you guessed it, these three tunes are hot all across the country. They're on the Hit Parade, naturally, and on the trade best-seller lists.

"Now here's the kicker, and it's a big yock. The d.j. who started the snowball rolling gets called up on the carpet by his boss at the station. Seems some publisher—I ain't saying whom—buzzes the boss that his boy is getting greased. This, you understand, is not kosher and the boss is plenty steamed. So when he calls in this jock and tells him he's been fingered for payola, this jock acts real hurt. He picks up *Variety*, *Billboard* and the *Cash Box* and flips the pages to those ratings. Then he grabs copies of his program clearances for the past couple of weeks and shoves them under the boss' nose.

" 'How can you say I'm playing payola tunes?' he asks. 'Am I playing dogs? Look for yourself. I'm playing what the public is buying. I'm playing the money platters in the jukes. I'm playing the Hit Parade!'

"So what could I—I mean, what could this publisher say? That these tunes wouldn't of got on the Hit Parade unless the d.j. hypo'd them? In the boss' eyes that would be like accusing his boy of being good at his job and blaming the station for being important. That's bad?"

The publishers who lament the loudest over disk jockey avarice are sensible to the fact that they have only themselves—or, rather, all those *other* publishers—to blame. Disk jockeys do not start out in their jobs seeking additional rewards from music publishers. Rewards are given to them, usually after they have demonstrated that they do their jobs effectively. The insidious element is that such rewards carry with them reassurance of personal importance and, in the afterglow of reassurance, the bribery motive is obscured.

"It seems I did the guy a favor without realizing it," a disk jockey is likely to think. "I played a record I happened to like, and it caught on. Nice of him to take the trouble to thank me."

Thus begins a subtle seduction. Having been rewarded for doing something voluntarily, the disk jockey is later asked to do the same thing in accordance with the "grateful" publisher's direction. "You did a great job with 'Pink Pebble,' " he is flattered.

"Give me the same break on 'Purple Rock' and I'll make it worth your while."

This is the line of demarcation between normal performance of his job and payola. If he recognizes it, the disk jockey has two courses open to him. He can refuse to be bought, either tactfully or indignantly, or he can justify his acceptance of a bribe by convincing himself it would be foolish to turn it down. The publishers are importunate, hinting that the "other fellows" are playing ball. His ego is nourished by the exhilirating thought that he, by the simple gesture of placing needle to record and speaking a few enthusiastic words from time to time, can mold public opinion.

Although most publishers' ready answer to the disk jockey payola question is "Who can afford disk jockeys?" off-the-cuff confessions cite case after case of payola on the platters. The smart jocks, they say, "take" only from firms whose material is good, thereby avoiding accusations of trying to foist poor material on the public.

A publisher points out that he can seldom get to the top men in the field, either because he knows they are incorruptible, or rich enough already, or too expensive. But, he hints, the word gets around when a new disk jockey starts getting hot. The trick is to get to him while he's building, before he gets the idea that he's important.

The story of Plato Jones, a purely fictitious name for a composite hero, is a case in point.

In a medium-sized city on the Eastern Seaboard, as one of the teachers in the music department of a local high school, Plato gave a series of lectures on contemporary popular music, illustrating his talk with records. One of his students spoke so enthusiastically at home about the course that her father, an executive for one of the area's radio stations, became interested. He invited the teacher to repeat his lecture series over the air.

Audience response to the program prompted the station to offer Plato a permanent job as a disk jockey, with programs scheduled throughout the day. Plato was flattered by the offer, but he was also considerably upset by it. His entire background had been directed toward the profession of teaching, and he was happy enough in his job.

Because the radio station offer meant a sizable increase in income over his teacher's pay, he found himself in grave conflict. He had a wife and two young children, a large mortgage on a small house and a time-payment contract for the only luxury he permitted himself—a good hi-fi set. The family car was paid for, but only because it had been a wedding gift, seven years earlier, from his father.

The prospect of more money with which to insure his family's security loomed large in Plato's thoughts, but it was offset to a degree by his hesitancy to break with academic life and his uncertainty about his qualifications as a disk jockey. "I'm a good teacher," he reflected, "but how do I know I'll be a good disk jockey? How do I even know if I'll like it?" He decided to seek advice from his department head at the school.

Somewhat to his surprise, the older man swept his doubts away. "Take it," he said. "You're a fine teacher and you'll go as far in this school as the system will allow you to. But when you reach the top bracket, in another five or six years, you'll still be earning less than the radio job offers you now. If you study for your doctorate and, in time, rise to the highest administrative position in education that this state promises, you may still be far behind what you may earn in the field of communications within a very short time. Forget about the so-called security of a teaching job. Take the plunge and see what happens. You can always come back to teaching."

Plato's duties as a disk jockey included the playing of records from the station's library and from a selection of new releases which reached his office daily. Between recordings, he was to read prepared messages supplied to him by local sponsors' advertising agencies, play transcribed commercials from national advertisers and make announcements as they were given to him by the station's copy and news departments.

Plato's training as a teacher had taught him to organize his material in advance of each day's classes and to speak with wit and conviction. As he grew more confident in front of the microphone, he began to inject into his program some of the dramatic interest he had created in the classroom. He built special programs around grouped recordings, interpolating brief critical or instructive comments between playings.

The first indications of Plato's personal popularity among his listeners came one day when something went wrong with the mechanism of his studio turntable. Unable to proceed with his scheduled recordings, Plato ad-libbed a running commentary on a miscellany of subjects and read a few local notices. During an advance announcement of a forthcoming musical program to be held in the city's town hall, he mentioned casually that he and his wife were disappointed that they would be unable to attend because they had not been able to find a baby-sitter for that night. When the turntable mechanism was repaired, he returned to his scheduled notes and finished out his working day.

As he prepared to turn the studio over to the newscaster who followed him, Plato was summoned to the executive offices by the station manager.

The manager motioned for him to sit down.

"How long have you been with us, Mr. Jones?" the executive asked.

"About three months," Plato said.

The manager toyed with some papers in front of him. "Do you make it a habit to keep stand-by scripts handy in case of emergency? Don't you know that all prepared material should be cleared first with our legal department?"

"But that wasn't a script," Plato explained. "When the mechanism failed, I didn't quite know what to do. So I just kept talking."

"I see," the manager said. "I understand that you and your wife would like to go to the Town Hall concert next Tuesday if you can arrange for a baby-sitter."

"Well, yes. I guess I must have said that on the air. I'm sorry."

The manager smiled. "Don't apologize. The baby-sitter situation is pretty tough in these parts. However, if you really want to go to that concert I think you can manage. I imagine you'll be able to choose a satisfactory baby-sitter from these."

The manager patted the papers in front of him.

"So far," he said, "the switchboard has received 276 phone calls from people who think you ought to go to that concert. They've offered their services as baby-sitters—276 baby-sitters—and I understand the calls are still coming in. I suspect there'll be a number of write-ins, too."

"I—I don't know what to say," Plato stammered. "If I caused the station any trouble—"

"Trouble! Young man, the life-blood of a radio station is the personal rapport its programs establish with listeners. The industry spends a fortune on pilot shows and surveys to find out what the public wants. Apparently something you said—or the way you said it—reached people and made them want to respond. We've had some reaction from our advertisers recently on that score, too, even though three months isn't a very long testing period.

"Now, I didn't call you in here just to tell you we found a baby-sitter for you. I want you to sign a new contract with us. It will guarantee you certain things, including a bonus and periodic raises, and it will bind you to this station for two years, with options to renew. We plan to spend some money on a promotional campaign built around your time, and we have to protect our investment.

"Starting tomorrow, we're setting up appointments for you with some of the sponsors who buy—or we hope will buy—time on your program. I want you to get familiar with their products. From time to time, instead of using the prepared commercials the agencies send you, do a little ad-lib pitching on your own, the way you did today. Is everything clear?"

Plato nodded. "There's one thing, though," he said. "When I buy the sponsors' products, should I keep a record of what I spend? Or will I have a petty cash account?"

"Uh—you won't have to lay out money for the products," the manager said. "The advertising department will see to it that samples are sent to your home. Now, the higher salary you'll be getting will rate more of your time. I want you to take full charge of the new record releases that come in. Set up your own system—play what you like and say what you think about them. But play more of the new things than you have been doing. You're inclined to get a little too longhair every so often—probably the teacher in you. We want to attract more young listeners in the after-school time slots, so give them what they want. Okay?"

"Okay," Plato said. "But do you mind if I take some of the new records home with me to try out before I put them on the air? So many of them come in that one reason I haven't played them is, I don't get a chance to review them first."

"Good idea, I guess," the manager said. "But don't you read the advance record reviews in the trade papers?"

"Well, no," Plato said. "To tell you the truth, I don't understand the way they express things."

The manager hid a smile. "Well, I have an idea you'll be catching on to the lingo soon. Meantime, keep on the way you've been doing up to now. You have a future here."

That night, there was great joy in the Jones household. With pencil and paper, Plato and his wife figured out that they could now pay off the balance remaining for their hi-fi set, plan to reduce the mortgage and start a college fund for the children. They speculated on whether they could start thinking in terms of a new car.

Within the next few weeks, Plato's household began to resemble a warehouse as advertisers' products began to pour in. He tested them conscientiously. Once, a shipment caused a temporary flurry of concern. This was a case of a new client's frozen blintzes—forty-eight packages of them. The reason for the concern was that Plato did not have a freezer. Hastily, the Jones family canvassed their neighborhood and presented packages of frozen blintzes to their friends.

When it came time for the commercial the next day, Plato broadcast a humorous account of the previous evening's experience, describing his family's and his neighbors' delight with the product and urging his listeners to try Bilko's blintzes without delay for a new taste thrill.

A week after this broadcast, Plato arrived home to find a gleaming new freezer on the back porch.

"Isn't it wonderful?" his wife exclaimed. "They monitored your commercial the day you said we didn't have any freezer, and this came today."

"Who's 'they'?" Plato asked.

"Open it up—you'll see."

Plato opened the freezer and saw that its twenty-four cubic feet were loaded to capacity with familiar packages of Bilko blintzes—all five varieties—as well as Bilko pizzas and Bilko berry pies.

"Well, gosh," Plato marveled. "Isn't that nice!"

His wife continued, excitedly. "One of the agency men came along when it was delivered. He said that the day after you told that funny story about us running around the neighborhood with blintzes, the client's distributor opened up seventeen new accounts and the factory had to put on extra shifts."

Baby-sitters and blintzes introduced Plato to the peripheral advantages of his job. In the weeks that followed, the ex-schoolteacher discovered that there was about his program some magic Aladdin's-lamp quality.

The day after he speculated idly on whether or not he should allow his little daughter to get a permanent wave for her straight hair, he was besieged by phone calls and letters. Half of these pleaded with him not to tamper with nature, and half of them urged him not to force his child to a life of misery without curls. He also received several notes from beauty parlors in the city with certificates enclosed entitling both his daughter and his wife to free permanents.

A casual mention of his difficulty in adding a column of figures right the first time brought him three pocket computing gadgets and a full-size adding machine from local office-equipment shops.

A chance remark that his skin was allergic to wool brought a formal protest from the local woolen plant's publicity director and a variety of haberdashery fashioned from nonallergic materials.

He acknowledged receipt of the gifts graciously during his programs. One day it occurred to him that this might be wrong. The station sold its time, and he was giving away what amounted to free advertising. He decided to consult the head of the sales department.

"Don't worry about it," he was told. "We'll let you know if you get out of line. We've been keeping tabs on those free plugs. We figure them as investments. It doesn't always follow, but often enough we can covert a free plug into a time contract. Matter of fact, we signed up two beauty parlors for spot announcements, and we're working out a program idea for the City Sweater Mill. They make nylon and orlon sweaters. Nonallergic."

Plato had put into practice his planned idea of previewing new record releases at home. During one of his listening sessions, he came across one that caught his fancy. Although it was an unknown label and the singing artist was unfamiliar to him, he liked it.

When he put the disk on his player for the first time in the radio studio, he said over the microphone: "I've never heard of this singer, and the label is new to me, too. But see if you don't agree with me that this record has something special about it."

It became apparent almost immediately that his listeners agreed with him. The station's switchboard was jammed as hundreds of requests were phoned in by people who wanted to hear the record again. During the week that followed, Plato played it several times a day "by popular demand."

Although he was not aware of it, his repeated spinnings of the obscure disk was causing a mounting excitement that started in his city and, arcing the miles, stirred up matching activity in New York.

Because the record was on a minor label with an unknown singer, the music dealers in town did not have it on their shelves. As customer requests poured in, dealers wired or phoned their distributors, ordering from ten to fifty copies each. The distributors got in touch with the recording company.

A small outfit operating independently on a low budget but high hopes, the company gleefully began to order pressings of its record to fill the orders.

One of the company's officials phoned the song's publisher and told him what was happening. Agreeably surprised—the song had been turned down by the top dozen or so record companies before finding the small diskery—the publisher ordered his contact man to push sheet music of the song to jobbers. In this business, he reflected, you certainly never know.

"We've got a sleeper," he said to his staff. "Who kicked it off?"

One of the contact men, who had traced the excitement to its origin, answered: "Some new jock in the sticks."

"Is it worth a trip?" the publisher asked.

"Seems as if," the song-plugger said. "If he could do it once, he could probably repeat."

"Okay," the publisher said. "*Popover* is cutting that new ballad of Joe's this week with some new gal. Get him."

"It's a Pullman hop," the plugger reminded him. "What about —uh—traveling expenses?"

The publisher glanced at him sharply.

"Anything within reason," he decided. "Use your head—this is a new jock."

Plato was pleased and flattered when he was visited, at the studio, by a man who traveled all the way up from a New York City music-publishing house to meet him personally. He invited his visitor home for dinner, politely declining an invitation to go on the town.

When the song-plugger arrived at Plato's house, he brought an armful of packages. There was a walking, talking, singing doll for the small daughter, a space suit and disintegrator gun for the son, a pair of handsome earrings for their mother and, for Plato, a fine leather wallet. Inside the wallet were two crisp fifty-dollar bills.

Plato tried to express his family's thanks.

"Don't thank me," the song-plugger grinned. "You've earned it. You did a great thing with that song of ours, and we're grateful."

"Pete's sake," Plato said. "All I did was play a record I liked."

"Don't knock it, you're a hit-picker," the song-plugger said. "That's pretty rare. Everybody in our business *thinks* he can pick hits, but not many can. Trouble with this racket today is that people don't realize the people who can really pick the hits are the people with experience. My firm has been in business for a long time, and the chief is a man who can spot a hit a mile away. He spotted this one, of course, but the business being what it is today, it would have died quietly if you hadn't kicked it off up here. You were able to recognize a hit that was turned down by the top A. & R. men—and they're supposed to be experts."

Plato turned his head to look at the pile of new releases on his table.

Noticing his glance, the song-plugger said:

"I brought a couple of new songs for you. Matter of fact, the New York office just sent me the records today. One of them is a big label, the other is a minor with a great new bunch of teen-agers with a song we can latch onto if it's got what we think it has. Do me a favor, Plato. Start plugging them. Don't stop playing the sleeper—your first discovery, I mean. We figure it has another month, being a ballad. The big labels are starting to cover it, and one of them is bound to make it. But start plugging these new ones right away. Let's have a couple of hits in a row, how about it? We'll make it worth your while."

Plato Jones, ex-schoolteacher and rising young disk jockey with a houseful of gifts from appreciative advertisers, held out his hand for the records. He played them, listening critically. Then he handed them back to the song-plugger.

"I can't do it," he said. "They're not very good. You probably know that already. But even if they were terrific, I couldn't accept your terms. I'd be getting myself into a situation I don't like, and that's something you can't make worth my while. If the songs your firm publishes are good, and they reach me on good recordings, I'll play them. You don't have to pay me to do that. It's my job. But I won't play a record that's in bad taste, or offensive. There are too many good ones coming through. Sure, I play a lot of things that I, personally, don't especially like—but not because I'm under obligation to play them to someone who wants them played. My audience is made up of all kinds of people, with all kinds of musical tastes, and I try to please them all. So far, I've been lucky. I'd be pressing that luck to hire out as some publisher's stooge, and sooner or later my program and my services to the station would be meaningless."

In this story, which most publishers will consider sheer fantasy, the payola did not engulf Plato. It could have. Ways to supplement their legitimate salaries are made so easy and attractive for disk jockeys with the ability to "kick off" records that many of them accept the palatable bribes willingly and gladly, considering the extra income as a normal advantage of their trade. They feel they are doing no real harm. If the publishers are foolish enough to pay, they would be foolish to refuse.

But the trade journals, the contact men's union and the popular press seldom hear about the Plato Joneses. Even when they do, the stories do not constitute news, for there is nothing very exciting about the exploits of an honest man. There is, however, constant if muted agitation about payola practices among disk jockeys, and occasionally the mutterings flare up in print. When this happens, the entire brotherhood becomes suspect until the fuss dies down. It always does, usually without any conclusive actions or resolutions other than an occasional firing if a disk jockey has been indiscreet.

Like any other minority group under public scrutiny, disk jockeys in general are often blamed for the sins of the few. There is at least one gentleman who has evolved a simple system for acquiring some of the material possessions he desires but cannot afford to buy on his modest salary as a disk jockey. He keeps a file box on his desk at home with cards coded as to publishers, record companies, ambitious singers and agents who, in his opinion, should be logical sources of tribute. He analyzes the best-seller charts, assessing the amount of his subjects' business during the year.

A month or so before Christmas, he spends some time with illustrated catalogs, scissors, paste pot and post cards. The individuals on his list have learned what to expect. To one, he sends a pasted picture of, for example, a tape recorder—or a boy's bicycle—or an electric shaver. He mentions the brand names he prefers. To others he sends illustrations of suits, hats, shoes, socks —complete with itemized information about sizes, colors and other pertinent data.

The "Santa Claus lists" from an opportunistic disk jockey are usually thrown into the nearest waste basket but sometimes, astonishingly, they are handed over to a secretary for fulfillment. One annual recipient likes to save his list from year to year. "I must be getting successful," he commented when the latest one was received. "Last year he sent a picture of a Sears, Roebuck garden cart—$7.95 plus shipping charges. This year it's a reclining leather chair. *Real* leather, not plastic!"

11. *Copyrights, Copycats and Con Men*

IF MENTION OF PAYOLA makes music pubishers nervous, mention of amateur songwriters makes them hysterical. They say they can smell an unsolicited manuscript at twenty paces and an amateur songwriter at fifty.

If you have never written a song, you are unusual. If you have never given so much as a passing thought to the idea that you *could* write a song, you are phenomenal and some music publisher would gladly hire you just for the exquisite relief of having someone around who won't whip a manuscript out of a pocket.

It is perfectly normal to write a song, or want to. Some people do it out of disgust or defiance when they hear a nonsensical tune being played interminably and selling a million records which earn masses of money for some fellow with no talent. Others do it when they feel happy, or sad, or after the third drink.

When someone who is not a professional songwriter writes a song and lets it go at that, he is just like anyone else. Sooner or later, however, a chemical change takes place and he begins to believe that, given the right breaks, he can *sell* his song and make a fortune. It is at this point that he becomes an amateur songwriter, a music trade term that is the equivalent of "boll weevil" to a Texas cotton rancher.

Amateur poets, painters or novelists are regarded in a kindly light by their professional counterparts and even enjoy a smattering of prestige among their workaday contemporaries. Amateur songwriters, on the other hand, are generally considered unworthy of equal billing with the human race by any member of the music business fraternity.

Steve Allen has a soothing answer for any amateur songwriter who, in pain and yearning, wants to crash Tin Pan Alley.

"There's nothing to stop you," Mr. Allen says. "But why don't you decide to be President of the United States instead—or go out in your back yard with a two-dollar uranium detector and become a millionaire? It's easier."

The voracious record business, by ignoring the former traditions and taboos of popular music, has pried open a narrow slit in what used to be a door tightly sealed against newcomers. Nevertheless, hordes of aspiring songwriters are left wailing outside, futilely beating against it with the American formula for success which is compounded of ability, ambition and determined effort. The formula does not seem to work in the popular-music industry.

Publishers' maneuvers to avoid coming in contact with eager-eyed men and women with a new song to sell are hardly more absurd—or adroit—than the amateurs' maneuvers to make that contact. Amateur songwriters have been known to disguise themselves as elevator operators, waiters, delivery men and baby-sitters in order to gain access to publishers' ears. Their unpublished manuscripts are likely to turn up in laundry bundles, candy boxes and under the napkins on luncheon trays sent up to Brill Building offices.

Particularly loathsome to publishers are the incredible numbers of fanatics who call themselves by a variety of pretentious names —"Victor Herbert Smith," "Stephen Foster Jones," "Irving Berlin

Kelly"—in order to attract attention to themselves. Some would-be songwriters spend all their earnings from less glamorous pursuits on a succession of four-dollar "unpublished copyrights," printing their songs at their own expense and swamping publishers' incoming mail baskets with impressive, bragging brochures. They bombard publishers with importunate letters and telegrams. They sit or stand for hours in tiny reception rooms, portfolios under their arms, waiting for someone—anyone—to notice them, steadfast in their belief that the instant their songs are heard they will be hailed as successors to Rodgers and Hammerstein and given lifetime contracts.

But all letters, packages and hollow objects sent as gifts and suspected of containing unsolicited manuscripts are returned to their senders unopened, if a return address is given, thrown into the wastebasket (unopened) if not. Visitors to publishing offices who are not known or unable to present convincing credentials explaining their presence are turned away or stalled by well-trained receptionists.

Some of the practical jokers among publishers have, when cornered, a habit of bouncing amateurs off each other. "See Mills," a man at Feist may say to an obvious novice. "They're looking for songwriters over there." At Mills, the perspiring amateur is advised to "see Miller," a firm which shares an address and policy with Feist. One of the biggest jokes is the tip to "see Vogel." This is a firm whose telephone operator answers incoming calls by caroling: "The *old* songs are the *best* songs, good *morning!*" This game of musical chairs can keep an amateur songwriter hopping for months. There are, roughly, three thousand music publishers.

One man, who runs his small publishing firm unaided by office assistants, has invented a series of defenses that would do credit to security agencies. He keeps his office door in the Brill Building locked, opening it only to persons equipped with the proper knock and password, changed daily. If an amateur should manage to reach him by telephone, he hisses: "So sorry. Mr. Boss gone to Japan to hire geisha girl song-pluggers. Not come back for two-three months."

Musical publishers' harsh treatment of aspiring songwriters might seem unreasonable and un-American except for the fact that a great deal of trouble can be traced to the amateurs. An avalanche of amateur-incited lawsuits descends upon publishers year after year. Some few of these are instituted by sincere novices who either mistakenly believe they have a grievance, or who have been convinced of it by less sincere but no less mistaken lawyers. Most of them, however, are trumped up by legal opportunists who chase fees the way, in former years, their brethren chased ambulances.

Unfortunately, law enactment officials are not always entirely clear in their understanding of musical copyright, and lawsuits which reach the courts depend for their disposition on the interpretation of the judges sitting on the cases. A local judge in a local court may rule in favor of a local boy as opposed to "big city" businessmen (the publishers). Out of this muddle has arisen a vicious nuisance in the music industry which is difficult to control. Thousands of undeserved dollars have gone, by court decree, into the pockets of people who did nothing to earn them except to plead their cause before tone-deaf judges.

One such case, narrated by Sigmund Spaeth in his *History of Popular Music in America* (Random House, 1948) tells of a 1931 song, "Starlight," with words by Joe Young and music by Bernice Petkere. Mr. Young was no mean lyricist, having penned the words to a number of outstanding popular works including "Five Foot Two, Eyes of Blue," "I'm Gonna Sit Right Down and Write Myself a Letter," "Dinah" and "In a Little Spanish Town." Miss Petkere, also a professional of high caliber, had to her credit the scores for top Broadway productions and the music for dozens of successful songs, among them the perennial standard, "Lullaby of the Leaves."

"Starlight" was pounced upon by a California amateur. He brandished a dated manuscript which showed that *his* melody (unpublished, but bearing a copyright stamp) had been written earlier than Miss Petkere's.

Mr. Spaeth, who has earned the title of "America's Tune Detective" over many years of tracing melodic origins for copyright litigants, stated that the published song and the amateur's manuscript had a common ancestor in an old melody, "Violets," composed by Ellen Wright and published by G. Ricordi & Company in 1900. Comparisons revealed that both melodies—Miss Petkere's as well as the amateur's—were almost note-for-note identical with the older tune, whose original copyright had lapsed.

The amateur was awarded $10,000 by the judge who—Mr. Spaeth writes—"admitted that he knew nothing about music . . . handed down the absurd verdict that has opened the door to innumerable suits of the same kind, mostly representing blackmail and attempted extortion."

According to Mr. Spaeth, the decision could as easily have gone to the defendants had Miss Petkere been willing to admit that she knew of the existence of "Violets," which her melody resembled so strikingly. She refused to admit it, however, and lost the case.

The earnest would-be songwriter who complains sourly that publishers brush him off without courtesy or consideration has dishonest—or, sometimes, just badly advised—amateurs to thank for his difficulties. He does not, however, realize that his own fellows have erected the wall which bars him from Tin Pan Alley. Instead, he blames the publishers.

But for corruption, the amateurs believe, they would be successful songwriters. In their minds the music publisher is an unforgivable creature—a man with no talent and of no particular charm who lives parasitically off the creative endeavors of others whom, no doubt about it, he cheats. He is detested as the sort of person who would confiscate an abundant natural resource—like water—and have the nerve to sell it to thirsty people. Moreover, he is suspected of protecting his monopoly on the water supply by ruthlessly poisoning hand-dug wells.

Here, now, is an odd thing. Ambitious aspirants to any other field of endeavor seldom condemn the field itself for their own failures. If they should, they are soon pegged, by their companions as projecting their own inadequacies by blaming someone or something else for their defeat. Men who wash out of aeronautics don't blame the aircraft industry for their personal inability to fly a plane. Men who flunk out of law or medical school don't accuse the professions of law and medicine of corruption. Aspiring artists, authors, actors or architects who are not successful turn their interests into hobbies and look for jobs. But frustrated amateur songwriters are unshakably convinced that the music business is a racket and all publishers are thieves. Some of them harbor the additional suspicion that the names appearing on title pages are not the names of real people at all, but of dummies invented by the publishers (for tax purposes). The songs were *really* written by amateurs.

For at least two generations there was a fable, recited by some professionals as well as amateurs, that Irving Berlin never wrote more than a tenth of the songs for which he is credited. It was whispered that Berlin kept a talented slave boy in a back room, turning out songs. During Berlin's most prolific years, the fiction expanded; he kept *three* boys in the back room.

Incomprehensively, even professionals in show business frequently act like amateurs when they add songwriting to their activities. Berlin, for one, learned this bitter truth the hard way. If given the choice of looking at an amateur's manuscript or diving into ice water in February, he would unhesitatingly choose the ice water.

Once, some years ago, a song-plugger who knew the famous composer-publisher well brought him a song written by a gainfully employed singer. He said, "Irving, I know you make it a rule not to look at outside manuscripts. But after all, this fellow is no amateur in show business. He's a pro. Besides, he sings your songs all the time—a good plug. He also plays ball with me, and I need him. Now, he's really written a song here that's got a good chance. We'll probably publish it ourselves, but he made me promise I'd show it to you. Please look at it. Or if you won't, at least write him a letter and he'll know I kept my promise."

Out of friendship for the song-plugger, Berlin dictated a polite note to the singer in which he expressed his hope that the song would be well received.

Five years later, Berlin wrote the score for a musical film. An infringement suit was promptly filed against him by the singer, whose song had not been published after all. The singer claimed that Berlin "stole" several bars of his song. As proof that the composer had had access to his work, he submitted the friendly note.

Berlin had to defend the suit. The judge ruled in his favor, declaring that no composer of Irving Berlin's stature need stoop to stealing a few bars of music from anyone.

Nevertheless, such lawsuits compound the generally held public superstition that larceny is rife in the music business. In 99 per cent of cases brought to trial, decisions go to the established copyright owners, but the cost of defending unwarranted lawsuits is high. Moreover, the damage is done when the suit is instigated. Public sympathy, if not judicial, is usually on the side of the underdog—the unknown or unsuccessful amateur who claims to have been exploited. Besides, the original announcement of a lawsuit is news; the settlement is anticlimactic and buried in the back pages of newspapers if it is mentioned at all.

Music publishers are not thieves. They don't have to steal songs. There are too many available, produced in prodigious numbers by seasoned professionals who, themselves, may write a hundred for every one that is published. Nevertheless, the myth persists. Like most superstitions, it had its genesis in certain tribal customs of the industry's remote past.

Before attempts were made to put popular music on an ethical business basis by trade associations, unscrupulous publishers did occasionally pirate unknown writers' songs. The copyright law was vague, and judicial interpretation of it subject to vagaries. "Borrowed" melodies for new lyrics were not only commonplace, they were acceptable. ("The Star-Spangled Banner" is based on a borrowed melody, and so are "The Battle Hymn of the Republic" and "Yankee Doodle," to name only three.)

But publishers were not the only ones with sticky fingers when Tin Pan Alley was young. Songwriters, too, found it a great lark to steal each other's tunes. Even innocent of outright larcenous intent, many songs of the past—and some of the present—have been bought for ridiculously low sums by professional songwriters who were either temporarily idea-barren, or quick to recognize commercial possibilities in a tune or lyric penned by an outsider, or merely kindhearted enough to shell out a few dollars to a down-at-the-heels colleague. Sometimes the songs acquired in this way were later monetary successes for the purchasers. In any other industry, such transactions would be considered shrewd business operations and the buyers would be congratulated for their astuteness. "Let the seller beware" is the new philosophy in this sophisticated, price-tag-conscious country. Not in the music industry. Word gets around that so-and-so "lifted" a derelict colleague's song and made a million while the poor slob he robbed was still mooching drinks.

In addition, there exists in popular music a tremendous amount of unconscious plagiarism; but the business and its almost infinite periphery are so aswarm with suspicious watchmen that the unconscious plagiarism does not remain in the dark for long. One of America's best known and most successful songwriters was involved in a lawsuit because of unintentional pilfering, and his troubles were far from unique.

The composer's melody, published in the 1940s, was a leader on all best-seller lists and piling up nice, fat royalty checks when his publisher received a legal document from a lawyer in a small Southwestern city announcing a client's intention to sue the publisher and the composer for half a million dollars, claiming plagiarism. Letters like this are not uncommon in publishing offices. Almost every hit song brings an afterwash of threatened lawsuits from cranks and crooks.

As a matter of routine, the composer was summoned and shown the claim, which he marked as preposterous. The plaintiff was the widow of a man the composer had never met but, according to her, the song was the original work of her late husband.

The publisher realized that the prominent names involved would mean unfavorable publicity if any truth in the claim could be proved, or even if an unfounded claim should reach the courts. He dispatched to the Southwestern city his lawyer and his editor, a man of prodigious musical memory and competence.

At the widow's home, the lawyer and editor listened to a well-worn homemade recording of a tune played, inexpertly, on a piano. Tearfully, the widow said that the record had been made during a happy gathering at her home while her husband was in his final illness. "He was tinkering at the piano," she said, "and this is what he played. He always played it. Used to whistle or hum it, too, when he was well enough to putter around outside. He didn't have long to live, and he said it made him feel better. When I heard my husband's song on the radio, I almost fainted. Then I got in touch with my cousin. He's the lawyer who sent you the letter."

The editor played the record again and examined a copy of the published hit song. Then he said, privately, to his firm's lawyer. "The melody line is almost identical. Can't understand it. God knows our boy doesn't have to steal a tune—he's got a million of them."

Under later questioning, the composer recalled that, years before, he had spent a few days in the Southwestern town. It was quite possible, he admitted, that he could have been somewhere in the vicinity of the widow's house and heard her husband whistling or humming. He had no conscious recollection of it.

Many years later, as he was working on a new song, it was possible that his brain's memory grooves loosed the melody they had stored so long.

Here was an obvious case of unintentional, unconscious plagiarism. What should be done about it? The chances were that if the case went into court, any judge hearing the testimony on both sides would have handed down a decision in favor of the copyright owners. The widow's property had never been copyrighted and enough years had passed for the statute of limitations to protect the composer.

However, the publisher and songwriter had unblemished reputations at stake and the story, if given publicity, was full of pathos which far outweighed its legal elements. Both of them agreed, moreover, that there was a moral principle involved. Acting on the advice of their attorneys, they offered to settle out of court. The widow was given a large check, for which she waived all claims to her husband's song.

Now a familiar standard, this is one song whose frequent playing brings no prideful pleasure to the composer.

Ironically, the reputation that music publishers are larcenous has been fostered not only by the legions of frustrated amateurs and their cronies, or by litigations brought by injured songwriters and their heirs, but also by the publishers themselves. A publisher who will express sorrow, anger or indignation when an outsider accuses him of stealing a tune is the first one to jump into court when one of his properties makes its appearance under another firm's imprint.

One of the most famous cases of two publishers fighting over the same bone is the story of a fracas involving the lively 1950 melody, "Tzena, Tzena, Tzena."

The Weavers, a favored folk-singing group, used the song as part of their repertoire when they performed at a Greenwich Village bistro, where it attracted the attention of Howard Richmond, head of several New York publishing firms.

Richmond instituted a search for the title, which he found in a book of collected Israeli folk songs. While the book bore the usual copyright, no notice could be found regarding the song itself. Mention was made that it had been arranged by Julius Grossman, an American schoolteacher.

On the assumption that an old folk song would be in the public domain, Richmond turned the melody over to composer Spencer Ross for doctoring, and to Gordon ("Manhattan Tower") Jenkins for lyrics.

Still jittery about the possibility of previous copyright, Richmond sent a copy of the revision to Israel for further clearance, meanwhile applying to Washington for an American copyright.

The Weavers, under contract to Decca, recorded the modernized version and backed it up with another adapted folk song, "Goodnight, Irene," a property of another of Richmond's publishing firms. The record was an instantaneous hit, and sheet music of the song enjoyed a lively sale.

Pending clarity on the copyright situation, Richmond's firm (Cromwell Music, Inc.) put aside composer royalties as they accrued, earmarking them for payment of possible future claims.

Suddenly, "Tzena, Tzena, Tzena" appeared on retail sheet music racks with a different title page and bearing the imprint of a different publisher, Mills Music, Inc. In this version, the words were by the celebrated lyricist, Mitchell Parish, while the music was attributed to Julius Grossman and Issacher Miron, a pseudonym for Michrovsky.

Hard on the heels of this appearance came notice to Richmond that Mills was bringing suit in behalf of the composer, Michrovsky. Basis for the suit was a contract between Mills and a representative who claimed to be Michrovsky's agent.

Michrovsky, a living Israeli, could establish that he was a composer of the song. Two sets of lyrics existed. Two publishers claimed title.

In his defense, Richmond pointed out that composer royalties were ready and waiting for Michrovsky. His firm had spent thousands of dollars to promote its version in good faith that the tune was either in the public domain or penned by a composer who did not come under the jurisdiction of the international copyright law.

When the case came to trial, the ruling favored Mills. The presiding judge said, in substance, "Even though Israel is not a member of the Berne Convention which set the reciprocal protection laws of international copyright, President Truman had, at the end of World War II, extended certain rights—including copyright protection—to Israel." This meant that the song's composer had the right to sell or assign his interests and, as Mills' spokesmen could prove, his agent had submitted the melody to them.

According to the court decision, Mills owned the publisher's copyright to the melody. It did not own the Gordon Jenkins words, but the firm had its own set of Parish lyrics. Jenkins tore up his lyrics and tried to forget the whole thing. The money Cromwell had expended in exploiting and popularizing the song was not recoverable. Now, in addition, the hit Decca record with the Jenkins lyrics constituted a copyright infringement and could not be sold or played on radio programs. All traceable copies of the recording as sung by The Weavers with the Jenkins lyrics and backed up by "Goodnight, Irene" were hastily recalled by Decca and destroyed. Cromwell's sheet music was similarly disposed of. If you should happen to have a copy of the Decca record, cherish it. It is a collector's item.

Despite the court decision which held that Mills Music, Inc., owned the copyright, there seems to remain some doubt about the affair. In the "*Variety* Music Cavalcade" the song is listed in the following manner:

Tzena, Tzena, Tzena. (1) w., Gordon Jenkins, m. arr. by Spencer Ross, Cromwell Music, Inc., copy. 1950; (2) w., Mitchell Parish, m. Issacher Miron (Michrovsky) and Julius Grossman, Mills Music, Inc., copy. 1950.

The entire scope of popular-music copyright is jealously and vigilantly policed, but the close-to-the-chest operations of the music publishers make it possible for an infringement to travel the total distance to publication and exploitation before it becomes apparent. Once detected, it has only one place to go—court.

As if music publishers didn't get into enough legal entanglements with amateurs and with other publishers, they also have an occasional rough time of it with some of their own most professional songwriters.

Sometimes out of mischievousness and sometimes out of bottled amnesia, songwriters of the colorful Tin Pan Alley days had a habit of selling the same song to more than one firm, then sitting back to enjoy the fireworks.

The irrepressible Jim Thornton (1861-1938) sold "When You Were Sweet Sixteen" outright to the publishing firm partnered by Edward B. Marks and Joseph W. Stern, which filed it away. Some time later, Thornton sold the same song to the Witmarks, who published it. They were promptly sued by Marks and Stern, who claimed prior ownership. This case never came to court, all parties knowing Thornton well. Witmark, with a bona fide bill of sale on file, signed by Thornton, forfeited $5,000 to Marks and Stern, who possessed a similiar—but earlier—document. Witmark had paid Thornton a total of $15 for the song, and Marks and Stern not much more. When the original copyright lapsed, its renewal was assigned by Thornton's widow to Shapiro-Bernstein, Inc. A hit when it was first published in 1898, it remained a barroom and barbershop favorite until it was revived in the 1944 film, *The Great John L.* and became a hit for the third time when Perry Como recorded it for Victor.

Another songwriting star who twinkled roguishly along Tin Pan Alley was Walter Donaldson (1893-1947) who, between escapades, turned out a steady stream of outstanding hits—"Mammy," "Little White Lies," "My Blue Heaven," "Love Me or Leave Me" and dozens more.

Donaldson was an enthusiastic devotee of horse racing. It is said that if music publishers wanted to know what Donaldson's most recent ASCAP royalty check amounted to, all they had to do was get in touch with his bookmaker.

Once, according to a favorite Donaldson yarn, the songwriter found himself simultaneously out of salable song material and funds. Realizing that he could easily remedy the former lack but requiring immediate cash to invest in a sure tip, the story goes, he phoned his friend Louis Bernstein, one of the principals of the publishing firm of Shapiro-Bernstein, Inc.

After exchanging greetings, Donaldson coughed dramatically and said, "I just finished a great song, Louis, but the doctor won't let me out of the house. Tell you what—you send me $500 and I'll let you have it."

Because a Walter Donaldson song was always a good risk, Bernstein sent the money by messenger.

After a few discouraging and unprofitable hours at the race track, Donaldson phoned the publisher again, saying he needed another $500. Suspecting a ruse, Bernstein refused to advance any more money without seeing the song.

Rebuffed but not unresourceful, Donaldson phoned a rival publisher and reprised his coughing monologue about having a great new song but being confined to bed and needing immediate cash. The second publisher, more than happy to anticipate acquiring a Donaldson song, made haste to comply.

Donaldson was a seasoned professional with enormous talent, and he was by no means a swindler. He made good his prevarication about having written a good new song by the simple act of writing one when he returned from the track. Still ruffled by Bernstein's caginess, which he considered unfriendly, he brought his song to the second publisher. When it was released, announced to the trade as Walter Donaldson's newest hit, Bernstein recalled that he had advanced $500 against the songwriter's promise to deliver his next tune. He promptly sued both Donaldson and the rival publisher. He lost his case. There was no way to prove that the song he put a prior claim on was actually the one for which he had advanced $500, sight unseen.

Not all of publishers' litigations are intramural or anti-amateur-songwriter. Hard-won copyright protections are so jealously and insistently cherished by the publishing fraternity that its legal departments are staffed by busy sleuths constantly on the lookout for infringements, intentional or otherwise.

A short story writer or novelist unfamiliar with the music industry's watchdog vigilance frequently runs into a snag when submitting for publication material which quotes the lyrics of songs. Editors know that not one line of lyric may be quoted without the written permission of the copyright owners. Such permissions may be obtained gratis, but usually they are given only if paid for. The fees are not standardized, their size depending largely on the individual publisher's disposition and particularly on the manner in which the permission is requested. Never, never tell a publisher that the quoting of his lyrics in a story of yours that needs them to advance the plot or establish mood will be "good publicity" for his song. *Nothing* is good publicity for a song except performances that lead to sales and royalties.

Publishers feel that they have spent a lot of money popularizing a song's lyrics. They see no reason why they should give away a precious part of their property for someone else's profit. A single line of familiar lyric, because of its frequent repetition within a song's framework, may represent as much as twenty per cent of the total content.

Advertising agencies are constant offenders as illegal lyric-quoters, and are just as constantly hit with demands for payment if they cause to be printed any part of copyrighted material, lyrics or music, as part of their campaigns.

Agencies aware of the situation are careful to apply for permissions before they show their layouts to clients, who may otherwise later be sued for copyright infringement. The publisher of "Don't Fence Me In," when the Cole Porter song was initially popular, turned down dozens of requests from ad agencies handling girdle accounts for permission to use the title. An astonished blouse manufacturer was sharply rapped for illustrating his advertisements with a few random music notes and the headline, "Wagon Wheels." There *were* wagon wheels printed on the blouse material, but the publisher won out.

Such infringements are a matter of judicial interpretation. Defendants, when hailed into court, indignantly protest that *titles*, using correct spellings of actual English words, are not covered by copyright. The music industry's lawyers, however, point out that the titles were used in ads only because they represented an association with popular songs, and therefore the advertisers are attempting to capitalize unlawfully on copyrighted material.

When you hear a singing commercial on radio or television that uses a familiar tune with new lyrics extolling the virtues of tooth paste, automobiles, soda pop or soap flakes, you may be sure that money has been paid to the publisher, composer and author for a license to parody.

In recent years, with many of the country's long-time ballad-writing composers unable (or unwilling) to compete on equal terms with the newer writers of the "crazy sounds" permeating the air-waves, more and more of these licenses are being issued. In earlier days, songwriters declined to lend their works to any-thing that might tend to cheapen them, but the fees forthcoming from well-heeled advertisers have proved too attractive to spurn.

Irving Caesar, the celebrated lyricist ("Swanee," "Tea for Two," "Crazy Rhythm," "Imagination") chuckles wryly over the music business situation which made the licensing of lyrics for commercials a welcome auxiliary income. In 1956, he sold the commercial rights to "Is It True What They Say About Dixie," which contains an appropriate line of lyric, to the manufacturers of Swanee Toilet Tissue.

The shadow of the copyright law falls on a number of assorted violators. Importers of music boxes, chiming watches and chil-dren's music-playing toys are under surveillance. When the tin-kling mechanisms play copyrighted tunes which have not been licensed for cigarette boxes, timepieces or teddy bears, their purveyors are subject to fines.

Sunday school teachers are unknowing lawbreakers when, lov-ingly but illegally, they reproduce on bits of tinted paper the lyrics of copyrighted spiritual songs for their pious little pupils to sing.

Most illicit users of music are guileless, but the industry feels it must clamp down on all violations in order to protect itself from the deliberate derelictions perpetrated by "lyric bootleggers" who peddle the words to popular songs in sheet or pamphlet form on city street-corners without paying royalties. This vice is a con-stant irritation to publishers, who are upset when the bootleggers —usually small printers—rake in profits on material in which they have no investment.

What with one thing and another, music publishers spend a

great deal of time bringing or defending lawsuits. And all this fun and frolicking in the courts, reported solemnly in the trade journals and sometimes hilariously in the popular press, have done little to rid the general public's mind of a suspicion that publishers must be an untrustworthy, slippery lot.

Publishers' reputations are further assailed by a matter of loose language. Through the Music Publishers Protective Association and running public relations effort, reputable publishers keep trying desperately to put one simple thought across to the public, especially to the songwriting public. This is: Not all people who *say* they are publishers, are. The warning is issued repetitively to milling throngs of would-be songwriters who get swindled annually by illegitimate "publishers" who belong to a group known as "song sharks."

Amateur songwriters are a gold mine for song sharks, many of whom manage to operate trickily within the letter of the law and are, therefore, hard to curb. They know that amateur songwriters, bruised by the repeated rebuffs they get on Tin Pan Alley, are sucker-bait for a promise that their songs will be looked at, read, evaluated and *published*.

They run small ads with big headlines in some of the music industry's trade papers and in the back pages of sensation or "confession" magazines, promising free examination and criticism of lyrics or melodies or both, adding that there are millions of dollars to be made in songwriting (as if the amateurs didn't know!). Some go so far as to identify themselves as publishers and recording companies in search of new material, hinting that if a songwriter has not yet succeeded in his ambition it is probably because he has not had the proper promotion.

When an amateur lyricist rises to the bait and sends his creations to such an advertiser, he receives—with dizzying promptness—a reply that sends his hopes soaring. "Your song poem is wonderful," the letter encourages. "You are fortunate—our staff comprises a professional composer who is willing to set your words to music! Please send $50 to cover expenses. We will copyright your song, send you printed copies, and *promote it*. Good luck! You are on your way to success!"

Not knowing that it costs several thousand dollars to promote a popular song properly, the amateur "invests" his fifty dollars. For his money he receives, as promised, a "musical setting," printed copies duly copyrighted and formal notice that the song has been sent to a "select list" of music publishers, disk jockeys, recording companies and performers.

In this way, the song shark has kept to the letter of his advertised word and is not subject to legal action. His "promotion" stops here, after an expenditure of from ten to fifteen dollars, which pay for an employee's time in copying some music, a few dozen photo-offset or photostatic copies, a United States unpublished copyright (which anyone can get for four dollars) and however many postage stamps it takes to get the amateur's song to the select list, made up of names easily acquired from any trade paper or music directory.

The song shark business, incredibly, mulcts millions of dollars a year from songwriting housewives, sales clerks, white collar workers and students who, when they realize they have been misled, have no legal recourse. They get what they pay for—"musical settings" (or, if they are composers rather than authors, "lyrics"), copyright, sheet music (in some cases, even demonstration records; these come higher) and certain vague "professional services." The song sharks call themselves "publishers" and they call their victimized clients the "ego trade." They have deceived so many hundreds of thousands of Americans over the years that to a sizable segment of the general public an impression remains that *all* publishers operate on a pay-as-you-go basis. This, added to everything else, does nothing to remove the smudges from the legitimate publishers' reputations.

No active, bona fide publisher asks—or accepts—payment for publishing a song, or advertises for music or lyrics. But how can the amateur songwriter know or believe this when he can't get close enough to an active, bona fide publisher to find out?

From inside as well as outside the professional ranks of the industry, the continuing existence of the song shark operation is occasionally blamed on the industry itself for its cavalier treatment of all amateurs. The suggestion has been made that they could be eliminated if legitimate publishers would embark on a program to give beginners an opportunity to be heard. A few halfhearted proposals have been made along these lines, including the feasibility of establishing a clearing-house agency for amateur-written songs or conducting regular nationwide contests open to aspiring nonprofessional songwriters. These plans would have to operate on an industry-wide basis, however, and the music business is seldom willing to join forces, preferring its Macy's-doesn't-tell-Gimbels policy. Besides, publishers are far too frightened of amateurs to take a chance on voluntary contact of any kind with them.

Song sharks, however, have no such hesitancies or fears. They have distorted and used for their own benefit the thoughtful suggestions put forth by observers of the amateur songwriters' misery. Self-styled "agents" run advertisements in which they offer to represent beginning songwriters with *guaranteed* results. Fees are on a sliding scale, running from $25 to $200 depending on shrewd analysis of what the traffic will bear. The "agents" state on printed contract forms that if they are unable to place the amateur's song (title given) within thirty or sixty days with a legitimate publisher, every cent of the fee will be returned. Another cause states that if the song is published and is commercially successful, the agent is to receive 10 per cent of royalties and other earnings *above the first $1,000*. This aptly worded phrase is tantalizing bait, hinting falsely that earnings will or may be forthcoming in four-figure amounts.

The "agent" very cleverly returns an occasional fee in congested metropolitan areas, thus creating a deceitful impression that he is strictly honest and aboveboard. The calculated gesture usually results in priceless word-of-mouth advertising which brings hundreds of new customers. For those whose fees are not returned, the "agent" performs a service which invariably ends in a cul-de-sac. Having made a business arrangement with an inactive, usually hungry, publisher, he hands over a percentage of the amateurs' fees for signed contracts. These the publisher mails to the songwriters.

An amateur songwriter receiving such a contract in his morning mail is delirious with joy. His song has been "placed" with a "legitimate publisher." Look at the letterhead! Look at the contract! In time, however, the delirium flattens out into corrosive disappointment. The contract was the end of the song—and of the amateur's money. It is never printed (the contract didn't say it would be) and it is never exploited. The songwriter —still an amateur—chews his chagrin until his bitter juices convert it into further distrust of all publishers.

Because, nowadays, even amateur songwriters realize that a tune needs a record before it can go anyplace, a slick species of song shark sets up recording studios as sidelines to regular operations, offering to record a song with a singing group for a stiff fee far in excess of the cost and supplying the songwriter with a dozen to fifty records which he is supposed to tout to disk jockeys, publishers and A. & R. men. This operation is so close to legitimate small-studio procedure that unwary amateurs are often trapped into paying more for one side of a record than it normally costs to record four sides at a regular session. With four amateurs paying studio, "artist" and production fees, the shady operator pockets a 75 per cent profit.

The "contest" idea has been twisted into a racket of heroic proportions. This one works in several ways, a favorite being to advertise for song-poem entries in a national lyric-writing contest . . . no obligation. This is a contest in which everyone wins. Each contestant is notified that *his* poem has been selected by the judges as the best example of fresh new talent. The prize is the once-in-a-lifetime opportunity for the amateur to collaborate with a "topnotch professional composer"—absolutely free of charge. There is, to be sure, the matter of publicity and exploitation, so necessary to promote a song. If the contest winner will send $50 to help defray expenses . . .

A slightly more elaborate and less individually expensive deception is perpetrated in another sort of "contest." This time, advertisements proclaim that lyrics are being sought for existing melodies which have been recorded in an album. All the contestant has to do is buy the album (a bargain at $2.98), write lyrics for one or more of the tunes therein and submit them for judging. Those who follow these rules are deceived into believing that any such contest exists. None does. The "sponsors" are satisfied with $2.98 each from thousands of aspiring amateur lyric-writers.

There are, of course, any number of amateur songwriters to whom the mere act of seeing their creations in print is a thrill. They do not have to pay the exorbitant fees exacted by the song sharks in order to accomplish this. Listed in the telephone book in most metropolitan areas are legitimate song printers, engravers and offset lithographers who will, at standard rates, strike off as many music sheets as are ordered. They make no promises other than to deliver clean copies.

Most communities, also, have amusement-park or penny-arcade "Hear-Your-Own-Voice" recording booths where, for a quarter or so, anything audible can be reproduced on a playable disk. More professional records are obtainable from genuine studios which have sources of talent supply as well as equipment for pressing quantities of disks from a master record. These make no pretense about exploitation, either.

A song seems such a simple thing to write, and promises so much in return for what seems like such little effort, that a career in popular music holds a fascination for thousands of well-meaning and talented people who are convinced that they could do as well as—if not better than—the few hundreds who manage to make a good living by writing, professionally, the nation's melodies and lyrics. But there are no short cuts to fame and riches in songwriting, and no "how to" books can chart the way to success in Tin Pan Alley.

Despite all barriers that confront newcomers, it is obvious that some hope must exist—for *beginners*, however, as opposed to "amateurs." There is a world of difference between the two; the difference is largely one of realistic self-evaluation and a willingness to work hard and stubbornly in the face of unusually hard and stubborn opposition. There is little room in the music business for the out-and-out amateur who dabbles in music as a hobby from which he would like to strike it rich, like a lucky quiz show winner on television or the holder of the wininng ticket in a raffle. New songwriters join the professional ranks regularly, adding their fresh talents to the continuing parade of popular music. Nobody can stop them.

12. *A Songwriter Has Two Heads*

TIN PAN ALLEY is no longer the closed corporation it used to be, but there is still a great deal more to becoming a professional author or composer of popular songs than the ability to write inspired words and pleasant—or provocative—melodies.

Even the most successful modern songwriters are haunted by gremlins who perch on their shoulders muttering doleful predictions of failure. With a dozen or a hundred published and recorded title credits to his name, many of them sensational hits or immortal standards, a songwriter never knows if his next one may not be a total flop, or even whether or not he can continue to write salable songs. The competition is rough, the pace is frantic and the well of creativity is subject to drought.

Irving Berlin once told a reporter, "It is much more difficult for me to write successes now because people expect so much from me on account of my previous hits." The interview appeared in the *Christian Science Monitor* in 1919, when Mr. Berlin was genuinely worried about his ability to go on writing such hits as "Alexander's Ragtime Band," "My Wife's Gone to the Country" and "I'll See You in C-U-B-A."

Songwriting is no ivory-tower pursuit, and a songwriter cannot afford the luxury of waiting for a touch of inspiration's wand.

He must be as productive as a farmer and as resilient as a door-to-door salesman with doors slamming in his face. He must be temperamentally equipped to reconcile artistry with accounting, craftsmanship with craftiness, self-effacement with self-aggrandizement. Ideas for lyrics and phrases of melodies may fly to him like swallows to Capistrano, but he examines them critically for commercial pinfeathers before he makes them welcome.

In recent years, there have been a number of successful popular songs in a cycle which Tin Pan Alley now calls "inspirational." These are songs written in current idiom with tempos and styles ranging from slow waltz to hillbilly or rock 'n roll, having in common sets of lyrics which suggest prayerfully folded hands and stained-glass windows. A decade or so ago, such songs—then labeled Bible-belt or gospel—would have been relegated to maidenly glee clubs or Sunday morning radio sermons with organ accompaniment. Lately they have reached the popular best-seller lists in company with considerably less pious hits.

On the trail of a story about the nation's growing spiritual awareness as expressed in its popular songs, a reporter interviewed the writers of a jazzy hymn which had flown like an angel to exalted levels of the Hit Parade, where it hovered for several weeks. Anticipating a reverent response to the question, "And what inspired you to write your song?" the reporter was somewhat discomfited when the spokesman of the songwriting team said, "Man, we needed the money."

There is hardly an idea the human mind is capable of understanding which has not been used in the building of a popular song, and sometimes even human understanding is not requisite. Where do the ideas come from? What, to use a word nonprofessionals are fond of associating with creative production, "inspires" them?

Songwriters can spin yarns by the hour to entertain willing listeners, telling of the deeply felt emotion, the unusual circumstance, the sudden flash of mystical perception from which blossomed each of their successful songs. Sometimes these tales have a nodding acquaintance with truth, like the love story in an historical movie spectacular. More often they confirm the song-writers' imaginative personalities.

It is said that Irving Berlin wrote one of his greatest hits of all time because of a typical Florenz Ziegfeld extravagance.

Three or four days before the 1919 *Follies* was scheduled to open, Ziegfeld cornered Berlin and confessed that he had ordered dozens of lavish costumes for which there was no spot in the show.

"My bookkeeper will kill me," Ziegfeld said. "Can you write a song I can use around them?"

Berlin said he didn't know, but he'd try. When the *Follies* opened, one of the show-stoppers was a parade of gorgeously gowned showgirls who glided across the stage while a baritone sang "A Pretty Girl Is Like a Melody."

Al Dubin said he wrote the words for "Dancing with Tears in My Eyes" because he wondered what beautiful young girls thought about when they were wrestled around a night club floor in the embrace of paunchy, pawing old men.

Jimmy McHugh, struggling to produce melodies for the movie *Higher and Higher* worked out a tune while he was tossing sleeplessly in bed. He sketched the melody on his bed sheet with a crayon but forgot all about it the next day when he turned up on the lot to work with his collaborator, Harold Adamson.

By way of greeting, McHugh said, "I couldn't sleep a wink last night." Adamson said, "Hey—that's a great song title." Mc-Hugh said, "I've got the music for it—I think." McHugh's housekeeper received a breathless telephone call from her employer, who startled her by asking that his sheet be sent over to the studio right away. It was rescued from the laundry in the nick of time.

Harry MacGregor Woods, determined to break into songwriting despite repeated rejections, took to prettying up his manuscripts by giving them artistic covers which he hand-painted, hoping that their attractiveness would impress a publisher. It did. He was offered a job as a title-page artist. Combining his talent with his love for the sea, he spent his last cent on a leaky boat that slept two, and moored it in a Cape Cod harbor. He sat on his bunk and wrote songs until the water lapped around his knees, when he would stop writing long enough to bail out. One day, in the throes of concentrated creation, he neglected to stop. Fortunately, there was a dinghy tied to the boat. A few days later, he wrote "Paddlin' Madeline Home."

Lyricist Charlie Tobias retained in his memory for forty years the sight of an old man who traveled the streets of the New England town where he lived as a child, turning the street lamps on at dusk and off at dawn. In 1947, he wrote "The Old Lamplighter" with composer Nat Simon.

For about twenty years, Vincent Lopez has kept two files—one metal, one mental—jammed with the "stories behind the songs." One day, it is to be hoped, he will write his long-planned book about songwriters.

It may be well, at this point, to define a songwriter. It is a misleading word. A songwriter may be one of three people: A writer of a song's lyrics; a writer of a song's melody, or a writer of both. If the first, he is also called an author. If the second, he is also called a composer. If the third, he is called Cole Porter.

Whether he is the writer of a song's words or of its music, he is rarely introduced in public as either an author or a composer. He is called a songwriter, and this leads to confusion.

From time to time television personalities with hour-long variety shows have fed into some of their programs a segment devoted to a representative from that almost anonymous group which creates America's popular songs.

On cue, a sedately dressed stranger walks from the wings to center stage and has his outstretched hand grasped by the show's star master of ceremonies. The studio audience peers restlessly at the stranger because they have not, as yet, been told who he is and why he is there. Is he the governor of a Midwestern state? A candidate for the All-American bowling championship team? The bearer of another award for the star?

When a name is mentioned, there is a polite patter of handclapping from an enlightened few, but the majority of the audience retains its frowning restlessness because the name is not yet recognized as belonging to a real celebrity. Prompted from the stage, the audience dutifully applauds, then settles back to wait suspiciously for the fellow to prove he's somebody.

Now the star of the show says with as much awe and affection as he can put into voice, ". . . who has given to people of all ages all over America and all over the world some of the greatest and most beloved songs of all time."

At this, the man walks deliberately to a grand piano on the stage. He sits in a position turned slightly away from the piano, as if he didn't really notice it. His legs are crossed, his hands folded loosely over the uppermost knee. He smiles with shy expectancy at his host, who is now leaning casually with one elbow on the piano.

"Won't you play some of your great songs for us?" the M.C. pleads.

Nodding and smiling modestly, the songwriter (*that's* what he is!) faces the piano and uncurls his fingers toward the keyboard. The audience stirs and quickens. They sit in readiness and eagerness to give their approval, whispering to each other, "What did he say the name was?" They're sure he wrote something they'll recognize. They're waiting to find out what.

As the man at the piano runs through a preliminary arpeggio, the applause starts again. There are always several people in any audience who pride themselves on being able to spot a song's full title from its introductory chords. A hum of appreciation and delight spreads through the studio as the song actually *is* recognized by everybody, and the applause and cheers mount to an ovation if the song is an especially well-known old-time favorite.

This pageant is sometimes called the "nostalgia bit" or, less respectfully, the "and-then-I-wrote routine."

Everybody knows and loves the songs, just as the M.C. said they would, and they are delighted to pay well-deserved tribute to the man at the piano who, they just discovered, *wrote* them.

There exists a solemn ritual of formal courtesy in the affiliated businesses of music and entertainment which regards it as tactless to describe a songwriter as either a lyricist or melodist. Consequently, habitual viewers of variety shows on television are puzzled, especially if they have good memories.

It could happen, for example, that such a program is arranged to honor songwriter Jimmy McHugh, one of the profession's most dignified and respected members, and one of its most prolific. While playing excerpts from his long list of song hits, he is rewarded with sincere, spontaneous applause when the repertoire reaches "I Can't Give You Anything but Love" and "Lovely to Look At," both greatly admired favorites for two generations.

It could happen at a later date that another of these programs honors songwriter Dorothy Fields, whose distinguished work is also greatly admired. Miss Fields might not allow herself to be coaxed to the piano, but she would smilingly and appreciatively receive the crowd's plaudits as the studio orchestra plays a medley of her songs—including "I Can't Give You Anything but Love" and "Lovely to Look At."

Somewhere in the audience, either present in the studio or home in the family room, will be someone with a memory. He'll say, "Hey—I thought Jimmy McHugh wrote 'I Can't Give You Anything but Love.' Heard him on Sullivan's show a few months ago."

"Yeah," someone else with a memory will say. "And what about 'Lovely to Look At'? First McCoy writes it, and now this Doris Fielding writes it. That's what they say. But the fact is, I happen to have seen the movie *Roberta* with Irene Dunne, and that song's from *Roberta*. And do you know who wrote *Roberta? Jerome Cohen.*"

It's too bad if the argument gets out of hand without a reference book for verification, because everybody's almost right.

Jimmy McHugh wrote the music for "I Can't Give You Anything but Love" and he collaborated in writing the words for "Lovely to Look At." Dorothy Fields wrote all the words for the former. On any program honoring the works of Jerome

Kern, "Lovely to Look At" is always played as one of the great composer's outstanding show tunes. It's from *Roberta*.

So thoroughly does everybody in the music business insist that a song's words and melody are inseparable that equal credit, billing and royalties are given to each of the two or more collaborators who wrote it.

While it is not an inflexible rule, the author is usually listed first on title pages and in book credits, the composer second. Sometimes, however, the listing is given as "words and music by"—followed by two or more names. This usually means that each of the people had a hand in both. To further the confusion, equal or proportionate credit, billing and royalties are often bestowed on people who had little or nothing to do with actually writing any part of either the words or the music of a particular song, but who have hitch-hiked a profitable ride because of some valuable exploitive or personal service they were able to perform for the true authors, composers and/or publisher.

Perhaps the infrangible fusion of dual or fractional elements is not only justified, but just. It is a controversial subject among even many professionals, who insist that in a popular vote about which is the greater contribution to a popular song—the melody or the lyric—the composer's role would win by a landslide. People tend to remember tunes more accurately and more permanently than they do words, except perhaps for some catchy titles. It is argued that "Star Dust" is identified with composer Hoagy Carmichael, not with lyricist Mitchell Parish.

The argument is neither strictly valid nor fair. When a composer and a lyricist "find" each other and settle down to work as a temporary or permanent team, it is their mutual compatibility of ideas and workmanship as much as their individual talents which enables them to write successful songs. The lyricist alone is a solitary poet whose words have no home. The composer alone is similarly lost and ineffectual without someone to weave words through the threads of his melody and make them durable. Songs are meant to be sung, and in the history of Tin Pan Alley there are remarkably few wordless tunes which have become lastingly popular.

Moreover, contrary to general belief, the composer is not necessarily the more important half of the song-writing team. It is harder to find a good lyric writer than it is to find a good composer. A competent and talented writer of melodies with experience and training in handling the mathematics of popular music notation can deftly arrange and rearrange the standard scale in such a way as to emerge with a pleasant or even a memorable melody. The lyricist roams around in the wide world of ideas and has to select from the entire English language words that are singable, believable and simple in their message. Whereas the composer does not even have to be able to read, write or speak the language in order to construct a song out of the universal symbols that make up musical notation—and, in some cases, does not even have to be able to write the notes down—the expert lyricist usually must have some practical knowledge of music in his background.

Should all this raise contradictions or scornful doubt in a reader's mind, it is recommended that he listen critically to the songs he hears today on radio or television, paying particular attention to the words. More often than not, he will find, a cute tune or pretty ballad is saddled with words that are woefully trite or even downright slovenly in meaning, grammar or continuity.

The prevalent combination of palatable melodies with unappetizing words is not brought about by trade indifference or by intended insult to intelligent ears. Established publishers, recording companies and popular singers would much rather offer up a steady stream of songs which blend structurally good melodies with sensible, singable, even splendid words. They are not easy to come by.

It is a happy day for the music industry, for the music-loving public and for the songwriters themselves when a truly good author and a truly good composer meet and merge their talents. When this happens, the world is enriched with unforgettable songs, like those written by the teams of Lorenz Hart or Oscar

Hammerstein II and Richard Rodgers; by Howard Dietz or Frank Loesser and Arthur Schwartz; by Dorothy Fields or Harold Adamson and Jimmy McHugh; by Sammy Cahn and Jule Styne; by Johnny Mercer, Ted Koehler or E. Y. Harburg and Harold Arlen; by Ira and George Gershwin; by Irving Caesar and Vincent Youmans; by Ned Washington and Hoagy Carmichael; by Mitchell Parish and Peter DeRose, Duke Ellington or Sammy Fain.

Not a complete or even representative list, these are only a few names skimmed off the top of the great song-writing teams whose works, immediately successful when they were introduced, have survived as standards. Their fine quality and undiminished popularity have earned continuing performances in a highly competitive and forgetful field. When it becomes a standard, a song with roots or tendrils in Tin Pan Alley is just about as classical as it can get—whether it was written for a stage production, a motion picture or an independent publisher.

Often, and for many more reasons than there are reasons for divorce, successful song-writing teams split up and form other partnerships. Sometimes the new teams produce even better songs than either member was identified with before, sometimes they do not.

Whether lyricist or composer, a songwriter is a creative person; but he is set apart from other creative people by an occupational difference as well as by a difference in psychological climate.

Most of the world's creative personalities are recognizable in the eyes of sensitive noncreative observers as outcasts from the common mold. For this they may be accorded respect tinged with distrust. Professional writers, painters and sculptors are accustomed to imprisonment in a private world. They have sorrowfully learned that they are clumsy about sharing their deepest feelings with other people except through the communication of their art. Whether it is committed to paper, canvas or clay, creative expression is dredged up from a diabolic amalgam of anguish and delight that is experienced only in solitude.

The writer who writes for a living knows how terribly alone and frightened he feels when he faces a blank page. His office or scribbling corner is a terrifying vacuum, his desk a loathsome trap. Even away from the physical shackles of his self-imposed imprisonment, when he emerges into society he is still invisibly chained. He cannot turn off the sputtering spigot of his mind. He suffers from mental flatulence as problems of plot or characterization continue to ferment in his consciousness. He is nervous about markets, contracts and deadlines. Always suspicious of his own thoughts and words, he is constantly involved with incompetent self-analysis.

The artist or sculptor with color and form for companions and tools to occupy his hands is perhaps a little less desolate, as is the serious composer with the grandiose sounds of orchestras in his head. All, however, are physically and temperamentally isolated while they work.

Popular songs are not works of art? The popular songwriter is not an artist? The serious writer, artist or composer—no less than the originator of juke box favorites—wants the selfsame rewards for his work: recognition and success. But popular songwriters could not exist in the same climate, could not function in so solitary an arena. They must work in close partnership, and to do this successfully they must be able to set aside their individual doubts, conflicts and hostilities.

Creative personalities in fields other than popular song writing reveal themselves, to a greater or lesser extent, in their work. Self-revelation is denied the writer of a song's lyric or melody, both of which are written according to almost inflexible limitations imposed by publishers, the public and the current trend. Except for novelties and special material, a popular song is rigidly bounded on four sides by the exacting demands of form, content, construction and simplicity. It is circumscribed as to melodic range, all-over and internal measurements and allowable language.

Unless it is intended as part of a musical-show plot, a motion picture theme or is custom-tailored material for a specific performer, the popular song is composed of a short verse (required, even though seldom used) and a chorus of thirty-two measures written in one of the acceptable tempos.

There are shorter popular songs, and longer ones, but the standard is thirty-two bars which follow a format that Nick Kenny describes as "A-A-B-A" in his book, *How to Write, Sing and Sell Popular Songs* (Hermitage Press, 1946). Mr. Kenny explains the format as follows: "(A) Eight measures of the main theme; (A) a repetition of the eight measures of the main theme (with a possible slight change in the last measure so as to lead naturally to the next eight measures); (B) the release, or middle eight measures, which should be of a different nature and pattern from the main theme; then follow with (A) eight measures of the first or main theme (with a possible change in the last measure or two to give the feeling of finality). The reason for using the main theme three times is that it can be easily memorized."

Because singers of popular songs are not usually trained for operatic vocal reaches, the melody's range is prudently confined to about ten notes or less whose pivot point is somewhere in the immediate vicinity of middle C. The lyrics cleave to the melody and follow where it goes, syllables skillfully matched to tonal accents until, to the ears of a listener, the music speaks the words and the words sing the music.

The songwriters work within these cramped quarters with incredible imagination and originality to achieve results which must, on performance, appear effortless, fresh and natural. To be acceptable for public performance on air or screen, the song's lyric must remain within the (adjustable) margins of good taste as interpreted by the Federal Communications Commission. It must combine resourceful and ingenious rhymes that allow a singer to keep his or her mouth open as much as possible.

These are the rules. It is like roping off a four-foot square area and saying to a choreographer, "Here is where the *corps de ballet* will dance."

After they have written their song under these inelastic conditions, the songwriters do not retire modestly behind an agent's protective shield. Far from being sheltered from traffic with crass commercialism, they venture out into the middle of it. They are in the embarrassing position of having to sell their own work, meeting their market face to face.

First they must sell a flint-hearted publisher on the idea of buying their creation and working on it, dickering shrewdly for as much advance money as they can extract. They cannot accomplish either result by placing a neat manuscript in the hands of a publisher who, more often than not, reads musical notation about as easily as a first-grader reads Chaucer. They must "warm up" the publisher the way a television comic warms up his audience before air time. They go into an act calculated to generate a contagion of enthusiasm before the publisher hears so much as the opening bars of their song.

This requires salesmanship of a very special nature. The publisher uses the same technique himself when he tries to sell a song to an A. & R. man, and he is only too familiar with the plot. Fortunately for everyone concerned, even publishers are susceptible to the ubiquitous Tin Pan Alley virus of enthusiasm.

Once past the hurdle of a publisher, songwriters continue their aggressive selling tactics on all strata of the music business. They frequently put in their own eloquent pitch to the A. & R. men. They confide to one popular singing star after another that this song was inspired by *her* unique style and talent, or written with *his* popular television show in mind.

When the song has been published and recorded, they are not satisfied to leave song-plugging to the song pluggers. Many of America's most prolific and successful songwriters find it expedient and profitable to become paid-up members of the Music Publishers' Contact Employees Union of Greater New York. Unless they do, they put themselves and their publishers in union disfavor when they plug their songs to performers, bandleaders, program directors and disk jockeys—which is whenever they see one.

Most songwriters belong also to either the West Coast's Composers and Lyricists Guild of America, representing film background cleffers, or Songwriters Protective Association.

The story of SPA's beginnings is interesting because it is so typical of the music business in which, for some perverse reason, trade associations always seem to have a much harder time getting internal endorsements from the people they are designed to help than would appear reasonable.

Although all professional songwriters realized in the 1920s that they had many problems in common and should probably join together in order to tackle them as a group, the efforts of songwriters Billy Rose, Edgar Leslie and George W. Meyer to form an organization to deal effectively with publishers met luke-warm response and some outright opposition. It took until 1931 to form SPA—with only fifty members who were willing to admit that handling their own affairs with publishers was giving them ulcers.

In his last report as SPA's president, published in 1948, three years before his death, Sigmund Romberg wrote:

"Prior to the organization of SPA, the songwriter was a faceless and featureless individual compelled to deal as an individual, in most intensely imaginable struggle for recognition by, and the favor of, the sole entity through which he might hope that his creation would reach the public—the music publisher.

"Hat in hand and humbly, the songwriter of those days, with few exceptions, ventured to submit his composition to what he hoped would be the gracious, merciful and generous consideration of the publisher. Quite generally he accepted whatever terms were offered, as the only alternative to complete failure of his work to reach the stage of publication.

"The publisher . . . usually drove a hard bargain, and had his unchallenged way with the writer."

By 1957, SPA boasted a regular membership of approximately two thousand willing professional songwriters (regular members) and nine hundred persuaded music publishers. In addition, the organization embraced about one thousand associate members and one hundred special associate members.

The distinctions are significant. A "regular member," further classified as belonging to group AA, A, BB, B, CC, C, DD or D, is described by SPA as a songwriter who has had at least one song published or recorded by a recognized company. The alphabetical class-marks are subtle evaluations of the songwriter's stature and productivity. They also indicate by key the amount of membership dues payable to SPA, scaling from $200 per year (Class AA—very prolific, very big) to $24 per year for Class D (professional, but not markedly successful or noteworthy).

An "associate member," dues $20 per year, is gently defined by SPA as "a writer who has not yet achieved professional status." This is a euphemism for amateur songwriter. While SPA does not aggressively seek out this membership, and denies it a vote in association matters, it nevertheless does not refuse to accept annual dues from "all persons of earnest intention in the field of musical composition or authorship" who, in filing their applications, signify their readiness to be bound by the Articles of Agreement and pledge obedience to, and performance of, all obligations.

However, the association hastens to emphasize, "aspiring beginners, and others, should clearly understand that the Association does not act as an agency for placing works with publishers; will not act as advisor in matters relating to the musical or artistic merit of the works of its members or others, or serve as an agent for securing the collaboration of other writers in completing a musical work."

At least a thousand of America's hopeful amateur songwriters find it comforting to be able to write "Assoc. Member, SPA" after their names when submitting their foredoomed manuscripts to publishers or recording companies. Payment of annual dues entitles them to an impressive listing of their names in SPA's printed membership roster, alphabetically, sharing print if not prestige with the top-ranking songwriters of the country.

"Special Associate" members include the successors in interest of deceased songwriters, with dues ranging from $10 to $30 annually depending on the size and activity of the departed songwriters' catalogs of copyrights which, of course, continue to earn royalties and fees for a lifetime total of fifty-six years under federal copyright laws.

One of SPA's functions is to notify members when copyrights are due for renewal and, on request, to obtain the renewal certificates at no cost other than the copyright office charge. While this may seem to be an insignificant and gratuitous service, it keeps a large staff of competent clerical workers busy with a mass of details that are actually very important.

Songwriters are likely to be forgetful of songs they wrote and had published twenty-eight years ago, and the heirs of deceased songwriters may not even know of songs still in copyright but long since fallen into limbo.

The importance of copyright renewals (with the original publisher or a new assignee) has grown considerably in recent years. Revived or even long-delayed hits, called "sleepers," happen along so often that no copyright can ever be considered completely worthless. Sometimes the revival is deliberately sparked by a publisher, song-plugger or songwriter who sees in a forthcoming movie or television show a likely spot for what the trade lovingly calls an "oldie."

The system of planting nostalgic or otherwise appropriate songs in the fertile soil of Hollywood studios and coast-to-coast networks can reap a bumper crop of new records, performances and interest for a sleeping copyright. It is one reason why the movie-makers farsightedly paid millions of dollars to buy out, or into, several of the nation's top publishing outfits when films were equipped with sound.

If MGM, for example, had a picture in the making that would be atmospherically or artistically embellished by the inclusion of a nineteenth-century bucolic melody, MGM's musical director would choose the most pertinent nineteenth-century bucolic melody in the catalog of MGM's music-publishing affiliate.

This is less a matter of patronage than economy. Should the director insist on a more germane copyright owned by an independent publisher or by a rival movie studio's musical subsidy, the license fee would most likely be exorbitant. Studio-subsidized publishers set a minimum price on their songs requested by the parent company. This calculated generosity is not without its rewards to the publishers. Any exploitable new songs written for the picture usually become the property of the studio's musical affiliate—provided, of course, they are not written by songwriters with tamper-proof commitments to other publishers. If the new songs are good, the movie plugs are bound to help their exploitation—and records—and performances—and sales.

The frequency with which supposedly defunct songs re-emerge as fresh new hits causes many a publisher to speculate about reincarnation.

In their endless search for songs to stylize, popularize and make peculiarly their own, the singing stars of television, radio and records often "discover" old, forgotten tunes which have not lapsed into public domain and raise them anew to the best-seller lists.

When Nick Kenny's 1931 copyright, "Love Letters in the Sand," was re-issued in 1957 because of a hit Pat Boone record, it was a brand-new song to millions of teen-agers whose approval of it put it on the Hit Parade and awakened sentimental memories in their parents. And, a year or so before, two precocious and vocal little girls somehow got their dimpled hands on an old and definitely unchildlike lyric penned in 1926 by Billy Rose to music composed by Lee David. Rose had almost forgotten he had ever written ("Although you belong to somebody else) Tonight You Belong to Me," but, fortunately, he had not neglected to renew it when the original copyright lapsed in 1954.

When it was first published, "Tonight" was only a moderate success. When it was recorded as a refreshingly arranged duet and delivered in sisterly harmony by two treble voices, it became a smashing hit. Commenting on its retarded success, Mr. Rose said, "I just hope those kids didn't understand what they were singing about."

SPA has done more than just protect copyrights from lapsing into public domain through failure of their owners to renew. It has standardized the popular songwriters' contract agreement to a formidable document containing more than seven thousand impressively legal words. Before SPA grew teeth and bared them effectively, there were as many forms of songwriter contracts with publishers as there were publishers. There was no uniformity, not even much similarity. Sometimes a single publisher had several contract forms in his desk, and he would reach for the one his shrewd appraisal informed him the songwriter would accept without question. The appraisal was made on the basis of how hungry the publisher estimated the songwriter to be.

Until SPA was empowered to act in their behalf, creators of popular songs were limited by their personal bargaining ability. Contracts, written by the publishers strictly for their own protection and interests, frequently omitted to mention many potential sources of a song's income and consequently did not include the writers as shareholders. The SPA contract made it very clear that *all* income was to be shared with the writers, specifying royalty rates and payment periods and assuring allocation of at least 50 per cent of the gross fees earned from channels outside the publisher's regular operations.

Some unscrupulous firms had made it a practice of promising a writer a high percentage of royalties from the sales of song books they published containing his work. When such a song book appeared, the writer would rush happily to the publisher's office to collect his royalties, only to be told that none was due. If he produced his contract and pointed to the clause that substantiated his claim, the publisher blandly informed him that *he* did not publish the book but had licensed an outside firm to do so and was therefore not obligated. The contract clearly stated that royalties would be paid only on books "published by this firm or an affiliate."

Knowing its membership, SPA insists that even the carefully worded contract form is not effective until it is countersigned by an SPA official. "Thus," states the organization's booklet, "What Every Songwriter Should Know," "the writer is protected—*even in spite of himself*."

Why is such a stipulation necessary? SPA knowingly foresees that a songwriter might try to induce a vacillating publisher to accept his song by offering to give up some of his rights. How does SPA happen to be so clairvoyant? Its officers and council members are songwriters.

As you see, professional songwriters have many problems—but the publisher brush-off is not one of them. *They* are not left forever cooling their heels in Brill Building offices. *Their* manuscripts are not returned unopened. How, amateurs yearn to know, did they make it to that wonderful, enviable place in the sun as published, professional, SPA-protected, royalty-receiving songwriters?

Professional songwriters do not act like amateurs. They were never far away from a professional approach to song writing. As children they showed an overwhelming interest in music or literature or both. As they matured, they gravitated toward show business. With very few exceptions, they did not willingly embark on parent-approved careers. Or, if they did, once a song came into their hearts they had no stomach for any other means of livelihood. Their stomachs were frequently empty, but their hearts overflowed. Even those to whom song writing was originally a cultural pursuit or a distraction from the serious business of life dropped everything else when Tin Pan Alley beckoned. (Cole Porter and Hoagy Carmichael were once honor law students and Arthur Schwartz a full-fledged lawyer with a Phi Beta Kappa key; Sigmund Romberg was an engineer, Vincent Youmans a stockbroker, Frank Loesser a newspaperman.)

From Stephen Foster onward (he flouted his family's modest ambitions to make a respectable bookkeeper out of him) the authors and composers of America's favorite popular music have become professionals because they could not be otherwise.

Glance through the *ASCAP Biographical Dictionary of Composers, Authors and Publishers*" (edited by Daniel I. McNamara; Thomas Y. Crowell Company, 1952), or *The Blue Book of Tin Pan Alley* (by Jack Burton; Century House, 1950). After each songwriter's name you will usually find a notation about early musical, theatrical or literary training. Their brief biographies are studded with the stepping stones to songwriting: "Got job as pianist." "Joined a road company." "Sang in restaurants as a waiter after school." "Wrote high school plays and skits." "Was a roving reporter." "Went to work for publishing firm as a song-plugger." "Sold musical instruments."

Even at the beginning of their relationships with publishers, professional songwriters never made one common mistake which invariably and indelibly marks the amateur. They knew that there are at least three main divisions of publishing houses and that each main division is further subdivided into components which remain more or less consistent.

A writer of sexy short stories would know better than to submit work to a magazine devoted exclusively to theological non-fiction. A science-fiction novelist would hardly dispatch his latest adventure in outer space to a publisher of college textbooks. Yet, in a sense, this is what an incredible number of amateur songwriters do.

There are publishers who concentrate exclusively on songs from either motion pictures or the musical-comedy stage. There are publishers who specialize in children's "art," gospel and part songs or even in music intended for specific instruments. Amateurs waste mountains of postage stamps and emotional energy because they ignore, disregard or are unaware of these distinctions. Most outsiders, all publishers believe, make their decisions as to where to send their manuscripts the way children pick a playmate to be "It."

One especially amateur-harassed publisher has thought seriously of changing the name of his firm from his own to one beginning with X or Z. His name starts with A, and he is convinced that this fact alone accounts for the three thousand unsolicited manuscripts which arrive at his office every week, sent by aspiring amateurs from all over the country who know where they can get their eager hands on a classified Manhattan telephone directory.

"If my name began farther back in the alphabet," he says wistfully, "maybe they'd run out of postage money before they got to me."

13. *A Publisher Wears Three Hats*

Today, music publishers have lost their dignity along with their control of the music business. Where once they selected, groomed and published songs winnowed from professional sources, they are now in the ignominious position of acting as go-betweens, scrambling like fiddler crabs to collect anything at all the recording companies will accept.

The richly catalogued old independent firms are disenchanted. Disgusted with "those crazy sounds" and faced with the futility of trying to interest A. & R. men in their sedate copyrights without resorting to rascally procedures, they are resigned to sitting it out until sanity and melody return to popular music. Meanwhile, they continue in business on the bountiful harvest of royalties forthcoming from ASCAP for their hundreds of standard ballad favorites which even the new discordant sounds cannot drown out.

To publishers who respect their title, "performance money" is paltry recompense despite the fact that their ledgers show increasing profits from year to year as record sales boom and more entertainment is beamed out to an increasing population. The money's there, but for these publishers the thrill has gone, leaving in its wake nostalgic sorrow and a sense of irretrievable loss.

The publisher who was an important cog in the music business in the "good old days," before coast-to-coast communications almost completely transformed song-plugging, is wistful in his memories of how it used to be. When you realize that the "good old days" are only twenty years or so back in recent history, the picture you get is not of oldsters mumbling about bygone glories, but of still-young, vigorous but bewildered men for whom the fun of song merchandising has departed forever.

As one young old-timer says, "There *is* no music business any more. All we do nowadays is clip coupons like a bunch of bankers. If my firm never published another song we'd still be rich because of our backlog of standards."

"There's no glamour in this business now," another complains. "No kick that comes from getting out and plugging a song to the headliners who could put it over for you. In the old days, I'd get a call that Jolson, say, just got back to town from a twenty-six-week tour of the country, hitting all the towns between here and 'Frisco.

"Jolson was a pal, see, and he'd want to know what the boys were turning out in the way of songs, so naturally he'd come up to my office and I'd get a few of the fellows together and we'd roll up our sleeves and play poker all night. We'd send out for sandwiches and drinks and sit around between hands, just talking. We'd get all the backstage gossip—like who laid an egg in Paducah, and who brought the house down in Davenport, Iowa, and why our new number about Texas was selling like wildfire everyplace but Texas.

"We were buddies with the headliners in those days, and they were great people. They depended on us for their material, and we knocked ourselves out to see that they got the best. Now? Phah! What's the glamour in talking to some new trick-voice gal's agent? Or in phoning some A. & R. man who don't know a damned thing about this business but can deliver songs to the public's living room because the big combine he's connected with has the TV stars under contract?

"In the old days, this guy was just a mechanical man. He'd

come around panting, with his tongue hanging out, coaxing us to give him our new copyrights for waxing. He'd make records out of the tunes *we* told him were good because *we* were the ones who had experience—and taste.

"But nowadays! He's a big shot. He thinks he's a genius. You have to beg for an appointment when he's got a few minutes to listen to your stuff between taking bows. Today you got to be a psychologist, not a song publisher. You got to know you shouldn't send your plugger to see this A. & R. man before lunch because he's grouchy in the morning. Or you shouldn't contact that A. & R. man after four p.m. because by then he's song-shocked and wouldn't recognize a good tune if it was 'Macushla.'"

Added to publishers' troubles with A. & R. men is the fact that they are frequently in the position of having to peddle their songs to rival publishers. In recent years, popular performing and recording stars have found it profitable to go into the business of publishing songs for themselves.

Top stars like Perry Como, Eddie Fisher, Julius LaRosa, Frank Sinatra, Elvis Presley and a score of big-name bandleaders have at one time or another set up their own music-publishing companies. Why? Why not? The songs they publish may not be great or even good songs, but artists who reach the top have a lot to say about the songs they record. Some listen respectfully to the A. & R. men when it comes to choosing the titles intended for vigorous sales exploitation, because most performers are notoriously inept about picking their own songs. But while a star may realize that even his expert rendition of a bad or indifferent song won't necessarily make it a hit, if it is recorded on the flip side of a disk which *is* a hit the publisher's royalties make a very nice showing at the end of a year. The performer-publisher is a painful thorn in the side of the full-time publisher with no other source of income except his copyrights, but he has to go along with the tide because he desperately needs the performer for his own plugs.

Although the publishers attached to the motion picture studios are not as distressed as the independents, because their income is virtually assured by film music, they have other gnawing dissatisfactions. Chief among these is their resentment about being administrators rather than creative leaders.

"We're called publishers but we're hardly more than glorified, high-salaried office boys," they complain.

"Sure, we can and do submit oldies from our catalogs that are in keeping with a picture's story line. But when it comes to *new* songs, we're publishers in name only. The film producer is supreme, taking over functions that would be performed better by a music publisher. It's the producer who assigns songwriters to a script. The songs are sent to us only after they have been okayed in Hollywood. Oh, sure, once in a while—as a gesture—the publishers and record men are invited to the studio for firsthand previewing of the music. Our recommendations to change or discard tunes don't mean much. Sometimes a song the publisher and the record man recognize as a good commercial song is cut out of the picture, God knows why. So instead of having a plug tune we know we can sell, we're forced to plug the dogs the producer wants."

About Hollywood's effect on popular music, the late Harry Link had this to say: "Out there, they've lost sight of the real message of a pop song. That goes for the songwriters, too. They write their songs to please the producer or fit the story when they should be writing for the *public*. Well, I suppose you can't really blame them. The big money they get—steady—as big-shot songwriters with fat contracts probably makes the thought of royalties seem like pretty small potatoes."

Link said it took him thirteen years to convince a film studio of the value of a song's bearing the same title as the film in which it appeared.

"Nobody out there would listen to me," he said, "until radio and TV proved that a picture-title song is a picture plug. Every time the song is performed, the film gets a free ad. Sure, they caught on early enough that *theme songs* would sell. Remember 'Diane' from *Seventh Heaven* and 'Charmaine' from *What Price*

Glory? What would have been wrong with picture title song titles? Two years after 'Diane' from *Seventh Heaven* became a smash, DeSylva, Brown and Henderson—and Al Jolson—thought enough of the picture title to write a song. And what was the song 'Seventh Heaven' from? The picture *Little Pal!*"

All this has changed, of course. Picture executives love picture-song titles, now—even if the film has no integral music in it, only interpolated themes or mood backgrounds (which most film musical directors agree should be unobtrusive). There isn't a major, minor or fledgling film studio in Hollywood which does not own, control, direct or have some kind of an understanding with one or more music-publishing houses. An interpolated theme or mood-background excerpt, no less than a deliberately written song, can rack up substantial profits long after the film it appeared in has been released for the late late show.

Another important music-publishing category is the one which concentrates on the songs and scores of stage plays and musicals. Occasionally, a Broadway musical's creative or production staff hits on the idea of publishing the show's tunes independently, by-passing the established publishers.

And, lately, several television producers have thought it a good idea to join the publishing ranks, adding further despair to those already there.

The mixed-up catalog situation arising from copyright sales or reassignments, contract severances or shifts in loyalty is so complicated that hardly any one publisher can claim to own the entire output of any one celebrated songwriter or song-writing team. Even publisher Irving Berlin, who bought back as many of songwriter Irving Berlin's creations as he could, is the author and composer of several important copyrights controlled by publishers who won't give them up.

A few years ago, anyone checking the trade journal best-seller lists would have found that the largest percentage of successful new popular songs were published under the imprints of the large, long-established houses—with or without film or stage connections. Names like Bourne; Bregman, Vocco & Conn; Chappell,

Feist, Fischer, Harms, Leeds, Marks, Miller, Mills, Morris, Remick, Robbins, Santly-Joy, Schirmer, Shapiro-Bernstein, Vogel, Williamson, Witmark, Yellen, appeared so regularly they were regarded as the ones to follow. Today, new publishers' names make their appearance on the lists so often and in such large numbers that even men who have grown up in the music business and presumably know everyone connected with it feel as though their ranks have been invaded by strangers from Mars.

The still-active, independent, old-line music firms with roots in old Tin Pan Alley number fewer than a dozen. Together with the movie and stage affiliates, they represent a small percentage of the alphabetically listed "music publishers" whose names can be found in any recent annual edition of a handy directory called "The Musician's Guide."

Who, then, are the remaining multitudes?

They are largely a new army of brash individuals who swarm like shock troops along an embattled Tin Pan Alley. Some have acquired rights to only a single song apiece, which they tout aggressively. Others arrive at their claim to publisher status simply by being related to, or friendly with, a new or established artist, a powerful disk jockey or A. & R. man.

With one of these important personages in his pocket, it is a simple matter for anyone wishing to be a "publisher" to find a wandering song, write or borrow one or, if absolutely necessary, buy one. It is not in the least difficult for an untrained "publisher" of this type to make money regardless of a song's origins or quality.

Serious publishers regard these fly-by-nights with fear and loathing. "Even a plumber has to have some training, a set of tools and a license to set up business," they say. "But all anyone needs to be a publisher, these days, is a song. These fellows aren't publishers, they're curbstone brokers. The hell of it is, they come up with something that catches on, they make money, they attract the younger songwriters who don't realize they still need grooming, and they lower the standards of the industry.

"Without a staff, without knowing how to prepare a manuscript for a printer, sometimes without even an office, they reap the profits while we sit around under our expensive overhead paying out salaries without anything coming in except record and performance money on old titles. Unless we indulge in their tactics, we're left out in the cold. You can't be a successful publisher today without records, and you can't get records without the A. & R. man. And he don't care where a tune comes from as long as it's something he can slap onto a disk ahead of the other A. & R. men. What if a tune is badly written or in lousy taste? His echo-chambers and trick arrangements and top singers and merchandising setup can sell records of a Czerny exercise set with lyrics out of Mother Goose."

The fly-by-night publishers risk nothing by their shoddy methods, their established contemporaries complain. They resort to payola practices. They hand over illegal exclusive rights. They have no reputations to uphold, and they care nothing about tradition. They are unconcerned about the jobs and welfare of employees because they are usually one-man operations.

But between the two extremes of music publishers—the sorrowing founding-fathers and the boisterous gate-crashers—there is a small but important group of young firms who are the future hope of America's popular music.

Descended in spirit and sometimes in substance from the hoary publishing firms which outgrew the creative motivation of hunger as they engorged rich catalogs, these vital new publishing firms are working against incredible odds in their valiant determination to uphold the standards and honor of music-publishing traditions.

Unlike the footling frenetics who live a hand-to-mouth existence on the fringe of Tin Pan Alley, and also unlike the music moguls who can afford to loll complacently on their cash-stuffed cushions of massed copyrights, these new firms are dedicated to the principle that a publisher's first concern is the development and grooming of talented new writers. This may seem to be emphasizing the obvious. Actually, it is so simple a law that its value has been overlooked during several years of music's evaluation by juke-box juries composed of dungaree dolls and their blue-jean escorts.

These few young publishers, standing between the disenchantment of surfeit and the opportunism of greed, are keeping alive the romance and ideals of the music-publishing industry. Although there are marked differences of approach among them as individuals, they share in common a background of sound music business know-how which has enabled them to adapt orthodox song-plugging to the streamlined techniques demanded by modern resources.

While they are no less ardent in their pursuit of records via the potent A. & R. men, they are more likely than either the rich or the rapacious publishers to feel a sense of social and creative obligation about their work. They are not living nostalgically in the past or haphazardly in the present, but are building constructively for the future. As a result, to the frequent chagrin of the older men, they are steadily adding to their now comparatively slim catalogs of copyrights hit after popular hit, many with the caliber and substance that will enable them to survive as tomorrow's standards.

Of this group, one man openly admits to having an ideal. Publisher Tommy Valando is trying, in self-confessed humility, to carry on in the tradition of Max Dreyfus, known in the industry as the Dean of American Popular Music.

Dreyfus, a musical man of much sweetness and shyness, devoted his lifetime to befriending and understanding young composers and lyricists, in many instances sponsoring them out of his own pocket until they could support themselves. He was fond of going to the musical plays and revues put on by students at colleges and universities where, he believed, outstanding song-writing talent was in bud.

It was Dreyfus who first recognized creative genius in an eighteen-year-old piano player employed as a pianist by another firm and gave him a weekly salary and contract as a composer. By the time the boy was twenty-one he had more than justified

the publisher's faith in him by writing his first popular song hit—
"Swanee." The boy, of course, was George Gershwin.

(Herman Starr, of Warner's Music Publishers Holding Corporation, tried to emulate Dreyfus when he put another young
composer on a salary of $25 a week. Under the name of Lenny
Amber, Starr's protégé dutifully turned out a few pop tunes, but
he was interested in other kinds of music as well. While he was
still with Witmark, he wrote—under his own name, Leonard Bernstein—his ballet *Fancy Free*, the *Jeremiah* Symphony, the song
cycle "I Hate Music" and the score for *On the Town*.)

Tommy Valando has no grandiose illusions that he will discover another Gershwin or Bernstein; he also realizes that Dreyfus' stage music entrée to publishing success is not so readily
available to a newcomer, for nowadays show producers—like
movie producers—prefer to select their own writers instead of re-
lying on publishers' recommendations. In Dreyfus' day, because
of his musicianly sponsorship of show-caliber songwriters and
intimate involvement with stage productions, his firms (Chappell,
Williamson, T. B. Harms) shared with Witmark the bulk of
theater music. Nevertheless, the Dreyfus pattern of working with
songwriters with patience and understanding has rewarded Valando in this regard, too, for several of his "boys" are writing the
music for Broadway shows.

Modeling his operations after Dreyfus means for Valando prin-
cipally that he looks for and sponsors new writers, whereas most
publishers shun them. He spends his life with them, puts them
under contract or on salary and works with them for several
years, if necessary, before expecting returns. He exerts no pressure on his writers to turn out hits; they can work in their own
way, in offices assigned to them if they like, and create one song
a year—or one a day. He gives his composers and lyricists free
rein, does not tell them how or what to write, never asks them
to imitate a popular trend in the current market.

Although Valando has never attempted to write a song himself,
his experience qualifies him to do frequent jobs of doctoring,
and his advice to new writers is that they must learn early to

accept a seasoned publisher's judgment. If he thinks the public won't understand or will be offended by a line of lyric, he insists that it be deleted or changed.

Valando likes to give his firms the names of trees because, he says, "I want them well rooted." Two of them are called "Laurel" and "Aspen."

The newer firms which are upholding publishing traditions in a field whose traditions are declining fast are, for the most part, splinters from the main trunk. Valando was a song-plugger and professional manager for the older firm of Santly-Joy. He started in the music business by accident—or fate—when he wandered into Tin Pan Alley one summer looking for a job to help pay for his pre-medical courses at Columbia University. Medicine lost him to music, and, after fifteen years, he went into business for himself with—as he describes it—"song Number One," lacking a catalog of standards or, for that matter, of anything. Modestly, he says he got lucky. Within a year he had five hits in a row and at one time, three out of the Hit Parade's top seven tunes bore his firms' imprints.

Another in the splinter group is Bob Mellin, who started out in the music business as a singer, left the stage to work for publishers, wrote a few songs. After years of picking hits for his employers, he decided he might as well do it for himself.

Each of the younger firms has its own way of adapting old-time procedures to new techniques. Whereas Valando's operations are essentially streamlined versions of a familiar Tin Pan Alley routine, Mellin has hit upon a unique method of song-plugging.

Instead of making the ordinary demonstration record for A. & R. men's appraisal, he packs rough manuscripts of unpublished songs in a briefcase and travels to Europe several times during the year. Using Continental talent, he records master records in overseas studios. The facilities are excellent in countries like the Netherlands, Germany, France and Italy, and costs are a fraction of what they would be in the United States. For the price of an American demonstration record with a single voice and piano accompaniment, he can record a new song in Europe with a vocalist, chorus and forty-piece orchestra. They are, he feels, far more impressive. Besides, American recording companies often buy the masters to use as albums, sometimes extracting individual songs to exploit in the Stateside manner.

Still another method is used by publisher Al Brackman who, with Howard Richmond, heads up no fewer than fourteen separate companies. While this is reminiscent of the long-established houses who acquire firm after firm by inheritance or purchase, Brackman's operation differs in that several of the companies under his office roof are only boarders. That is to say, Brackman and his partners do not own these firms or their copyrights, but act as consignees, handling the details of licenses, printing and merchandising on a fee or percentage basis.

It is the opinion of the younger men that the fat, rich, old-time firms will ultimately atrophy insofar as new popular music is concerned; because of their lucrative backlogs of standards, they do not have to struggle for existence. The vital new publishing firms feel also that the opportunistic, disorganized hit-chasing operations of the fly-by-night publishers without experience or integrity will eventually cause them to outsmart themselves and fade from the scene.

The serious young publishers do not worry themselves excessively about teen-age fads and wildfire trends. They feel that popular music will always maintain a basic equilibrium, temporary evidence to the contrary. They point out that each trend leaves something worth-while behind it. There have always been outbreaks of "crazy music," they say, but the beautiful ballad goes on forever.

14. *Hits Aren't Made...*
They "Happen"

No POPULAR SONG is a spontaneous hit.

Many seem to be, bursting as they do through the sound barrier of all others and making impact on your awareness the first time you hear them. Your response to a new song, immediate and emotional, is the goal toward which people in the music business have been working hard and hopefully, some of them for many years.

The spontaneity is yours—not the song's, not the people's who labored to bring it to your ears.

Unless the song that forces your attention has qualities of endurance, you may never hear it again after next month. But if it has those qualities and you are either in love or unhappy when it was first a hit, you may never hear it again without a lurch in your heart.

Popular songs are like that. They are personal, and they pack a wallop to the vital organs. A song that makes your sister run sobbing from the room may fill you with dreamy-eyed reminiscence at the same time it impels your father to snarl and reach for a blunt instrument.

238

Such a song "happened" last week. It was one out of several million written this year by professional songwriters and amateurs. It was one out of ten thousand that were published within the past month or so. It was recorded and released along with three hundred others in the same week.

But this one—these thirty-two bars of lilting but limited melody, these unremarkable words performed together on a vinyl disk by a girl with a pleasant but unexceptional voice—this one is the one that happened.

You rushed out to buy a record, and perhaps even a copy of the sheet music. You heard it all day long on disk jockey shows and in the juke boxes. Every time you turned on the television set, somebody was singing it.

And while all this was going on, a spasm of happy excitement was electrifying a few offices along Tin Pan Alley and Record Row.

Word got around that the song was happening, and each of the participants with a stake in either the song or the record hastened to heap compliments on everyone else.

The publisher congratulated the writers. "Greatest song you ever wrote," he exulted. "Greatest song *anybody* ever wrote! It's another 'Star Dust'! You're the greatest!"

Later, in the A. & R. man's office, he slapped this gentleman on the back. "Greatest disk in years!" he said. "Brother, *you're* the one who made it happen. Took a song—not a bad song, but no 'Star Dust,' of course—and gave it that million-dollar treatment. Man, you're the greatest!"

The A. & R. man countered with congratulations of his own. He couldn't have done it without the writers, the publisher, the arranger and especially the girl singer, who is the greatest.

The artist was busy congratulating everybody else, not neglecting for one moment the disk jockeys.

The writers ran out of superlatives in their eagerness to glorify the publisher for infallible hit-picking, the A. & R. man for genius and the artist for brilliance.

While all this promiscuous praise was being thrown like confetti within the charmed circle somewhere near the Brill Building, you began to wonder what made the song "happen" in the first place. What magic combination of ingredients transformed it into a sound that saturated an entire nation within a few days of its first public exposure?

It's a good question.

For an answer, naturally, you'll go to these same people, so wildly joyous in the midst of the excitement generated by the hit that set you to wondering. But by the time you get to them, another song will have "happened" in which, most likely, none of the same personnel is involved. So you'll tactfully refrain from asking about *that* old hit, specifically, but ask instead about hits in general.

"What makes a song a hit?"

You decide to extend your research beyond the personages connected with last month's—or last week's—hit. You will, you determine, see a lot of publishers, A. & R. men, songwriters, singers, disk jockeys. They ought to have the answer.

They have. They have a hatful of answers. You collect them all and tabulate them. The common denominator seems to be a shrug which, freely translated, means, "Who knows?"

The manager of one of Tin Pan Alley's oldest and most respected music-publishing firms is unshaken in his belief that, to succeed, a song must embody a perfect marriage between poetic lyrics and a skillfully constructed melody.

"Above all," he maintains, "a song must have a beautiful thought. Take 'Tea for Two,' for instance. There's a standard gets more performances year in, year out, than any other song on the books. It was a hit when it came out, and it still is. And why? Because it's got a beautiful thought in it. The tune's fresh and simple. You can sing it, anybody can sing it. But the most important thing is, the lyrics are timeless and universal. There's this fellow, he practically paints a gorgeous picture how he and his girl will have a romantic life together. Now, everybody likes that idea. And the beauty is, the *girl* can sing it, too, only by changing a couple of words. Once a firm I was connected with professionally published a song called 'Murder at Midnight.' Swell tune, real pro. We plugged it hard in all the right places, but it flopped. The *thought* wasn't beautiful, see?"

Ask him to explain the phenomenal success of certain hit songs, past and current, whose garbled gibberish and sonic harshness are somewhat less than beautiful, and he dismisses them in a lump with a deprecatory gesture. "Just freaks, is all," he says.

So you go to a publisher of successful "freaks" and learn that all a song needs is a message for American teen-agers. The message can be a beat—an offbeat—an effect—a silly word—an unaccustomed sound—anything at all. The song that's got it ("don't ask *me* what it is") is a ready-made hit.

Disenchanted members of the music-publishing fraternity sneer at any attempt to credit merit or even teen-age appeal for a popular song's success. Their unanimous answer to your question is: "Money. That's all it takes to make a song happen. With enough money to butter the right bread, any song can be a hit, if you follow me. Without a record, you're dead. Without a top singer, you're mediocre. Without the disk jockeys and the jukes —well, you get the picture. Just leave it to the little old payola."

More decorously, the publisher with a current hit will insist that, primarily, professional know-how is responsible for a song's success.

"A bona fide, conscientious publisher recognizes a potential hit when he hears it," one such gentleman tells you. "He has years of experience behind him. When he starts working on a song property which his instinct and intellect tell him is great, his solid reputation as an expert—plus his shrewd knowledge of procedures and the market, of course—can raise that song to the hit status. It's in knowing things like the fact Como doesn't care much for a song with 'I' in its lyric, and Eckstine won't sing the word 'dark' and Crosby never liked a pop song that mentions God. It's knowing you don't ever plug a *song* to Lombardo, you talk about motorboats. You can depend on it . . . a publisher with know-how and particularly know-who is the one who makes hits."

You ask him why, then, his firm's bulging catalog of copyrights is not limited exclusively to titles you recognize as having been hits. He says, "Well, of course, you've got to get the breaks. Understand?"

Music publishers are not alone in subjective analyses of the hit-song formula.

The A. & R. men are convinced that a song's success depends largely, if not entirely, on their unique genius for linking it with its most compatible performing artist.

The artists, for their part, privately equate a song's success with brilliant performance and personal charm, in either order. Their managers and agents go along with this equation, adding the Q.E.D. of their own participation in having sold the public beforehand on how brilliant and charming the artists are.

Disk jockeys consider that they, collectively and sometimes individually, can make or break a song by their exposure or neglect of it.

Somewhere along the line, the writers who created the hit song are given a grudging portion of the total credit *they* claim.

The question about what makes a song "happen" does not lack answers after it has become a hit. Second-guessing is occupational routine in the music business. Predicting, however, is an occupational hazard.

A song's success or failure presents a fascinating deviation from mathematical doctrines of probability. In theory, the anticipation is infinite. In practice, the reckoning is infinitesimal.

It would be interesting to feed into an electronic computing brain the known statistics about the resources available to any new song. The brain's answer should give enormous odds on its success-potential, for each song as it emerges from the minds and hands of its creators has in its favor approximately:

3,000 music publishers—some deserving the title and some not, but each one capable of starting it on its way.

1,000 recording companies—large, small and fleeting, any or all of whom might record it.

3,500 radio stations, many of them operating twenty-four hours a day and hungry for new songs.

3,000 disk jockeys, each with one to six hours of air time daily in which to play records old and new.

1,000,000,000 radio receiving sets in American homes, automobiles and public places.

45,000,000 television homes.

30,000,000 record players from hand-cranked to hi-fi, for which the American public buys an estimated $300,000,000 worth of popular records annually.

There are, furthermore, hundreds of thousands of supermarkets, stores, restaurants, factories, hospitals and other public institutions which have music piped into them on contract with one or more of the transcription services to provide continuous musical entertainment.

Record stores, bookstores, department stores, music stores, drugstores, chain stores and newsstands sell records or sheet music, or both.

The nation's public and private schools have bands, orchestras and glee clubs which use a great deal of published music, popular as well as classical. So do the nation's industrial plants, its civic organizations and social clubs and its armed forces.

There are dozens of top-flight professional dance bands, hundreds of lesser ones and thousands of amateur groups making harmonies and rhythms of various tonal qualities but sharing in common a need for music to play.

There are juke boxes.

Now add to this aggregate of outlets for popular music the uncounted and terrifying numbers of adults and children who play, professionally or for self-expression, some musical instrument. Don't forget ukuleles.

If any mathematician or electronic brain cares to calculate the number of performances and sales a single popular song *might* get out of these astronomical figures, he or it is welcome to do so.

With such dizzying numbers floating around in the music industry's awareness, winged with little dollar signs, it is hardly any wonder that each song is breathed into life by enthusiasm and borne aloft on the buoyant hope that it is headed straight for the Hit Parade, a gold record and a niche in the revered company of immortals . . . a "standard."

The sad and sobering reality is that the chances of a song's reaching the modern-day pinnacle of success are about on a par with those of a tourist in Las Vegas hitting the jackpot in a silver-dollar slot machine. It's done, but not every day.

By current standards, a recorded song is an all-out, triumphant hit when it sells a million records. When it does this, the achievement is symbolized by the presentation to the recording artist of a solid gold record, suitably inscribed. Except for the phenomenon of meteoritic personalities who so captivate teen-age worshipers that they could intone thirty-two bars of the telephone book and be sure of a hit, gold records are not handed out so often that their recipients get bored with them.

Between the humble beginnings of a new popular song and its glorious climax as a gold-record hit there is the same thrill of uncertainty, hope and enthusiasm that charges through the veins of the Las Vegas tourist as he drops his heavy coin into the slot machine and pulls its lever. The music business is a very big slot machine, and launching a new song is always a gamble.

Why? With so many known factors in the possession of experienced men and women in the music business, why should a new song be dependent on luck for its course and outcome?

One answer is that nobody really needs a new popular song.

People eat, clothe themselves, crave possessions and like to be entertained. They buy food, garments, furniture, automobiles, houses, luxuries and do-it-yourself kits—and their entertainment consists of many things, including songs. Food is consumed, clothes and machines and furniture wear out, houses depreciate or are outgrown, luxuries beget a desire for more luxuries, and homemade coffee tables and tie racks come to dusty roost in attics and rummage sales.

But a song is indestructible.

If another one is never written, published or recorded, there are surely enough already on paper, vinyl, tape or wire or in people's memories to last for years to come. Unlike tangible and more friable products, the older a song is the better it's liked. Even wine and cheese which improve with age are ultimately consumed, and antiques loved for their oldness are vulnerable to the elements. All flesh is grass, all matter is reducible to ash.

But once it has been released into the surrounding atmosphere, a song cannot be destroyed as long as anyone remains to keep it alive. Its temporal abode on vinyl or paper may disintegrate, but its spirit can be revived on a young girl's lips, in an old man's memory. Popular songs which were never written down have passed to succeeding generations and survive as folk songs.

The music business, however, like all other American business, is umbilically tied to the production line and nurtured on formulas compounded to promote quantity and profit. Theoretically and philosophically it may be true that the consuming public does not need a new popular song. Those inside the music business, and those who provide it with materials and services, are not abstract thinkers. They most certainly do need new popular songs. That is why so many are thrust at you twenty-four hours a day, every day, until some of them become epidemic.

The man at the slot machine does not stop after risking one silver dollar. Sooner or later, he is sure, one of them will pay off. In the music business, sooner or later, one of the new songs will pay off, too, for its writers—its publisher—one or more recording companies—one or more performers.

Like this, for instance.

The song-writing team of Rip Cord and Andy Mann (whose names are fictitious) had worked together on more than eighty songs, thirty of which had been published, twenty of them on records. None had been a hit.

Cord and Mann have evolved a satisfactory routine. Some teams work best when the author writes words to which the composer later writes a tune. Others prefer the order of music first, words later. Cord and Mann produce their material cooperatively, which is to say that they both contribute title and lyric ideas and work out the melody together. They have found this system is best for them, as each of them knows something about music and both of them know a great deal about the physical structure and language demands of a commercially acceptable song.

About three months ago, Cord and Mann were working in their small office in the Brill Building suite occupied by the Torrey Publishing Company (fictitious). Earlier that day, Timothy Torrey had poked his head through their door and smiled widely at them.

"Fellows, 'Snap' is on its way. That Mink record is being plugged all over Rochester, New York. Thought you'd like to know."

"Snap" was the office nickname for "All I've Got Left of You Is a Kodak S-s-snapshot," a novelty the team had turned out a few months before.

"Gee, that's great, Timmy. Thanks," Mann said. "We'll have something else for you before long. Got a great lyric."

"You *always* have great ideas, boys. Best in the business."

As Timmy closed the door again, the two songwriters looked at each other.

"That Timmy," Mann said. "Tries to make you feel good."

"Yeah. What's the great lyric we've got for the new song?"

"Well, let's bat a few into the outfield, like they say on Madison Avenue. Got any ideas?"

"At the moment, the only idea I have is that 'Snap' will never make it outside of Rochester, New York, where they make Kodaks. The Mink record was lousy and you know it. A novelty like 'Snap' should of had a jump group like the Pogo Sticks and a solid rhythm background. Why Mink gave it to Tay I'll never know. Not that Tay isn't great. She's great for ballads. But a novelty?"

Mann shrugged. "So that was last week. Now suppose we ride. We haven't had a hit since breakfast."

Cord closed his eyes. "Well, I was thinking. Since Sputnik,

there haven't been many songs around with a—you know—an outer-space idea. Maybe we ought to kick it around."

"You been swinging that science-fiction stuff again?" Mann asked.

Cord looked hurt. "Listen, if Washington takes it seriously, why knock it?"

"I'm not knocking it," Mann said. "But is it commercial?"

Cord looked eager. "We'll *make* it commercial," he said. "Listen, they said 'Star Dust' wasn't commercial."

"That's because it was too long."

"Okay. So we'll write a *short* song. How about a girl who lives on like Venus? Get it? Venus—goddess of love."

"Oh, great."

"Come on, Andy. Start cooking. We can try it, can't we?"

Andy sat at the piano. "All right, Captain Video. How's this?"

He struck a dissonant chord and, with eyes rolled upwards, warbled:

"Interstellar Stella, I've been jet-propelled since I beheld ya,

"You're my star-girl, my way-up-far girl. . . ."

"Cut it out, Andy," Cord said. "But you give me an idea. How *about* that star bit . . . like wishing on one, for instance?"

"Great idea, Rip. We'll call it 'When You Wish Upon a Star' and get Washington and Harline to collaborate. Berlin won't mind publishing it again, and maybe Disney will put it in a picture."

"Oh, yeah. That from *Snow White?*"

"No. *Pinocchio.*"

Andy swung around and reached across the few feet to the cluttered desk for a lined yellow pad and a block of manuscript paper. He retrieved a pencil from its nest above his ear and looked intently at his partner.

"Okay," he said quietly, "let's pitch."

After several hours and six containers of coffee apiece, Cord and Mann had sketched a lyric and melody with which they were almost satisfied. By a long process of argument and trial, they had agreed to drop the idea of outer space and had come up with a song based on another modern phenomenon. They called their song "Univac Says You Love Me (and Univac ought to know").

Arm in arm, the boys walked down the hall to Timmy's office. The door was open. Timmy, perched on the corner of his desk and talking rapidly into the telephone, beckoned them in with a wide sweep of his free arm. Into the phone he was saying, "Listen, they love it in Rochester. I wish you'd just play it once. You'll flip. Besides, I need your opinion."

Andy seated himself at the upright and Rip stood next to him. When Timmy was finished talking, he walked around the desk to a leather chair next to the piano and sat on its broad arm.

The boys demonstrated their song, and looked at Timmy inquiringly.

"Hey, that's cute!" Timmy said. "What's that line again—the something something dream?"

Andy played and sang the line, glancing upward at Rip as he did so with an "I-told-you-so" lift of his eyebrows.

Timmy frowned slightly.

"That bothers me—rhyming dream with machine. It's offbeat."

"It bothered us, too," Rip admitted. "Then we figured if Jason and Burton could rhyme aloof with truth in 'Penthouse' we could get away with it. And how about that bit that goes 'for just you and I?' Man, that's always fractured me."

"Well, maybe we can blow around it," Timmy said. "Mind a suggestion? The tune's right. It's just that end rhyme that bugs me. Suppose instead of 'something's wrong with the machine' you say 'the machine is off the beam'? Same beat, and it gives you a sort of middle rhyme. What do you think?"

"Great!"

"That does it!"

"Okay," Timmy said. "I'll get Minnie to cut a demo for Fletch."

"You think it's for Fletch?" Rip asked. "We kind of thought Nate. He's got that new boy."

"Well, Fletch is a great man with sound effects, and this song could be a knockout with some clickety-clacks. Suppose I try him first?"

Within minutes, Timmy had put through a call to Minnie Minton, known along Tin Pan Alley as the most competent demonstration artist in the business. She can "sell" a song. She can sell other products, also, and is so skillful a musician that she can sing with conviction as she sight-reads, requiring little rehearsal time. She is in great demand among publishers, advertising agencies and producers of singing commercials. She is not a celebrity, but she is successful. At $10 a side, she can cut as many as ten or fifteen demonstration records a day. She also receives top AFTRA pay (American Federation of Television and Radio Artists) for spot commercials. She makes so much money at this steady employment that she is not especially concerned about a glamorous career. As she says, she doesn't have to be nervous about losing her rating.

At one of the numerous recording studios in New York, Timmy arranged for a demonstration session the following day. After brief rehearsal, Minnie sang "Univac" with Andy at the piano. Timmy had ordered six copies, which meant that Minnie and Andy performed the song six times for six "takes." Demonstration records are original copies and not, as in commercially sold records, pressings from master negatives.

When he okayed the demos, Timmy telephoned A. & R. man Fletch Fuller and said excitedly: "Fletch, the boys have just come up with the hottest novelty of the year. You'll flip. I need your opinion on it. Nobody has heard it yet."

Thus diplomatically, Timmy let it be known that, according to the unwritten rules, he was offering the A. & R. man first choice on a new song.

Luck played a hand when Fuller heard the "Univac" demo. The night before, he had happened to watch a television drama in which an electronic brain solved a murder mystery that baffled Scotland Yard. He had enjoyed it thoroughly. He liked to play hunches.

Also—as luck would have it—he had recently signed a new girl singer with an extremely wide vocal range. She would be a natural for some of the tonal effects, following first a bassoon, then a clarinet, then a flute in the coda.

When "Univac" with its flip side—a revived ballad from a public-domain Spanish-American-war album—was routinely sent to the disk jockeys for previewing, nothing happened.

The singer was unknown, the song timely but not extraordinary. Besides, the disk jockeys had received that same week a new Armstrong album, two new Como disks and two by Damone, a reissue of all the songs associated in the public's sentimental memory with the big name bands of the '40s, sixty new Rockabilly incantations by downy-cheeked high school students with guitars.

But, somewhere in Texas, a disk jockey's grandfather was having a birthday. He was a veteran of the Spanish-American war and, primarily to please him, his grandson played the flip side of "Univac" around the old man's suppertime. He received a few telephone calls from other oldsters in the area, and scheduled it to be played again. On one of the occasions when he reached for the disk, he inadvertently put it on the turntable wrong side up. As soon as he realized his mistake he apologized over the microphone, but allowed "Univac" to be played through.

The rest, of course, is history.

What made it a hit?

You did.

Index